study guide with programed units

STUDY GUIDE

with programed units for
Hilgard, Atkinson, and Atkinson's
introduction to PSYCHOLOGY FIFTH EDITION

Rita L. Atkinson
Stanford University

Richard C. Atkinson
Stanford University

HBJ | HARCOURT BRACE JOVANOVICH, INC.
New York   Chicago   San Francisco   Atlanta

Study Guide with Programed Units
for Hilgard, Atkinson, and Atkinson's *Introduction to Psychology,* Fifth Edition

ISBN: 0-15-543650-3

Printed in the United States of America

TO THE INSTRUCTOR

The *Study Guide* is designed to assist the student in mastering the content of the introductory course. In preparing the *Guide* consideration was given to three major difficulties that the student may encounter: In the first place, he may fail to learn the meanings of key concepts and terms used in the course. Second, he may have no satisfactory way of knowing how well he has mastered the material until he takes an examination (which often is too late). Third, he frequently finds it difficult to understand or appreciate the role that research plays in psychology.

Parts of this *Guide* have been designed to help the student in each of these areas. Each chapter contains three divisions. First, there is a programed unit, which gives the student a preliminary acquaintance with some of the important terms and concepts used in the text. The student should work on this unit *before* he reads the corresponding text chapter. (For further discussion of the programed units, see the *Instructor's Manual*.) Next, there is a multiple-choice quiz, which provides the student with an opportunity to practice exam-taking and, at the same time, shows him his areas of weakness. Finally, there are individual and class exercises, which give the student a closer look at one or more of the concepts discussed in the chapter and a feeling for the way that information is derived from research. A few of the exercises must be done in class, but most have been planned so that the student can carry them out on his own if the instructor does not want to take class time. The usual procedure is for the student to collect his own data, which he can then analyze on his own or bring to class, where it can be combined with those of the other students for analysis and discussion.

TO THE STUDENT:
HOW TO USE THIS GUIDE

The *Study Guide* is designed to help you in three ways: It introduces the concepts and terms that you will encounter in the text; it provides examination questions that will enable you to determine just how much you have learned; and, finally, it suggests exercises that will give you an understanding of the interests of the psychologist and, in most cases, a look at psychological-research methods.

Each chapter in the *Guide* parallels one in the text, and there are three sections for each chapter. The first section of each chapter in the *Guide* uses a technique of learning called "programed instruction," a method of self-instruction. This technique, based on certain principles of learning that are explained in Chapter 10 of your text, aids in the understanding and mastery of material.

These programed units are intended as a *preview* of the text chapter. From each programed unit you will acquire an acquaintance with *some* of the key terms and concepts presented in the text; as a result, you should be able to read the text chapter with increased understanding. Although the programed units are intended chiefly as a preview of the text, they also may be profitably used later as a review before examinations.

A word of warning: The programed units cannot serve as a substitute for the text chapters. They do not treat all of the important ideas presented in the text—for the programed units to do so would require a book many times the size of this one. And even the ideas that they do cover are treated in much greater detail in the text. If you work through the programed units, however, and then go on to study the text, you will master the text treatment more easily than if you had not gone through the programed material.

The programed unit consists of a series of short steps called "frames." Each frame requires you to make a *response*—either by filling in a blank or by circling a choice between two words. To the left of the frame, on the same line as the blank, is the correct response.

You will find a cardboard strip, or slider, inserted in the *Guide*. Use it to cover the answer column to the left of the program. After you have written your answer in the appropriate blank in the frame, move the slider down only far enough to reveal the correct answer. If you have made a mistake, cross out your answer and write the correct one above it.

Once the programed unit has been completed, you should then read the corresponding chapter in the text. After studying the text chapter we recommend that you turn next to the self-quiz section of the *Study Guide* and answer all the questions. Check your answers against the answer key; for questions on which you made an error go back to the text and review the appropriate material.

The final section of each *Study Guide* chapter presents one or more exercises, which are designed to illustrate various aspects of psychological research. A few of the demonstrations require special equipment and must be presented by the instructor in class, but most are designed so that you can carry them out on your own. Sometimes you may be asked to do an exercise on your own but to bring the data to class so that the data from all students may be combined for analysis and discussion. The exercises in the *Guide* are designed to give you a better understanding of scientific methodology and a feeling for how psychologists investigate some of the problems presented in the chapters.

Let us now summarize. There are three sections in each chapter of the *Guide:* programed unit, self-quiz, and individual or class exercise(s). You first complete the programed unit for a chapter, then read the chapter, and then proceed to the self-quiz and the exercise(s). These sections are designed to help you understand the concepts in the text, to allow you to evaluate your learning, and, finally, to introduce you to the methods of psychology. It is important to remember, however, that the *Guide* is designed as a supplement, not a substitute, for the text. Used properly, the *Guide* will enhance your comprehension of the text's contents.

CONTENTS

study guide with programed units

1 psychology as a behavioral science

programed unit

Note: Before beginning this programed unit, make sure you have read and understood the instructions on pages vi–vii.

1. Psychology is the science that studies *behavior* and *mental activity*. By behavior we refer to those activities of an organism that can be *observed*. When

behavior   we observe a child laughing or talking, we are observing _____ .

2. Behavior can be observed unaided or by means of *instruments*. If we use a lie detector to measure physiological responses to questions, we are observ-

behavior   ing _____ .

measure (or observe)   3. Tests are another type of instrument that can be used to _____ behavior. When we give an intelligence test to a child and score the results,

behavior   we are observing _____ .

observed   4. Behavior refers to any activity of an organism that can be _____ ,

instruments   either directly by another person or by means of _____ .

behavior   5. We defined psychology as the science that studies _____ and

activity   mental _____ . You may be wondering at this point what is meant by mental activity and how it can be observed.

6. Mental activity refers to the many *conscious* and *unconscious processes* that go on within us and that may or may not be reflected in behavior. Conscious

processes   *pro*_____ are internal events of which we are *aware*. Emotions,

conscious   dreams, perceptions, and memories are all _____ processes of which we are aware.

1

conscious	**7.** If you are angry and are aware that you are angry, this is a _____ process. Your anger may or may not be reflected in your _____ .
behavior	
aware	**8.** Conscious processes are those internal events of which we are fully _____ .
cannot	**9.** Another person (*can/cannot*) directly observe your feelings of anger. He can only know about your conscious processes through what you *report* to him. Conscious processes cannot be directly *ob*_____ .
observed	
report	**10.** When certain events take place within you and you are able to _____ these events, they are called conscious processes. Your verbal or written report of a conscious process is a form of _____ that is directly observable.
behavior	
	11. Some internal events are unconscious; these are emotions, repressed memories, and desires of which we are not aware. Internal events of which we are
unconscious	not aware are called _____ processes.
	12. If you are angry at your mother but are not aware of this anger, then it is
unconscious	an _____ process. Since you are not aware of your
report (or synonym)	angry feelings, you cannot _____ them to others.
unconscious	**13.** Emotions and desires of which a person is not aware are called _____
reported	processes. Unconscious processes cannot be observed or _____ but must be *inferred* from gestures, slips of speech, dreams, and other behavior.
observed	**14.** Psychology, then, studies behavior that can be _____ directly or measured by appropriate instruments. It also studies mental
activity	_____ , which includes conscious processes, those internal
aware, reported	events of which the person is _____ , and which can be _____ to another person, and unconscious processes, internal events of which the
inferred	person is not aware and whose existence must be *in*_____ from behavior.
	15. The aim of a science of psychology is to discover *relationships among variables*. A *variable* is something that changes, something that can take on different values. "To change" means "to vary"; therefore a quality that is
variable	subject to change is called a _____ .
is	**16.** A person's rate of breathing in different situations (*is/is not*) likely to
variable	change. Breathing rate is thus a _____ .
	17. Many experiments in psychology study more than one variable. If we wished
two	to discover the effect of fear upon breathing rate, we would have _____ (*number*) variables in the study. We would be trying to discover the
relationship, rate	*rel*_____ between the variables of breathing _____
fear	and _____ .

18. *Time* is a variable in many experiments. If a psychologist wants to determine the effect of the passage of time upon forgetting, he might ask several subjects to memorize the same set of materials and then have them recall the materials after varying intervals of time. In this case the variable whose effect

time   the psychologist was trying to discover would be _____ .

19. When the psychologist studies the rate of forgetting by varying the passage of time, he is able to manipulate the time variable by deciding when he will test the memory of his subjects. A variable that is directly controlled or *manipulated* by the experimenter is called an *independent variable*. Time,

independent   in the experiment we have been describing, is a(n) _____ variable.

20. We call such a variable independent because its value does not depend upon

manipulated   the values of any other variable. Instead it is controlled or _____ by the experimenter.

21. The experimenter can control or manipulate time in an experiment, but he cannot directly control or manipulate forgetting. If he finds, however, that forgetting is affected by the passage of time, he can say that forgetting is *dependent* upon time. If time is called an independent variable, then forget-

dependent   ting can be called a(n) _____ variable.

22. The independent variable is the variable manipulated by the experimenter. The variable whose value may vary as a result of changes in the independent

dependent   variable is the _____ variable. In other words, the value of the dependent variable is dependent upon the value of the independent variable.

23. If we want to discover the effects of marijuana upon sexual behavior,

independent   marijuana is the _____ variable and sexual behavior is the dependent variable.

24. If we are concerned with the effect of age upon the accuracy of visual perception, age of the subject is the independent variable and the accuracy of

dependent   perception is the _____ variable.

25. If an experimenter varies the temperature in a classroom to determine its

independent   effect upon examination grades, the temperature level is the _____ variable and the examination grades of the students constitute the

dependent   _____ variable.

26. In a laboratory experiment the variable the experimenter manipulates, the

independent   _____ variable, can be varied with precision. Similarly, the variable that is a consequence of the subject's behavior, the

dependent   _____ variable, can be carefully measured. Other variables that the investigator does not want to influence the outcome of the experiment can be *controlled*.

27. For example, if we want to study the effect of sleep loss upon learning ability, we can select subjects of the same age and intelligence, provide them with the same diet and living conditions, and then see how their performance on a learning task (such as memorizing a poem) varies with the

sleep

amount of _____ they are permitted. In this situation, variables that we do not want to influence the results (such as age, intelligence, and diet)

controlled

are *con*_____ . We can thus be fairly confident that differences

dependent

in scores on the learning task, the _____ variable, result

independent

from different amounts of sleep, the _____ variable.

control

28. Laboratory experiments thus enable us to _____ variables that we do not wish to influence our results, as well as provide the means for

independent

careful manipulation of the _____ variable and pre-

dependent

cise measurement of the _____ variable.

29. But it is not possible to study all types of behavior in the laboratory. *Field observation* is another method psychologists use to study behavior. Suppose we want to know how a child's aggressiveness on the school playground is related to his behavior at home. If the mother answers a questionnaire to the effect that her child is quite "aggressive" at home, will he also exhibit aggressive behavior on the playground? We cannot answer this question in the

controlled

laboratory, where variables can be precisely _____ . Instead we must determine how the ratings provided by the mother cor-

field

respond to _____ observations made by trained observers who record notes on the child's behavior on the playground.

30. The relationship between home behavior and playground behavior in this

is not

case (*is/is not*) determined by manipulating aggressive behavior at home and studying the results on the playground; instead we observe both variables as they occur in nature and then look for a *relationship* between them.

observations

31. In field _____ we must find some method of

relationship

determining the _____ between the two variables. The relationship between two variables in situations in which we cannot

manipulate (or control)

experimentally _____ the variables is determined by *correlation*.

32. Suppose we want to know whether "cooperativeness" is a personality characteristic that persists throughout life; will a child who exhibits cooperative

cooperative

behavior in nursery school be judged _____ as an adult?

33. In this case we cannot use the experimental method to answer the question.

correlation

Instead we use the method of *cor*_____ to determine the relationship between some measure of cooperative behavior as a child and

cooperative

another measure of _____ behavior in adulthood.

cooperative

34. As a measure of _____ behavior in childhood we might use judgments by nursery school teachers, who rate each child as to the degree he cooperates in play as opposed to being aggressive or with-

measure

drawn. As a _____ of cooperative behavior in adulthood we

could look at the same individual when he is in college and note how his dormitory mates rate him on a scale of cooperativeness.

measures (or variables)

35. The figure on this page shows the relationship between these two _____ for ten different young men. A rating of 1 indicates very uncooperative be-

cooperative

havior, while a rating of 12 indicates extremely _____ behavior. Note that John received a rating of 2 in nursery school and the

2
uncooperative

same rating of _____ in college. Thus we would say that John's behavior has been consistently (*cooperative/uncooperative*) over the years.

11
cooperative

36. Jerry received a rating of _____ in nursery school and also in college. His behavior appears to be consistently (*cooperative/uncooperative*).

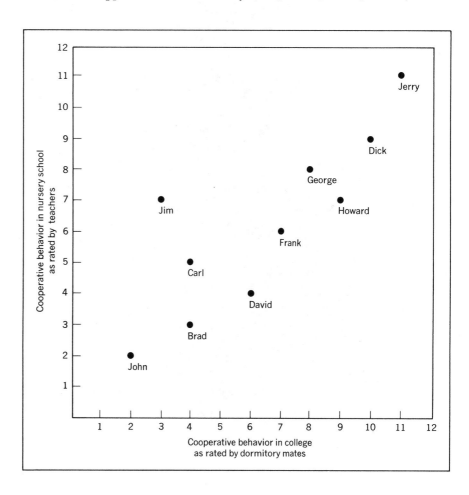

37. What can we say about Jim and Howard? They both received the same

7
less
Jim

rating of _____ in nursery school, but in adulthood Jim is rated as (*more/less*) cooperative than Howard. Both boys changed over the years, but the change was greatest for _____ .

38. The other subjects show some discrepancy between ratings in childhood and

ratings
correlation

_____ in adulthood. But their ratings are similar enough to indicate a close relationship, or *cor_____* , between cooperative behavior in childhood and cooperative behavior in adulthood.

correlation

39. If the *c_____* between child and adult behavior were perfect, then all the ratings would fall on a straight *diagonal* line when plotted on the graph; each person would have received the same ratings in

childhood

adulthood as he did in _____ .

correlation

40. If there were no relationship, or _____ , between adult and child cooperative behavior, then the scores would be scattered randomly all over the graph.

41. Since the scores in this hypothetical experiment fall very close to a straight

diagonal

*dia*_____ line, we can conclude that there is a close relationship, a

correlation

high _____ , between child and adult behavior.

42. The actual measure in a correlational study is the *coefficient of correlation,* signified by the lower-case letter *r,* which expresses the degree of relationship. If there had been a perfect correlation between cooperation in childhood and adulthood in the above study, then we would have a correlation

coefficient

*coef*_____ of *r* = +1.00.

43. The plus sign signifies that the relationship is *positive,* that a child who is cooperative will tend to be cooperative as an adult. A positive coefficient of

correlation

_____ , or *r,* indicates a positive relationship between the two variables; an increase in one variable is associated with an

increase

_____ in the other.

44. If, on the other hand, children who were cooperative in nursery school always turned out to be uncooperative adults, we would have a perfect *negative*

correlation

correlation. A negative _____ of *r* = −1.00 indicates

variable

that one variable increases as the other _____ decreases.

45. Life expectancy decreases as the amount a person smokes increases. This is

negative

an example of a (*positive/negative*) correlation.

46. Life expectancy increases as the adequacy of one's diet increases. This is an

positive

example of a _____ correlation.

positive

47. A correlation of +1.00 signifies a perfect (*positive/negative*) relationship

negative

between two variables. A correlation of −1.00 indicates a perfect _____ relationship.

coefficient

48. A correlation *coef*_____ of *r* = .00 signifies no relationship at all. If we tried to determine the relationship between hair color and grades in

r = .00

college, we would expect a correlation of (*r* = + *1.00/r* = *.00/r* = −*1.00*).

49. A correlation between *r* = .00 and either +1.00 or −1.00 indicates an im-

correlation

perfect relationship. The more closely the _____ approaches 1.00, either plus or minus, the greater the degree of relationship, either positive or negative. In our study on cooperativeness, for example, we

r

might expect a correlation in the neighborhood of _____ = +.86 be-

positive

tween childhood and adult behavior. There is a (*positive/negative*) rela-

is not

tionship between the two variables, which (*is/is not*) perfect.

50. Cause-and-effect relationships cannot always be inferred from high negative or high positive correlations. In laboratory experiments we can manipulate

the _____ variable and measure precisely its effect

independent

dependent

cannot

upon the _____ variable. In correlational studies we can only note that two variables vary together. We (*can/cannot*) say for certain that one variable *causes* the other.

51. For example, there is a high positive correlation between the softness of the asphalt in city streets during the summer and infant mortality rate. We do not assume that some poisonous vapor from the soft asphalt causes infants to die. Instead we attribute the relationship to a third variable—probably

heat (or synonym)

_____ .

52. Correlation implies the existence of a positive or negative relationship be-

causes

tween two variables. It does not necessarily mean that one _____ the other.

53. Two *modes of explanation* recur frequently in psychology. The *developmental* mode emphasizes the historical roots of present behavior; it focuses on the experiences of the individual as he grows up. The *interactive* mode stresses the influence of current motives and needs on behavior. When a psychoanalyst delves into the early childhood experiences of his patient to

developmental

explain a present conflict, he is using the _____ mode of explanation.

54. Steve feels very tense and anxious whenever he has a date with a girl. If we explain his behavior in terms of the present situation only, we are using the

interactive

_____ mode.

55. If we look back into his childhood to learn something about his relationship with his mother in attempt to explain his present behavior, we are using the

developmental

_____ mode of explanation.

historical

56. The developmental mode tries to determine the _____ roots of present behavior.

57. The interactive mode explains behavior in terms of the situation existing in

present

the _____ .

explanation

58. In many situations both modes of _____ are important. In treating a person's psychological conflicts it is frequently helpful to

developed

know how the conflicts *de*_____ as he grew up. But regardless of the origin of an individual's problems, his ability to resolve them depends

present (or current)

upon his _____ situation and the pressures imposed on him.

59. Now let's review. Psychology is concerned with the study of behavior and mental activity. By behavior we refer to those activities of an organism that

observed

can be _____ by another person.

60. Mental activity includes internal events, such as emotions and memories,

conscious	which we are aware of and can report; these are called _____
unconscious	processes. Internal events of which we are not aware are called _____ processes.
activity	**61.** In studying behavior and mental _____ psychologists often measure quantities that are subject to change. Any quantity subject to
variable	change is called a _____ .
independent	**62.** The variable under the control of the experimenter is called the _____ variable; by manipulating this variable the experimenter can observe its
behavior	effects upon the b_____ of the subject.
	63. The variable that the experimenter observes and that depends upon the
independent, dependent	value of the _____ variable is called the _____ variable.
independent	**64.** In laboratory experiments we find careful manipulation of the _____
measurement	variable, precise _____ of the dependent variable, and
control	_____ over variables that we do not wish to influence the experiment.
	65. In situations in which we cannot control the variables, such as in field
observations, correlation	_____ , we use the method of _____
variables	to determine the relationship between the _____ .
r	**66.** The coefficient of correlation, which is signified by the letter _____ , tells
relationship	us whether there is a rel_____ between the variables, and
positive, negative (either order)	whether the relationship is _____ or _____ .
causes	It does not necessarily imply that one variable _____ the other.
	67. Finally, there are two basic modes of explanation that are useful in psy-
developmental	chology. The _____ mode emphasizes the his-
interactive	torical roots of behavior; the _____ mode explains behavior in terms of present motives and situations.

A reminder: This programed unit is intended as an introduction to, not a substitute for, Chapter 1 of the text. If you have mastered the terms presented here, you will draw more meaning from the text itself. But you will find that the text presents more ideas, and goes deeper into the ideas presented here, than it is possible to do in this programed unit.

self-quiz

Select the alternative that best completes the thought.
In some cases several answers are fairly satisfactory;
you are to pick the *best* one.

_____ **1.** Correlational studies
a. establish a clear cause-effect relationship

b. systematically manipulate the independent variable
c. assemble correspondences without experimental control
d. are seldom used with large masses of data

_____ 2. Activities of an organism that can be observed are termed by psychologists as
a. behavior
b. action
c. field-Gestalts
d. reflexes

_____ 3. Contemporary cognitive psychologists
a. utilize objective methods to study mental activity
b. reject the idea of man as an information-processing organism similar to a computer
c. utilize the analogy of the reflex arc from S-R psychology
d. reject mental activity

_____ 4. The survey method does *not* usually include
a. a pretested questionnaire
b. groups of trained interviewers
c. a scientific biography
d. a carefully designed sample

_____ 5. The control group is the group
a. in which the experimental condition is present
b. in which the experimental condition is absent
c. in which the investigator carefully manipulates the variable
d. that is tested first

_____ 6. The individual's own consciousness and introspections
a. are ignored in psychology because they are too subjective
b. are materials for the artist, not the scientist
c. have come back into psychology through verbal reports
d. should be psychology's only concern

_____ 7. A coefficient of correlation turns out to be −.85. This means that
a. there is no relationship between the variables
b. a mistake has been made in its computation

c. causation of the relationship is determinable
d. there is a meaningful inverse relationship between the variables

_____ 8. If we attempt to discover the effect of varying degrees of hunger upon the amount a boy will eat, the amount eaten is the
a. dependent variable
b. intervening variable
c. antecedent variable
d. independent variable

_____ 9. Comparative psychology refers to
a. behaviorism
b. a comparison between theories of psychology
c. the study of the behavior of lower organisms
d. stimulus-response psychology

_____ 10. The area of psychology in which the largest percentage of people specialize is
a. social
b. experimental
c. counseling and guidance
d. clinical

_____ 11. The term "conditioned reflex"
a. is an important concept in comparative psychology
b. was invented by B. F. Skinner
c. refers to the constriction of the pupil in the presence of bright light
d. is synonymous with learned reflex

_____ 12. The experimental method is distinguished from other methods of observation
a. by its ability to control variables
b. because it attempts to find regular relationships among variables
c. because it usually takes place in a laboratory
d. because the data obtained from using this method is always valid

_____ 13. The school that emphasizes the importance of wholes over parts is called
a. Behaviorism
b. Structuralism
c. Gestalt psychology
d. Introspectionism

_____ 14. A correlation of $r = +1.00$ means

a. there is no relationship
b. a perfect negative correlation
c. a perfect positive correlation
d. it is twice as great as a correlation of $r = +.50$

_____ 15. The counseling psychologist
a. is quite different from the clinical psychologist
b. would typically be found working in a mental hospital or a prison
c. often deals with problems of vocational and educational guidance
d. deals with the mentally ill

_____ 16. Observations of chimpanzees in their native environment of Africa would be research using
a. field observations
b. the survey method
c. a longitudinal study
d. case histories

_____ 17. Unconscious processes
a. refer to circulation of the blood and the reflex constriction of the pupil
b. were brought to the attention of psychologists by Sigmund Freud
c. can be understood only through psychoanalysis
d. can usually be directly observed

_____ 18. We call the antecedent condition the
a. dependent variable
b. independent variable

c. results
d. consequence of the subject's behavior

_____ 19. The behavioral sciences
a. include only those fields of inquiry that have to do with individual behavior
b. are included among the social sciences
c. do not include economics and history
d. include those fields of inquiry that study man as an individual as well as the institutions under which he lives

_____ 20. An interactive explanation in psychology
a. stresses historical roots of present behavior
b. includes S-R psychology and psychoanalysis
c. cannot be logically accepted along with the developmental explanation
d. deals with the arousal and control of behavior in the present

key to self-quiz

20. d	15. c	10. d	5. b
19. d	14. c	9. c	4. c
18. b	13. c	8. a	3. a
17. b	12. a	7. d	2. a
16. a	11. d	6. c	1. c

individual exercise

THE SCIENTIFIC METHOD

introduction

The status of psychology as a science hinges upon its use of the experimental method. An experiment involves observation of some aspect of behavior (dependent variable) while one factor (independent variable) is systematically changed under certain specified conditions (controlled variables). In the experimental method all the factors producing a given result, except the one whose effects are being examined, are held constant. Before an experiment is performed, the experimenter generally states a hypothesis describing the process that he believes underlies the behavior under investigation.

Although the experimental method provides the most reliable source of scientific information and is the preferred method of science, difficulties are encountered even in simple experiments. Many experiments appear to have satisfied the fundamental requirement of controlling relevant variables, but careful analysis of the procedures used sometimes reveals the presence of overlooked, uncontrolled variables that may invalidate the results.

This simple experiment will provide you with an opportunity to criticize procedure and to become somewhat more familiar with the scientific method.

equipment needed

None

procedure

The results of a fictitious experimental study are given in Tables 1 and 2. Read carefully the experimental problem, the hypothesis, the procedures used, the results obtained, and the conclusions drawn. Then, using the concluding questions as an aid, make an analysis of the experiment.

1. EXPERIMENTAL PROBLEM: To investigate the effects of drinking coffee (which contains caffeine) on the achievement of college students on a final examination in general psychology.

2. HYPOTHESIS: Two cups of black coffee taken immediately before a task requiring mental exertion increase a student's academic efficiency.

3. PROCEDURE: Two groups of subjects were used. Group 1 consisted of 200 freshmen who were matched in age, intelligence, sex, and grade-point average with the 200 freshmen in group 2. Subjects in both groups were enrolled in the elementary course in psychology. All subjects in group 1 drank two cups of black coffee immediately before taking the final examination. All subjects in group 2 were instructed not to take any stimulants during the day the final examination was to be taken. For purposes of analysis, the grades of the students of both groups were converted into the following numerical equivalents (grade points): A = 4; B = 3; C = 2; D = 1; and F = 0. The average grade-point score for each of the two groups was then computed on this basis.

4. RESULTS: The results of the experiment are summarized in the tables. Table 1 indicates the number and percentage of students in each group obtaining each of the five letter grades as final grades in general psychology. Table 2 gives the average grade-point scores of the two groups.

These results indicate that the students in group 1 did consistently better than the students in group 2.

	Group 1 (took coffee)		Group 2 (did not take coffee)	
Grade	**Number**	**Percent**	**Number**	**Percent**
A	30	15	14	7
B	46	23	24	12
C	80	40	112	56
D	36	18	40	20
F	8	4	10	5

TABLE 1

Group	Average grade-point score
1 (coffee drinkers)	2.25
2 (non-coffee drinkers)	1.96

TABLE 2

5. CONCLUSIONS: Comparison of the final grades earned in general psychology by two groups of college students (a stimulant-taking group and a non-stimulant-taking group) indicates that the taking of a mild stimulant, such as two cups of black coffee, immediately before an examination increases the academic efficiency and achievement of freshmen college students in a general psychology course.

questions for discussion

1. What is the dependent variable in this experiment?

2. What is the independent variable in this experiment?

3. What are the limitations of the experiment?

4. How would *you* design an experiment to test the hypothesis that taking a mild stimulant before an examination increases academic efficiency?

2 the behaving organism

programed unit

1. In order to understand behavior we need to know something about the physiological processes that enable an organism to respond to its *environment*. Even the simplest organism could not survive if it were not sensitive

   environment   to *changes* in its *en*_____ . The specialized portions of the

   changes   body that are sensitive to environmental _____ are called *receptors*.

2. Different receptors are *sensitive* to, or excited by, different forms of *physical*

   energy   *energy*. The ear is sensitive to the physical _____ called sound

   receptor   waves. The ear is thus a _____ .

3. The eye is sensitive to the form of physical _____ called light

   energy   waves. The eye is thus a _____ .

   receptor

4. The body contains many other receptors, some much less obvious than the

   physical   traditional "five senses." Each is sensitive to a different form of _____

   sensitive   energy. There are receptors in the skin that are _____ to heat, pressure, and pain. Receptors in the muscles, tendons, and joints tell us about changes in our position in space and about movements of parts of our bodies. Receptors in our internal organs tell us about our state of hunger, thirst, or need for elimination.

   energy   5. The physical _____ that excites a receptor is called a *stimulus*

   stimuli   (plural, *stimuli*). Light waves are the _____ that excite the

   sound   eye; the stimuli that excite the ear are _____ waves. Both of these

   stimuli   receptors are sensitive to particular kinds of _____ .

6. A stimulus that excites a receptor produces an effect upon the organism. A bright light shines in your eyes, and you may respond by raising your hand to shield your eyes. The bright light serves as a _____ to initiate the response of hand-raising. The part of the body that carries out the response to a stimulus is called an *effector*.

stimulus

7. Since the response of hand-raising was carried out by the muscles, muscles must be one class of _____ . Another class of effectors is the various glands of the body.

effectors

8. The two classes of effectors are the _____ and the glands. Effectors carry out responses to _____ .

muscles
stimuli

9. The energy that excites the _____ is transmitted to the effector by means of the nervous system. We will consider the nervous system in a moment. Right now we are concerned with the effectors: the muscles and _____ .

receptor

glands

10. You are walking across the street when suddenly a car speeds toward you. The driver blows his horn as a warning. The noise from the horn is a _____ that registers on your ears, which serve as _____ .

stimulus
receptors

11. The energy from the stimulus impinging on the ears is transmitted by the nervous system to the _____ , the muscles and glands. The effectors enable you to respond to _____ .

effectors
stimuli

12. Nervous impulses activate the muscles, enabling you to run. They also activate the *adrenal gland,* an effector that prepares the body to respond quickly in an emergency. The adrenal _____ secretes *hormones* directly into the blood stream.

gland

13. The adrenal gland responds to _____ by secreting substances called _____ directly into the blood stream. These hormones influence our responses. The adrenal gland is thus classed as an _____ .

stimuli
hormones
effector

14. The adrenal gland is a *ductless,* or *endocrine,* gland. Ductless, or _____ , glands are glands that secrete their hormones *directly into the blood stream.* The *thyroid, parathyroids, thymus, pituitary, pancreas,* and *gonads* (sex glands) also secrete their hormones directly into the blood stream and must therefore be _____ glands.

endocrine

ductless (or endocrine)

15. There are two kinds of glands: *duct* glands and *ductless* glands. *Duct* glands, such as the *tear* glands and the *salivary* glands, are glands that secrete their products on the *surface* of the body or into the body *cavities,* but *not* directly into the blood stream. The adrenal gland, on the other hand, secretes its hormones directly into the blood stream and is therefore a(n) _____ gland.

ductless (or endocrine)

16. The duct glands, which include the _____ glands and salivary glands, secrete their products on the _____ of the body or into the body *cavities,* but *not* into the blood stream.

17. Ductless, or endocrine, glands secrete their hormones directly into the

_____ _____ , whereas duct glands secrete their products on the _____ of the body or into the body _____ .

18. Duct glands secrete their products on the _____ of the body or into the body _____ . Ductless, or _____ , glands secrete their hormones directly into the _____ _____ .

19. The text will tell you about the various endocrine glands and their functions. Here we shall discuss only the adrenal gland, which, being an endocrine

gland, secrets its hormones directly into the _____ _____ .

20. The *adrenal* gland has two major parts, each secreting its own

_____ . The *medulla* (inner layer) of this gland secretes the hormones *epinephrine* and *norepinephrine* into the blood stream when the organism is experiencing strong emotion. The *cortex* (outer layer) of this gland secretes a number of *adrenocortical* hormones, which are life-maintaining regulators, since they control both salt and carbohydrate metabolism.

21. *Epinephrine* and *norepinephrine* are hormones secreted by the *medulla* of

the _____ gland. Adrenocortical hormones, which are secreted by the _____ (outer layer) of this same gland, are life-maintaining regulators, since they control both salt and carbohydrate metabolism.

22. The adrenal gland has two major parts: the *medulla,* which secretes _____ and _____ during excited emotional states; and the *cortex,* which secretes _____ hormones, which control both *salt* and *carbohydrate* metabolism.

23. During intense emotional states the inner layer of the adrenal gland, called

the _____ , secretes the hormones epinephrine and norepinephrine. The cortex of this gland secretes the adrenocortical hormones, which

control _____ and _____ metabolism.

24. The *nervous system* provides connections by which impulses originating in the receptors are transmitted to the effectors. Energy transmitted by the

nervous _____ is called a *nervous impulse;* a nervous impulse is

transmitted via the nerves of the _____ system.

25. When a receptor is stimulated by energy from the environment, it converts that energy into chemical processes that in turn produce an electrochemical

impulse in the nervous _____ . This electrochemical impulse travels along the nerves and eventually initiates a response by one or more

_____ .

26. The nervous system thus serves as a connection between the _____
receptors

effectors   and _____ .

27. The basic units of the *nervous system* are specialized cells called *neurons.* Each neuron is a living cell with a *nucleus* and other parts common to all cells. The human nervous system contains many billions of these nerve cells,

neurons   or _____ .

28. Specialized cells that are the basic units of the nervous system and that serve
neurons   as the connectors between receptors and effectors are called _____ .

29. A nerve is a bundle of nerve fibers. Thus a single nerve may contain hun-
neurons   dreds of fibers, or specialized cells called _____ .

30. The elements of the nervous system may be divided into three classes: (1) incoming, or *afferent,* nerves; (2) *centers,* or connections between nerve cells; and (3) outgoing, or *efferent,* nerves. A convenient way to remember the difference between *af*ferent and *ef*ferent nerves is to remember that the

efferent   outgoing, or *ef*_____ , nerves make connections with the *effectors* (which in turn have an *ef*fect upon the environment).

31. The efferent nerves make connections with the effectors; the incoming, or
afferent   _____ , nerves make connections with the receptors.

32. The incoming, or afferent, nerves and the outgoing, or efferent, nerves are connected through various *centers.* The chief characteristic of the centers is that they contain *synapses,* or *junctions between neurons.* You might expect

neurons   the brain to contain large numbers of such junctions between _____ .

33. The *brain* and *spinal cord* are the chief centers in which junctions between
synapses   neurons, or *syn*_____ , occur. However, there are also certain centers called *ganglia,* located outside the spinal cord, at which synapses, or

junctions   _____ between neurons, occur.

spinal cord   **34.** The *brain,* the _____ _____ , and the *ganglia* make up the

synapses   centers at which junctions between neurons, or _____ , occur.

35. Receptors throughout the body are connected to nerve fibers over which impulses *come into* the central nervous system. These fibers must be in-

afferent   coming, or _____ , nerves.

36. Nerve fibers lead out from the *centers,* again in bundles called nerves, to connect with the *effectors,* the glands and muscles. These are the outgoing,

efferent   or _____ , nerves.

37. Each neuron has a specialized structure with three main parts: the *cell body,* containing the *nucleus;* the *dendrites;* and the *axon.* The dendrites and the cell body *receive* impulses from receptors or from other neurons; the axon *transmits* impulses to other neurons or effectors. Each neuron, you will

nucleus   remember, is a single living cell with a _____ and other parts common to all cells.

38. The *dendrites* and the *cell body* receive impulses from receptors or from other neurons; the *axon* _____ impulses to other neurons or to effectors.

transmits

39. The _____ and the cell body receive impulses from _____ or from other neurons, while the axon transmits impulses to other neurons or to _____ .

dendrites

receptors

effectors

40. Each neuron has a specialized structure with three main parts: the _____ _____ , containing the nucleus; the _____ ; and the _____ , which transmits impulses.

cell body, dendrites

axon

41. The _____ _____ and the _____ of the neuron receive impulses from receptors or from other neurons; the _____ transmits impulses to other neurons or to effectors.

cell body, dendrites

axon

42. Unlike lower animal life, such as the coelenterates, which have a *nerve net* with neural impulses traveling in *all* directions, man has a *polarized synaptic* nervous system with impulses conducted in only *one* direction. You recall that a synapse is a _____ between neurons.

junction

43. Organisms such as the coelenterates have a primitive nervous system called a nerve _____ , with impulses traveling in *all* directions. Man, on the other hand, has a highly developed nervous system, called a polarized _____*tic* nervous system, with neural impulses traveling in *one* direction.

net

synaptic

44. Another way of looking at man's nervous system is to divide it into two portions: the *central nervous system* and the *autonomic nervous system*. The autonomic nervous system is usually thought of as including the *efferent* (outgoing) nerves running to the *glands* and the *smooth muscles* (those found in the stomach, intestines, and other internal organs). Thus we would expect the efferent nerves leading to the salivary glands to be part of the (*central/autonomic*) nervous system.

autonomic

45. Many of the activities controlled by the autonomic nervous system are "autonomous," or "self-regulating." The process of digestion, for example, goes on without any conscious willing or *awareness* on the part of the individual. We might also assume that the secretions of the adrenal gland are regulated by the _____ nervous system.

autonomic

46. The self-regulating activities controlled by the autonomic nervous system can go on while a person is asleep or unconscious, that is, without his being _____ of them.

aware (or conscious)

47. The autonomic nervous system has two divisions: the *sympathetic* and the *parasympathetic* divisions. These two divisions are often opposite, or *antagonistic,* in their action. But both divisions operate through (*efferent/afferent*) nerves to the glands and _____ muscles.

efferent

smooth

48. The sympathetic division of the autonomic nervous system operates to *dilate* the blood vessels of the heart, while the parasympathetic division operates to *constrict* these blood vessels. This is an illustration of the fact

antagonistic

that the two divisions are often opposite, or _____, in their action.

49. The sympathetic division tends to act as a *unit* in *excited* states, while the parasympathetic division tends to act in a more *piecemeal* fashion and to be more important in *quiescent* states, or those activities that conserve and protect bodily resources. If you observe that a subject's heart rate has speeded up, that he is perspiring profusely, and that his pupils are dilated,

sympathetic

you might expect that the _____ division of the autonomic nervous system was playing a part in these responses.

50. Since the adrenal gland is dominant in excited states, it would be logical to

parasympathetic

conclude that the _____ division has no connection to this gland.

sympathetic
parasympathetic (either
order), sympathetic
parasympathetic

51. The two divisions of the autonomic nervous system are the _____ and the _____ divisions. The _____ division tends to act as a unit in excited states, whereas the _____ division tends to act in a more piecemeal fashion in quiescent states.

autonomic

antagonistic

52. The _____ nervous system has two divisions, the sympathetic and parasympathetic divisions, which are often _____ in their action. Now we must examine the *central* part of the nervous system, the *brain* and *spinal cord,* which contain nerve fibers interconnecting the receptors and effectors from the region outside the central nervous system. The ganglia of the autonomic nervous system are *not* considered part of the central nervous system.

brain

central

53. The _____ and spinal cord constitute the central part of the nervous system, or the *central nervous system.* The ganglia of the autonomic nervous system are not considered part of the _____ nervous system.

54. The central part of the nervous system consists of the brain and the

spinal cord

_____ _____ .

55. Let's review. The *autonomic nervous system* derives its name from the fact

autonomous

that many of its activities are _____ , or self-regulating,

aware

and occur without our being _____ of them. It has two divisions that

antagonistic, sympathetic
parasympathetic
(either order)
sympathetic

are often _____ in their action: the _____ division and the _____ division. The _____ division tends to act as a unit in excited states,

parasympathetic

whereas the _____ division tends to act

quiescent

in a more piecemeal fashion in _____ states. The *central*

brain, spinal cord

nervous system consists of the _____ and the _____ _____ and is generally distinguished from the autonomic nervous system.

56. In the text you will find several illustrations of neurons (nerve cells), of the autonomic nervous system, and of the central nervous system. You will learn something about the evolution of nerve cells, nerve networks, and the complex collection of neurons that we call the *brain*. The remainder of this unit will present some of the major structures of the human brain. The brain,

central

you will remember, is part of the _____ nervous system.

57. In very primitive animals, such as flatworms, there are concentrations of the cell bodies of neurons toward the head of the animal. The cells that make up the eyes at the front end of the flatworm are connected to the cell bodies of the neurons at the front end. Thus we might call this collection of neurons

central

a primitive brain, or the beginning of a _____ nervous system.

58. The text will explain that in the brains of vertebrate animals, such as the dogfish or the shrew, certain specialized parts are recognizable. These are the *hindbrain,* the *midbrain,* and the *forebrain.* These three main parts of the brain, though they have evolved in complicated ways, are still found in the human brain. Thus, in addition to the *hindbrain* and the *midbrain,*

forebrain

you would expect to find a _____ in man.

59. Since man is a more *complex* animal than a dogfish, however, you would

complex (or synonym)

expect man's forebrain to be more _____ than the forebrain of a dogfish.

60. We will largely skip the text explanation of how the simple three-part brain of the lower vertebrates has evolved into the complex human brain, and we will now discuss a cross section of the human brain. Remember, however,

hindbrain

that the human brain has developed from three parts—the _____ ,

forebrain (either order)

midbrain, and _____ —also found in other vertebrate animals.

61. The illustration of the human brain on page 19 is an adaptation of the illustration you will find in the text. In this programed unit you will begin to learn the names of the parts of the human brain shown here. Note that the text illustration, in addition to listing the labels shown here, provides lists of the various functions of each part of the brain. (These functions are also described in the text.) You will not learn all these functions from this programed unit, but you will get acquainted with some of them. (*Now look at the illustration and go on to the next frame. Refer to the illustration as necessary.*)

62. The first thing you should notice in the illustration is the *cerebrum*—the

forebrain

most highly developed portion of man's _____ brain. (*You can guess how to fill in this blank by remembering the three parts of the vertebrate brain. Which would be nearest the top of the human brain?*)

63. The surface of the *cerebrum* is highly wrinkled, or convoluted. The fact that this surface, known as the *cerebral cortex,* has so many wrinkles, or convolu-

greater

tions, means that the total surface area is much (*greater/smaller*) than it would be if the surface of the cerebrum were smooth.

64. Since the *cerebral cortex,* or surface, of the cerebrum is so large, it provides

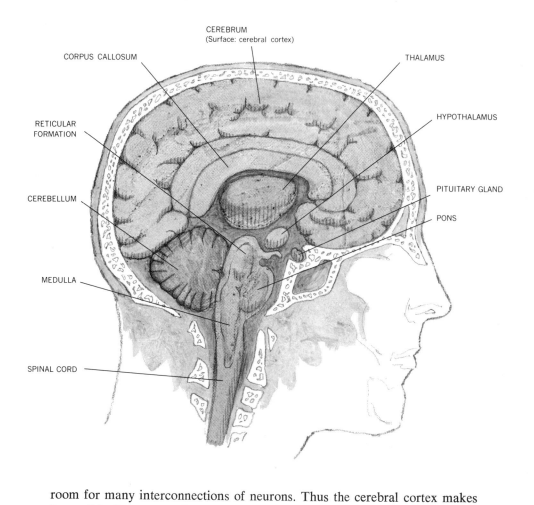

CEREBRUM
(Surface: cerebral cortex)

CORPUS CALLOSUM

THALAMUS

RETICULAR FORMATION

HYPOTHALAMUS

CEREBELLUM

PITUITARY GLAND

PONS

MEDULLA

SPINAL CORD

room for many interconnections of neurons. Thus the cerebral cortex makes it possible for man to learn, remember, think, and carry on many of the activities that distinguish him from the lower animals. You might expect the cerebral cortex of a fish to be (*more/less*) wrinkled, or convoluted, than that of a man.

less

cerebrum, cerebral

65. The _____ , with its wrinkled surface, the _____ cortex, is often called man's *"new brain"* to distinguish it from the primitive

forebrain

_____ *brain* of lower vertebrates.

new

66. Man's " _____ brain," the cerebrum with its surface, the cerebral cortex, makes possible many of the capacities that distinguish man from the lower animals. Man's capacity for *thinking* is based upon the development of his

cerebrum

_____ .

67. The central core of the brain includes parts of the primitive hindbrain and midbrain as well as other structures identified on the diagram. This central core is known as the *brain stem (not labeled on the illustration)*. Now locate

brain stem

the *hypothalamus,* which is part of this central core, or _____ _____ .

68. The *hypothalamus* functions as a thermostat and regulates such bodily functions as *temperature* and *metabolism*. When we begin to perspire after our

hypothalamus

temperature reaches a certain point, the _____ is presumably involved.

69. The hypothalamus, part of the central core, or brain stem, acts as a thermo-

the behaving organism   **19**

temperature

thinking (other answers
may be correct)

stat and controls such functions as _____ and metabolism. The cerebrum, by contrast, controls such higher activities as learning, remembering, and _____ .

hypothalamus

70. The general level of functioning characteristic of the healthy organism—such as maintaining a normal body temperature, a normal heart rate and normal blood pressure, and a standard concentration of salt in the blood—is called *homeostasis*. You recall that the _____ acts as a thermostat, or regulator of body temperature, and therefore helps the body maintain homeostasis as far as temperature is concerned.

homeostasis

71. If we are too warm we sweat, and if we are too cold we shiver. Our body attempts to maintain a state of normalcy or constancy. The term used to describe this optimal level of functioning is _____ .

thalamus

72. Now locate another part of the brain stem, the *thalamus*. This portion serves as a sensory relay station for impulses coming up from the spinal cord and down from the cerebrum. In any activity that requires the coordination of information from several receptors, the (*hypothalamus/thalamus*) is likely to be involved.

spinal cord

73. The thalamus is a sensory relay station for impulses coming up from the _____ _____ and down from the cerebrum.

hypothalamus

homeostasis

74. Such functions as temperature and metabolism are controlled by the _____ , which helps the body maintain a state of normalcy or constancy that is called _____ . Related to the functions of the hypothalamus are those of the *reticular formation* (*see illustration*), which, among other things, has to do with the state of *arousal* and *alertness* of the organism. When we move from a state of sleep

formation

to wakefulness, the reticular _____ is involved.

reticular formation

75. When we arouse from sleep, the _____ _____ is involved. Now locate the *cerebellum*, which controls *body balance, muscle tone,* and the ability to coordinate *voluntary movements,* such as those of our fingers and thumbs.

reticular formation

cerebellum

76. When we wake up in the morning, the _____ _____ is involved in the change from sleep to wakefulness. When we rub our eyes and step out of bed, however, the _____ is involved.

body

muscle

cerebellum

in front of

77. The part of the brain that makes it possible for us to maintain _____ balance and _____ tone and to coordinate voluntary movements is the _____ . The *pons,* which is located (*in front of/ behind*) the cerebellum, contains nerve fibers that connect the cerebellum with the brain stem.

hypothalamus

homeostasis

78. Temperature is regulated by the _____ , which helps the body maintain a state of normalcy that is called _____ .

79. Now locate the *medulla,* which helps control, among other activities, our

below

arousal (or alertness)

breathing, swallowing, and *digestion.* The medulla is located (*below/above*) the reticular formation, which has to do with the state of _____ of the organism.

80. Besides swallowing and digestion, another function controlled in part by the

breathing

cerebellum

pons

medulla is _____ . The brain structure that controls body balance is the _____ , which is connected to the brain stem by nerve fibers in the _____ .

medulla

cerebrum

81. Breathing is controlled by the _____ . Thinking is controlled by the _____ .

82. A top view of the brain, as distinguished from the side view shown here, would show that the *cerebrum* is divided into two halves, or hemispheres. (*Your text will make this clear.*) Now locate the *corpus callosum,* which contains fibers connecting the two cerebral hemispheres. The two cerebral

corpus callosum

hemispheres are connected by the _____ _____ .

83. Now locate the *pituitary* gland, which secretes its hormones directly into the

ductless (or endocrine)

blood stream and therefore must be a(n) _____ gland. It is often called the *"master gland"* because it exerts a complex and pervasive influence upon the other endocrine glands and upon many aspects of bodily *growth.*

pituitary, master

ductless (or endocrine)

84. The _____ gland is often referred to as the "_____ gland" because it exerts a strong influence upon the other _____ glands and upon many aspects of bodily growth.

85. Finally, locate the *spinal cord,* which provides conduction paths for *motor* impulses (those going to the effectors) and for *sensory* impulses (those com-

system

ing from the receptors). It, too, is part of the central nervous _____ .

cord, motor

86. The spinal _____ , which provides conduction paths for _____ impulses (to the effectors) and *sensory* impulses (from the receptors), is a

central

part of the _____ nervous system.

hypothalamus

87. The _____ controls such activities as temperature and metabolism. The process by which the body maintains an optimal level of

homeostasis, thalamus

functioning is known as _____ . The _____ is a sensory relay station to the cerebral cortex for impulses coming up from

reticular

the spinal cord and down from the cerebrum. The _____ formation has to do with the state of arousal or alertness of the organism, as in changing from sleep to wakefulness. Body balance, muscle tone, and

cerebellum

coordination are controlled by the _____ , which is

pons

connected to the brain stem by nerve fibers in the _____ . Such activities as breathing, swallowing, and digestion are controlled in part by the

medulla

_____ .

self-quiz

Select the alternative that best completes the thought. In some cases several answers are fairly satisfactory; you are to pick the *best* one.

_____ 1. The _____ gland is called the "master gland" because of its influence upon other endocrine glands.
   a. pituitary
   b. adrenal
   c. thymus
   d. parathyroid

_____ 2. The greatest change in the brain in higher vertebrate forms has been the development of
   a. the cerebral cortex
   b. a highly sensitized hypothalamus
   c. the size of the midbrain
   d. the limbic system

_____ 3. The transmission of a neural impulse along a nerve is best conceived as a(n)
   a. flow of electric current through a wire
   b. hydraulic process
   c. electrochemical process involving the interchange of ions
   d. timing device on an alarm

_____ 4. The parasympathetic division of the autonomic nervous system
   a. is dominant in excited emotional states
   b. tends to act as a unit
   c. tends to act in a piecemeal fashion, affecting one organ at a time
   d. usually acts in harmony with the sympathetic division

_____ 5. The antagonistic muscles
   a. are used in isometric exercises but are seldom used during normal activity
   b. are gradually disappearing through the evolutionary process
   c. are found in pairs and work so that if one of the pair contracts the other relaxes
   d. are utilized only when the organism is engaged in combat

_____ 6. An experiment by Penfield and Roberts revealed that vivid memories could be recalled when an association area of the temporal lobe was electrically stimulated. When this spot was surgically removed,
   a. the subject could no longer remember the event
   b. the subject could not remember common names of objects
   c. the subject had difficulty solving delayed-response problems
   d. the ability of the subject to remember the event was not destroyed

_____ 7. Experiments in which subjects have been kept in isolation under conditions of restricted stimulation have shown that
   a. inactivity has little effect upon the adaptive responses of a person
   b. active stimulation and response are necessary for normal functioning
   c. most people enjoyed the time spent under experimental conditions
   d. scores on intelligence tests increased markedly

_____ 8. Impulses are carried from the receptors to the central nervous system by
   a. efferent nerves
   b. afferent nerves
   c. connector neurons
   d. interstitial nerves

_____ 9. Damage to the motor area of the right hemisphere of the brain results in
   a. impairment of the left side of the body
   b. loss of the ability to tell the position of one's arms or hands with the eyes closed
   c. the inability to distinguish among tones
   d. impairment of the right side of the body

_____ 10. Transmission of a nerve impulse at a synapse is always in the direction of
   a. dendrite to axon or cell body
   b. dendrite to cell body
   c. axon to dendrite or cell body
   d. axon to dendrite

_____ 11. Physical reactions to psychological stress are

a. the result of a smoothly operating homeostatic mechanism
b. usually minor physiological changes that aid the organism in adapting to the environment
c. classified as psychosomatic disorders
d. most often localized in the limbic system

_____ 12. The neuron is the basic unit of the nervous system. Each neuron has
a. a cell body and a nerve fiber
b. glia cells and nerve fibers
c. a cell body, dendrites, and an axon
d. ganglia and axons

_____ 13. Myelinated fibers
a. are clearly present at birth because the infant acquires his sensory and motor abilities so rapidly
b. conduct impulses much more rapidly than nonmyelinated fibers
c. are insulated by the myelin sheath, which is very thick and provides good protection
d. constitute 30 percent of the muscle fibers

_____ 14. The adrenocortical hormones secreted by the adrenal cortex
a. produce many of the symptoms found in excited emotion
b. increase blood pressure
c. control salt and carbohydrate metabolism
d. quicken the rate of blood clotting

_____ 15. The human brain is composed of three concentric, interrelated structures:
a. a central core, an outer layer, and a new brain
b. an outer layer, an old brain, and the hypothalamus
c. a central core, the reticular formation, and an outer layer
d. a central core, an old brain, and an outer layer of new brain

_____ 16. The part of the brain that makes it possible for us to maintain body balance, muscle tone, and the ability to coordinate voluntary movements is the
a. medulla
b. thalamus
c. hypothalamus
d. cerebellum

_____ 17. The process by which the body adjusts to environmental conditions in order to maintain an optimal level of functioning is called
a. homeostasis
b. self-regulation
c. self-innervation
d. evolution

_____ 18. If an individual has extremely high muscle tone he is probably
a. athletic and energetic
b. on the verge of collapse
c. asleep
d. suffering from a condition known as spastic paralysis

_____ 19. The change in the state of arousal from waking to sleeping is controlled by the
a. adrenal cortex
b. hypothalamus
c. reticular formation
d. medulla

_____ 20. The role of the effectors in the reflex circuit is to
a. mediate the smooth-muscle and glandular responses within the body as well as responses to the environment
b. convert energy from the environment into chemical processes
c. act as a stimulus impinging upon the receptors
d. signal changes at the sense organ and regulate the amount of sensory input

key to self-quiz

20. a	15. d	10. a	5. c
19. c	14. c	9. a	4. c
18. d	13. b	8. b	3. c
17. a	12. c	7. b	2. a
16. d	11. c	6. d	1. a

class exercises

PHYSIOLOGICAL ASPECTS OF BEHAVIOR

introduction

The experiments described here will enable you to examine the general nature of two aspects of behavior, *reflex action* and *homeostasis*. *Reflex action* constitutes the simplest level of neural functioning and is generally of service to the organism in adaptation or protection. Thus we automatically blink our eyes when a foreign object endangers them. Likewise, we automatically slam our foot on the brake of our car when there is an impending collision. Such simple, automatic habits make up much of human behavior.

Another characteristic of the organism is its automatic striving to achieve and maintain an optimum equilibrium, or a "constant internal environment." Our biological functions may be thought of as regulatory mechanisms that enable the organism to maintain inner stability. This process has been described by Cannon as *homeostasis*. A simple illustration of this principle is the ability of the organism to develop antibodies to deal effectively with an infection in the blood stream.

A.   HOMEOSTASIS

equipment needed

Watch with second hand

procedure

Your class will be divided into two groups; half the class members will act as experimenters and the other half as subjects. Each experimenter is to take one subject's pulse for 1 minute. Record his normal pulse rate here: _____ . Now ask the subject to hop on one leg 100 times. Note the exact time when he finished the last hop here: _____ . Now take his accelerated pulse rate and write it here: _____ . Keep taking the subject's pulse until it returns to its normal rate. Write here the length of time it took the subject's homeostatic processes to bring about return to the normal pulse rate:

_____ .

treatment of data

Your instructor will ask the experimenters to submit the normal pulse rate, the accelerated pulse rate, and the time in minutes it took their subjects to achieve their normal pulse rates. The instructor will then give you these data for all the subjects tested so that you can fill in the chart on page 25.

questions for discussion

1. What was the average length of time it took the subjects to achieve homeostasis?

2. Was there much variability in normal pulse rate? In accelerated pulse rate?

3. How does this exercise demonstrate the principle of homeostasis?

4. After hopping on one foot 100 times, did most subjects desire to rest? Why?

5. What other examples of homeostasis can you think of?

B.   THE NORMAL KNEE-JERK REFLEX

equipment needed

None

procedure

Ask your subject to sit on a chair with one leg crossed over the other, so that his foot swings freely from the knee. Ask your subject to relax. Then briskly tap his leg just below the kneecap with the edge of your hand. Repeat several times.

RESULT: _____

_____

_____

Now vary the procedure slightly. Request your subject to tense the muscle of his swinging leg. Again briskly tap his leg.

RESULT: _____

_____

_____

Again, vary the procedure. Request your subject to try to prevent the knee jerk. Now briskly tap his leg.

RESULT: _____

_____

_____

This time ask your subject to relax his leg but to clasp his hands together behind his head and to pull on his clasped hands as hard as possible just before you briskly tap his leg.

RESULT: _____

_____

_____

questions for discussion

1. Were there differences in reflex activity during the four steps of this exercise?

2. If so, how do you explain the differences?

Subject	Normal pulse rate	Accelerated pulse rate	Number of minutes to achieve normal rate
1			
2			
3			
4			
5			
6			
7			
8			
9			
10			
11			
12			
13			
14			
15			
16			
17			
18			
19			
20			
21			
22			
23			
24			
25			
Sum			
Mean (sum divided by number of subjects)			

3 infancy and childhood

programed unit

1. An important concept in the study of development is *maturation*. Maturation refers to physical growth processes that result in orderly changes in behavior relatively independent of learning or experience. If certain behavior appears in all members of the same species at about the same time, without special training, we may suspect that the behavior is largely the result of

maturation   _____ .

2. Some species of birds reared in isolation, so that they never hear the song characteristic of their species, are still able to reproduce it properly at the appropriate stage of development. Thus we can reasonably say that singing

maturation   in these birds is controlled largely by _____ rather than by learning.

3. When behavior depends more upon physical *growth* processes than upon

maturation   *learning,* the process controlling the behavior is said to be _____ .

4. Maturation refers to growth processes that produce behavior changes that

learning (or experience)   are relatively independent of _____ . If the behavior change

learning   is due to training or experience, the process is called _____ rather than maturation.

5. The development of the fetus within the mother's body, which follows a fixed time schedule, provides a clear picture of what we mean by maturation. Fetal behavior, such as turning and kicking, follows an orderly sequence depending upon the growth stage of the fetus; fetal behavior is thus a result of

maturation   _____ .

6. Growth, of course, is not complete at birth. The motor development of the infant after birth follows such an orderly sequence (rolling over, sitting, standing, walking) that this behavior appears to be the result of continuing

growth, maturation

_____ processes, or _____ , rather than learning.

7. Maturation provides the readiness to learn, and most behavior depends upon both learning and maturation. A child will learn to talk only after he has

maturity (or synonym)
learning

reached the proper stage of _____ . The language he will speak is the one he hears, thus indicating the role of _____ .

8. Behavior during the early developmental years frequently reflects an inter-

maturation
learning (either order)

action between _____ and _____ .

9. Although the appearance of certain behavior may depend largely upon maturation, conditions of severe deprivation or unusual stimulation can influence the *rate* of *development*. Infants provided with a colorful mobile suspended above their crib will develop the eye-hand coordination necessary for reaching for an object earlier than infants who are kept in a bare crib with nothing to look at. Visually directed reaching is a response that develops in clearly specified maturational stages, but a more stimulating or enriched

rate

environment will accelerate the _____ of its development.

10. A deprived environment, on the other hand, can delay the rate of

development

_____ . Three-month-old monkeys raised from birth in darkness show serious deficiencies in visual behavior when first exposed to light. For example, they do not follow a moving object with their eyes or blink when threatened with a blow toward the face. In this case severe

deprivation

*dep*_____ of visual stimulation resulted in delayed

development

_____ .

11. Once the visually deprived monkeys were exposed to light, they acquired the appropriate behavior in a much shorter time than newborn monkeys. This

maturation

finding points up the importance of _____ .

maturation, learn

12. Both _____ and the opportunity to _____ are necessary for the development of visual-motor behavior.

13. Research on the effects of early experience suggests that there may be *critical periods* in development, during which favorable or unfavorable experiences may have lasting effects upon behavior. For example, monkeys that are raised in isolation for the first six months of life show abnormal social behavior as adults; they rarely interact with other monkeys and are difficult to mate. Regardless of the amount of subsequent exposure to other monkeys, these early-isolates never develop normal social behavior. For

critical

monkeys, then, the first six months of life may be a _____ period for the development of normal social behavior.

14. Some psychologists hypothesize that the first year of the human infant's life is critical for learning to trust other people. If the infant is cared for with warmth and affection, he learns that people are trustworthy; if he lacks affectionate care during his first year, he may grow up to distrust others. If

critical

trust

this hypothesis is true, the first year of life may be a _____

period for the development of _____ in others.

period

15. The critical _____ concept assumes that at a given stage of development some kinds of influences are unusually important. If they are lacking, later development may be stunted; if they are favorable, there is a

critical

greater chance for optimal development. Failures at a _____ period of development can be made up, if at all, only with great difficulty.

16. Puppies isolated between three and seven weeks of age grow fearful of both dogs and people, while isolation earlier or later does not have much influence on their behavior. This example illustrates the concept of a

critical period

_____ _____ .

17. Another way of looking at human development assumes that the individual passes through definable *stages* as he grows up. When we talk about infancy, childhood, adolescence, and adulthood, we are talking broadly about suc-

stages

cessive _____ in development.

periods

18. The concepts of stages and critical _____ are related but not identical. A failure in development at one stage need not be critical for future development.

19. For example, there is a period of time in the development of the young child when he is maturationally ready to learn to talk. (Age two to four is the time of most rapid language development.) Suppose the child were raised by deaf-mutes during this period and exposed to language for the first time as a teen-ager. If he learned to talk as a teen-ager, although with considerable difficulty, we would say that the two- to four-year period constituted a

stage

_____ of language development. If he never learned to talk despite

critical

intensive training, we would say that this period was a _____ period for language development.

20. The Swiss psychologist Piaget has proposed that the child progresses through a fixed sequence of stages in his *cognitive development*. The first stage, from

cognitive

birth to two years, is called the *sensorimotor stage* of _____

sensorimotor

development. During the *sensori*_____ stage the child does not use language or symbols but explores his environment by means of his senses and motor activities. At first he can study objects only visually, but he soon learns to reach for and explore them with his fingers and his mouth.

stage

21. One of the many things the child learns during the sensorimotor _____ is that an *object* is *constant,* or enduring, regardless of the angle from which it is viewed. His bottle is a source of milk whether it is presented with the nipple toward him or is seen propped against the side of the crib. His rattle

object

does not disappear when hidden by a blanket but is a constant _____ that will reappear when he lifts the blanket.

22. The concept of object constancy is achieved, according to Piaget, during the

sensorimotor

_____ stage of development, which occurs in the

two

first _____ years of life.

development	**23.** A later stage in cognitive _____ is called the stage of *preoperational thought,* which occurs between the ages of two and seven years. The child now possesses language and can begin to deal with problems by means of symbols and concepts. Objects become symbols that represent classes of things.
preoperational symbols thought, seven	**24.** During the stage of *pre*_____ thought, the child begins to use *sym*_____ to conceptualize his environment. The stage of preoperational _____ covers the period from two to _____ years.
preoperational has not	**25.** One of the concepts the child develops toward the end of the stage of *pre*_____ thought is that of *conservation;* he learns that the amount of a substance does not change—that is, it is conserved—when the substance is divided into parts or placed in different-sized containers. If a four year old is shown two identical short jars containing what he acknowledges to be an equal amount of beans and watches while the contents of one jar are poured into a tall, cylindrical jar, he will say that the tall jar contains more beans. The four year old (*has/has not*) attained the concept of conservation.
conservation	**26.** A six- or seven-year-old child presented with the same situation will say that the contents of the short and tall jars are equal. He has attained the concept of _____ .
conservation	**27.** If a child says that a ball of clay contains the same amount of material when it is rolled into a sausage shape as when it is a sphere, he has achieved the concept of _____ .
preoperational thought two, seven	**28.** The development of the concept of conservation occurs during the stage of _____ _____ , which covers the ages of _____ to _____ . Later stages of cognitive development during which the child's thought processes gradually approach those of an adult are discussed in the text.
are not	**29.** Piaget's stages (*are/are not*) critical periods because, although cognitive processes usually develop in the sequence specified, behavior that fails to occur at a particular age owing to lack of appropriate stimulation can occur later.
cognitive personality	**30.** Piaget's stages are concerned with _____ development. Other theorists, such as Freud and Erikson, have proposed stage theories dealing with *personality development.* Freud proposed five stages of _____ development that have to do with deriving pleasure from different parts of the body at different ages. He called these *psychosexual* stages, using a very broad definition of sexuality.
psychosexual oral	**31.** The first of Freud's _____ stages is the *oral* stage, during which the infant derives pleasure from stimulation of the lips and mouth region, as in nursing or thumb-sucking. According to Freud, frustration during feeding may lead to *fixation* at the _____ stage. By "fixation"

he meant that problems associated with unsatisfied needs at this stage might persist into later life.

32. If an adult who was severely frustrated as an infant during nursing shows a continual need for activities such as over-eating, smoking, and gum-chewing,

fixated, oral   Freud would say he was *fix*_____ at the _____ stage of psychosexual development.

33. During the oral stage the child derives pleasure from stimulation of the

lips, mouth, psychosexual   _____ and _____ region. Subsequent stages of *psycho*_____ development are the *anal* stage, during which the child secures pleasure from withholding and expelling feces; the *phallic* stage, in which gratification is obtained from fondling the sex organs; the *latent* stage, during which the elementary-school child turns his interests toward the environment so that sexual interests are no longer active; and the *genital* stage, at which point the sex organs are beginning to mature and the adolescent becomes interested in heterosexual relationships.

34. The second stage of psychosexual development, in which the child derives

anal   pleasure from withholding and expelling feces, is called the _____ stage.

35. As you might expect, the anal stage occurs during the second year of life while the parents are concerned with toilet training. According to Freud, a

fixation   rigid and harsh approach to toilet training may lead to *fix*_____ at

anal, psychosexual   the _____ stage of _____ development.

oral   **36.** The first stage of psychosexual development is the _____ stage, the

anal   second is the _____ stage, and the third is the *phallic stage,* during which the child derives pleasure from fondling the genitals.

37. If the parents are overly upset and punitive when they discover their four year old masturbating, we might expect the child to have some problems dur-

phallic, psychosexual   the _____ stage of _____

development   _____ .

38. It is also during the phallic stage that the *Oedipal* stage may occur. The Oedipal stage refers to a period during which the child develops a sexual interest in the parent of the opposite sex. The four-year-old boy who professes that he wants to marry "mommy" when he grows up and tries to compete with his father for the mother's attention is probably going through

Oedipal   the _____ stage, which is concurrent with the phallic stage of

psychosexual   _____ development.

Freud   **39.** The first three psychosexual stages of development proposed by _____

oral, anal, phallic   are the _____ , _____ , and _____ stages. Oedipal

phallic   feelings may appear during the _____ stage. Following these stages in the preschool child, there is a *latent* stage during which the elementary-school youngster's sexual interests are said to be dormant, or latent, and his concerns are directed toward the environment and the acquisition of

latent

knowledge and skills. The _____ stage lasts until puberty, at which point heterosexual interests arise and the genital stage begins.

psychosexual

40. Freud's theory of _____ stages has had considerable influence upon theories of personality, but it is not accepted by most psychologists as a precise statement of development. Erikson, a later psychoanalyst, proposed a theory of *psychosocial* stages of development that is con-

sexual

cerned with problems of *social* development rather than _____ development.

psychosocial

41. Erikson's stages of _____ development are con-

social

cerned with the _____ problems encountered at different ages. For example, Erikson claims that during the first year of life the infant learns to *trust or mistrust* other people, depending upon how well his needs are attended to during this period when he is helpless and totally dependent.

42. The infant's first social contact occurs while he is being fed. If the experience is a pleasant one and his needs are satisfied, he learns to associate his mother

trust

with satisfaction and relaxation. He learns that he can *tr*_____ other people to satisfy his needs.

43. If, on the other hand, the feeding situation is unpleasant and hurried, with the infant remaining hungry and uncomfortable much of the time, he may

mistrust

learn to *mis*_____ others as a source of satisfaction. We can see how

first

these experiences during the _____ year of life might well lead to a

trust, mistrust
(either order)

basic attitude of _____ or _____ toward people later in life.

44. During the second year of life the child has his first real encounter with discipline and self-control in connection with toilet training and in learning what not to touch or investigate as he begins walking. According to Erikson

psychosocial

the *psycho*_____ problem at this stage is one of *autonomy* and *self-control* versus feelings of *shame* and *self-doubt*.

45. The psychosocial stage during the second year of life concerns autonomy and

self-control, self-

_____-_____ versus feelings of shame and _____-

doubt

_____ . If parental discipline is warm but firm, the child learns pride in controlling his own impulses. If the parents try to discipline by shaming the child and making him feel that he does not live up to their expectations,

shame, doubt

he is likely to develop feelings of _____ and self-_____ .

46. Erikson has proposed a number of later stages that are concerned with

psychosocial

_____ problems. Freud's stages, in contrast, are

psychosexual
cognitive (or
intellectual)

concerned with _____ development, while Piaget's

stages have to do with _____ development.

47. We noted that the child's first social contact occurs while he is being fed. It would be reasonable to assume that the child's close attachment to his

food (or milk)

mother during the early years occurs because she provides his _____ . However, experiments with infant monkeys cast some doubt on this assumption. If a monkey is raised from birth in a cage containing two artificial "mothers," one constructed of wire but with a nipple providing milk and the other covered with soft terry cloth but with no milk supply, the monkey will spend most of its time clinging to the terry-cloth "mother."

48. The infant monkey will show greater attachment to the cuddly, terry-cloth

milk (or food)
is not

"mother" despite the fact that she is not a source of _____ . These results indicate that attachment to the mother (*is/is not*) solely dependent upon the fact that she is a source of food.

49. In humans, attachment to the mother becomes most apparent at the age of seven or eight months. Before this time the infant will usually smile at anyone who smiles at him. But beginning at about seven months he will evidence fear at the appearance of a strange face and frequently cry when he is separated from his mother. *Fear of strangers* thus appears at about the age

seven

of _____ months.

50. Prior to seven months the infant will smile indiscriminately at anyone. His responses during this time are not considered to be truly social. As he becomes able to discriminate between those who are familiar and those who

strange

are _____ , he begins to restrict his social responses to those who are familiar.

51. Bobby's mother is proud of her happy, friendly baby who smiles and coos whenever her friends come to admire him. She becomes upset when Bobby suddenly begins to cry when guests appear and frets whenever mother leaves the room. Bobby's mother would be less concerned if she realized that her son's apparent personality change is a natural stage of fear of

strangers
discriminate
seven

_____ , which occurs in most infants as they learn to

*dis*_____ between familiar and unfamiliar faces. We might guess that Bobby is (*five/seven*) months old.

fear

52. Although children soon outgrow the period of _____ of strangers, attachment to the parents and other members of the family remains close during the preschool years. Because the parents are the dominant figures in the child's life, they serve as models, or *identification figures,* for the child to copy. When we say that a child *identifies* with his parents, we mean that he unconsciously assumes many of their values and patterns of behavior as his own.

53. When Sarah bathes and diapers her doll using the same mannerisms and tone of voice that her mother uses in caring for her baby brother, we may assume

identifies

that she _____ with her mother.

54. When Tommy staggers around in his father's fishing boots casting an imaginary line into the bathtub, we may assume that Tommy's father serves as an

identification

_____ figure.

55. When we say that a person is identifying with another person, we mean that

like (or synonym)

whether he knows it or not, he is trying to become _____ the other person.

56. Identification is largely an *unconscious process*. It differs from conscious imitation, as in imitating someone who is trying to teach you to roller skate, in that you are largely (*aware/unaware*) that you are identifying with the person.

unaware

57. Unlike conscious imitation, identification is largely an _____ process.

unconscious

58. One of the major areas of behavior in which children identify with their parents is in the acquisition of *sex-role standards*. Sex-role _____ refer to the ways of behaving that a culture considers appropriate for men and women.

standards

59. A child acquires his *sex-*_____ _____ by identifying with the parent of the same sex. If a culture expects aggressive behavior from its male members, then aggression is a _____-_____ _____ for men in that culture.

sex-role standards

sex-role standard

60. A girl acquires her sex-role standards by identifying with her mother; a boy acquires his _____-_____ _____ by _____ with his father.

sex-role standards

identifying

61. Sex-role identification develops as the child perceives himself as similar to the parent of the (*same/opposite*) sex.

same

62. If a girl's mother is aggressive and domineering and rejects the sex-role standards of her culture, we would expect the girl to have difficulty in developing the appropriate sex-role *id*_____ .

identification

63. Many personal qualities, however, are not sex-typed. A sense of humor, personal warmth, and many moral qualities are shared by both men and women. These are *personal* or *non-sex-role identifications*. Personal or _____-_____-_____ identifications may be learned from either parent.

non-sex-role

64. A girl may acquire her father's dry sense of humor, and a boy may learn consideration from his mother. These are _____-_____-_____ identifications.

non-sex-role

65. Characteristics and behavior that are not sex-typed and may be learned from either parent are called _____-_____-_____ identifications. Learning behavior that is appropriate to one's sex is called _____-_____ identification.

non-sex-role

sex-role

self-quiz

Select the alternative that best completes the thought. In some cases several answers are fairly satisfactory; you are to pick the *best* one.

_____ **1.** The assumption that there is continuity from the past to the present, so that the present can be understood in terms of

the past, is most important in understanding
a. basic science
b. applied science
c. the developmental viewpoint
d. critical periods

2. The term "critical period" in development refers to
a. the continuity from the past to the present
b. the time when each individual goes through a period of criticizing all he finds around him
c. a fixed time period during which the organism is maximally sensitive to particular learning experiences
d. the idea that the timing and patterning of changes, beyond birth, are relatively independent of experience

3. Which is the correct order of Freud's stages of psychosexual development?
a. oral, latent, anal, phallic, genital
b. oral, anal, phallic, latent, genital
c. phallic, oral, anal, latent, genital
d. latent, oral, genital, anal, phallic

4. Infant rhesus monkeys were reared in darkness except for brief periods each day when they were exposed to light while wearing translucent, plastic goggles. When first exposed to light without goggles, they
a. were able to follow moving objects with their eyes
b. made appropriate reactions to threatened blows to the face
c. showed deficiencies in visual behavior but acquired the appropriate responses more quickly than newborn monkeys
d. were never able to perform as well as normal monkeys

5. Human infants who were provided with an enriched or more stimulating environment
a. showed accelerated development even when they were not maturationally ready
b. showed no more progress than the infants in a regular environment
c. were retarded in their development
d. showed that too much stimulation provided too early may be upsetting

6. If one of two equally large balls of clay is rolled into a sausage shape, a child of four will say that
a. the round one contains more
b. both are the "same"
c. both are the "same" only if he has seen the experimenter roll the second ball into a sausage
d. the longer one contains more

7. Correlations between stress in infancy and adult height in men showed that
a. there was no significant relationship
b. males stressed in infancy averaged several inches taller as adults than those not stressed
c. the Spartan explanation could be completely ruled out
d. adult stature appears to be affected most when the stress occurs later in childhood

8. A theory of stages in cognitive development has been proposed by
a. Erikson
b. Freud
c. Piaget
d. Kohlberg

9. Maturational principles apply to
a. prenatal development
b. the predictable, or orderly, changes in behavior during infancy
c. some changes in behavior during adolescence and adulthood
d. all of the above

10. The practice that is perhaps most harmful to development is
a. fondling
b. stress
c. stimulation
d. neglect

11. The best way to handle the feeding of an infant is to
a. satisfy the infant's hunger without undue delay and make the experience a pleasant one
b. let the infant cry so that he will learn to handle frustrating situations
c. bottle feed the baby
d. breast feed the baby

12. The best age to begin toilet training
a. is at three to four months

b. has not been determined

c. is at eighteen to twenty months

d. is independent of the child's maturational readiness

____ **13.** When young monkeys were kept in isolation but permitted to feed from and cling to artificial mothers, it was discovered that

a. monkeys raised in this sort of isolation develop normal social behavior

b. the monkeys grow up to be ideal mothers

c. the monkeys were most attached to the "mother" that was the food source

d. the monkeys were most attached to the "mother" that was soft and cuddly

____ **14.** Which of the following is detrimental to the son's adoption of his masculine role?

a. perceiving the father as supportive

b. perceiving the father as exercising power

c. the presence of a mother who is more dominant than the father

d. finding some objective basis for being similar to his father

____ **15.** Which of the following variables has the least influence upon speech development?

a. sex of the individual

b. weight of the individual

c. number of siblings

d. social class

____ **16.** The use of physical punishment by the parents

a. provides their child with an aggressive model to imitate

b. produces children with fewer feeding problems

c. produces children with high self-esteem

d. produces friendly children

____ **17.** The process by which the individual gradually comes to see himself as appropriately masculine or feminine is called

a. negativism

b. sex-role identification

c. psychosexual development

d. sibling rivalry

____ **18.** The child who is separated from his parents during early childhood

a. shows behavior unlike that of the infant monkey taken away from its mother

b. although initially disturbed, always makes an adequate adjustment

c. shows distress, then becomes withdrawn and may also show physical retardation

d. has a greater chance of becoming famous

____ **19.** The majority of the black children in a study involving preference for dolls of different colors

a. liked the brown doll best

b. liked the white doll best

c. rejected the prevailing stereotypes of their own race

d. proudly identified themselves as looking like the brown doll

____ **20.** A personality characteristic of a first-born child is that he

a. is responsible

b. is sociable and well liked

c. is spoiled

d. scores lower on intelligence and ability tests

key to self-quiz

20. a	15. b	10. d	5. d
19. b	9. d	8. c	4. c
18. c	13. d	8. c	3. b
17. b	12. c	7. b	2. c
16. a	11. a	6. d	1. c

individual and class exercise

BIRTH ORDER AND PERSONALITY CHARACTERISTICS

introduction

Research has shown that some aspects of an individual's personality are related to his order of birth. First-born or only children, in particular, tend to differ from other children. The text discusses several factors that make the first-born or only child's position in the family unique. This exercise will show whether personality differences among your acquaintances bear any relationship to birth order.

equipment needed

None

procedure

Write the names of ten people of your own sex whom you know quite well in the spaces provided at the left of the data sheet (page 37). Now rate each person on the personality traits listed at the bottom of the data sheet. Note that a rating of 1 means that the person possesses the trait to only a slight degree, while a rating of 5 indicates that he possesses the trait to a high degree. For example, a rating of 5 on the trait of "aggression" indicates a very dominant, aggressive person; a rating of 1 would describe someone who was quite meek and unassertive. After deciding which number best describes the aggressive or non-aggressive nature of your first subject, enter this number in the first column next to his name. Now rate him according to the remaining three traits. Carry out the same procedure for each acquaintance. Try to avoid the common tendency of rating everyone toward the middle of the scale.

treatment of data

After you have rated each of your ten acquaintances on all four traits, find out his birth order (if you do not already know it) and turn to the data tabulation sheet on page 38. List the name of each first-born or only child in the appropriate column and enter his rating for each trait. Do the same for those who were later born. Add the ratings for each trait and enter the total at the bottom of each column. Divide each total by the number of subjects in the column to find the average rating. Bring this sheet with you to class. Your instructor will tabulate the average ratings obtained by each class member for the four traits.

questions for discussion

1. Is there any difference in the average ratings for first-born or only children as compared to those for the later born? If so, which traits are most affected by birth order?

2. How do the circumstances of the study limit interpretation of the results? That is, might different results have been obtained if the subjects had been selected from the population at large rather than from a group of college students?

3. What are some of the factors stemming from the individual's position in the family that might explain the obtained results?

DATA SHEET

Name	Personality traits			
	Aggression	Conscientiousness	Intellectual ability	Sociability
1.				
2.				
3.				
4.				
5.				
6.				
7.				
8.				
9.				
10.				

Aggression

1. Very meek
2.
3. Moderately aggressive
4.
5. Very aggressive

Conscientiousness

1. Careless in attention to responsibilities
2.
3. Moderately conscientious
4.
5. Very conscientious

Intellectual ability

1. In lower 10% of class
2.
3. Average
4.
5. In upper 10% of class

Sociability

1. Withdrawn; a loner
2.
3. Moderately sociable
4.
5. Very outgoing and sociable

DATA TABULATION FOR BIRTH-ORDER STUDY

First-born or only child

Name	Aggression	Conscientiousness	Intellectual ability	Sociability
Total				
Average				

Later-born child

Name	Aggression	Conscientiousness	Intellectual ability	Sociability
Total				
Average				

4 adolescence and adulthood

programed unit

changes

1. *Adolescence,* the transitional period from childhood to adulthood, is a phase of development marked by *changes.* The most striking *ch*_____ are bodily changes in the *sex characteristics* and in *rate of growth.*

sex

rate

2. Mary is a typical thirteen-year-old adolescent girl. We would expect her to experience striking bodily changes in _____ characteristics and in _____ of growth.

changes

sex characteristics

rate of growth

3. The bodily _____ that occur during adolescence involve both _____ _____ and _____ _____ _____ .

primary

4. It is customary to distinguish between two kinds of sex characteristics. The *primary sex characteristics* are the *reproductive organs,* both internal and external. The testicles of the male would be a _____ sex characteristic.

secondary

5. The *secondary sex characteristics* are those physical features that distinguish a mature man from a mature woman in ways not directly related to the reproductive organs. A beard distinguishes a male from a female, but it is not directly related to the reproductive organs; therefore it is a _____ sex characteristic.

primary

6. The growth of the uterus in an adolescent girl is a change in a _____ sex characteristic, since a mature uterus is necessary for reproduction.

secondary

7. The deepening of the voice quality that occurs in adolescent boys is a _____ sex characteristic, since it is not directly related to the re-

secondary

productive organs. Breast development in girls is also a _____ sex characteristic.

8. While most secondary sex characteristics differ in males and females, some changes, such as the appearance of pubic hair, are common to both sexes. Since pubic hair is not essential to reproduction, it is considered a

secondary

_____ sex characteristic.

Primary

9. _____ sex characteristics refer to changes that take place in the

Secondary

reproductive organs, both internal and external. _____ sex characteristics refer to those physical features that distinguish a mature man from a mature woman in ways not directly related to the

reproductive

_____ organs.

10. The period of adolescence that is accompanied by the most rapid changes in height and weight and by the maturing of the primary and secondary sex characteristics is called *pubescence*. Margaret, who is eleven, suddenly begins to experience a rapid increase in height and weight and to develop breasts.

pubescence

She is in that stage of adolescence called _____ .

11. Pubescence lasts about two years and culminates in *puberty*, which is marked by *menstruation* in girls and the appearance of live *sperm cells* in the urine of boys. Puberty marks the end of the period of rapid growth known as

pubescence

_____ .

Puberty

12. _____ is the culmination of the two-year period of rapid growth

pubescence

and sexual development known as _____ .

menstruation

13. Puberty is marked by _____ in girls and the ap-

sperm cells

pearance of live _____ _____ in the urine of boys.

14. The average age for menstruation has dropped from 17 in 1830 to 12.6 in

puberty

1960. It appears, then, that _____ now occurs earlier for girls than it did 150 years ago.

15. Boys and girls average the same size until around age eleven, when the girls suddenly spurt ahead in both height and weight. Girls thus enter

pubescence

_____ , the period of marked physical growth, earlier than boys.

16. Girls tend to mature *two* years earlier than boys. The average age of maximum growth rate is twelve for girls and fourteen for boys. Thus if a girl achieves her maximum growth rate at age ten, she is more mature than the average girl her age, who achieves maximum growth rate at the age of

twelve

_____ years. A boy whose maximum growth rate occurs at age

more

thirteen is (*more/less*) mature than the average boy his age.

two

17. Although girls tend to achieve their maximum growth rate _____ years earlier than boys, there are large individual differences in rate of maturation. Some boys will mature earlier than some girls.

more

18. Boys and girls who mature markedly later than their classmates tend to have adjustment problems. Bob is a late maturer. He will probably have (*more/less*) difficulty in adjusting than his early-maturing classmates.

19. The bodily changes and newly intensified sexual urges that accompany *sexual maturity* are often a source of adolescent conflict. Some anthropologists suggest that one reason adolescents in our culture experience "storm and stress" is that our culture imposes too many *taboos* on *sexual expression* and that

sexual

marriage is postponed beyond the time when _____ maturity is attained.

20. Studies of some nonliterate cultures in which greater sexual freedom is permitted show that in these more permissive cultures the transition from childhood to adulthood is relatively *smooth*. This evidence suggests that our cul-

sexual

ture imposes too many taboos on _____ expression.

expression
smooth
taboos (or synonym)

21. Some nonliterate cultures permit freedom of sexual _____

and the transition from childhood to adulthood is relatively *sm_____* ,

whereas our culture imposes many _____ on sexual expression. Cultural differences may account in part for some of the "storm and stress" of the adolescent period.

22. Emancipation from parental authority and from emotional dependence upon parents begins in childhood, but the process of emancipation is greatly accelerated during adolescence. Adolescents tend to be *ambivalent* about *independence*. They want the freedom to do as they please, but are not always willing to assume the responsibilities that go along with being independent. David plans a beach party without consulting his parents but expects them to

ambivalent

provide the food and transportation. He is _____ in his attitude toward independence.

independence

23. Adolescents tend to be ambivalent about _____ .

24. If parents insist upon close supervision and control of a youngster during adolescence, they are apt to produce an adolescent who continues his dependence and is unable to make his own decisions. A certain amount of

independence

freedom is thus necessary for the development of _____ .

25. Studies have shown that a *"democratic* family," in which the adolescent is allowed a fair degree of autonomy and is included in important decisions, produces a more capable and well-adjusted youngster than an *"authoritarian* family," in which rules are arbitrarily set and freedom of behavior is limited. Parents who wish to encourage the development of a well-adjusted adoles-

democratic

cent, therefore, would seek to establish a(n) _____ family.

26. In their rebellion against authority some adolescents engage in activities that seriously violate the law. *Juvenile delinquency* is a major social problem. When we note that more than half of the serious crimes in the United States are committed by fifteen to nineteen year olds, we acknowledge the problem

delinquency

of juvenile _____ .

juvenile	**27.** It is customary to distinguish between two types of _____ delinquency. *Social delinquency* expresses itself in *gang activity* in which a group of adolescents engages in such activities as car theft, the use of illegal drugs, and robbery. Although the behavior of the gang violates the law, it may not violate the standards of the social group to which the adolescents belong.
gang	**28.** Social delinquency expresses itself in _____ activity, which may not violate the standards of the social group to which the gang belongs.
social delinquency	**29.** A group of adolescents from a slum neighborhood burglarizes for cash and salable items and uses the money to purchase marijuana and heroin. This type of delinquency would be called _____ _____ .
social delinquency	**30.** A gang from one neighborhood beats up two members of another gang. This is an example of _____ _____ .
gang	**31.** *Individual delinquency,* on the other hand, may appear in "good" families and neighborhoods as well as "bad" ones. The adolescent is not acting according to the standards of his group or _____ but in response to some *personal problem* of his own.
individual	**32.** Tom's father is a doctor, and both his parents are highly respected in the community. His theft of valuables from neighboring houses would be called _____ delinquency.
standards personal	**33.** Tom does not appear to be behaving according to the _____ of his social group; his actions are probably motivated by _____ problems.
social delinquency	**34.** When delinquent behavior is typical of the neighborhood in which one lives or the group with which one associates, it is called _____ _____ .
delinquency individual	**35.** Social _____ expresses the frustration of many adolescents from low-income and minority neighborhoods at their inability to attain jobs and status. Delinquency not associated with gang behavior or cultural conflict is referred to as _____ delinquency.
role	**36.** As the individual progresses through adolescence into adulthood, he learns to assume the appropriate *sex role.* Certain differences in behavior are expected of men and women, although it is difficult to determine whether the behavioral differences are to be attributed to *biological differences* or to *cultural influences.* The expectation in our culture that men should be more aggressive than women is an example of a sex _____ .
	37. Studies of nonliterate societies reveal the *wide range* of possibilities in the behavior of the two sexes. Men and women in the Arapesh tribe of New Guinea, for instance, are quite similar in their passivity, gentleness, mildness, and domesticity. From our point of view, both sexes exhibit behavior we would consider *feminine.* We might infer that these behavioral differences are

cultural

to be attributed to c_____ *influences* rather than to *biological differences.*

range

cultural

38. In nonliterate societies there is a wide _____ of possible behavior in sex roles; these variations are largely attributable to _____ influences rather than to biological differences.

39. Men and women of the Arapesh tribe exhibit behavior that is considered

feminine

_____ in our own culture.

40. Both men and women in the Mundugumor tribe of New Guinea tend to be ruthless, aggressive, and violent. From our point of view, both sexes are quite *masculine*. This sex-role behavior contrasts with that of the Arapesh tribe, in which both sexes tend to manifest traits that our culture would con-

feminine

sider _____ .

feminine

41. Whereas men and women of the Arapesh tribe are _____ by our standards of behavior, the men and women of the Mundugumor tribe

masculine

are quite _____ from our point of view.

42. The *sex roles* of the Tchambuli tribe of New Guinea offer the most dramatic contrast to those of our own culture. The Tchambuli *woman* tends to be the aggressive partner, the manager of business affairs, and the dominant person

roles

in the family. In other words, in terms of our own culture, sex _____ of the Tchambuli are reversed.

43. The aggressive partner and dominant person in the Tchambuli family is the

woman (or wife)

masculine

feminine

_____ . In the Mundugumor tribe both sexes manifest traits we con-

sider _____ . In the Arapesh tribe both sexes manifest traits we consider _____ .

44. Thus we see that cultural influences are more important than biological dif-

sex

ferences in determining what are considered appropriate _____ roles.

cultural influences

45. Traditionally men have been doctors and women nurses. This division of labor is the result of (*cultural influences/biological differences*).

46. *Problems in adjustment* may arise when cultural pressures force an individual into a role for which he is not suited or prevent him from achieving in a role he desires. A woman who prefers to forgo marriage and child rearing in order to devote all her energies to a career may have problems in

adjustment

_____ .

47. The adoption of appropriate sex roles by men and women is but one factor that may contribute to *success in marriage*. Many marriages are not successful; consequently, we are concerned with those factors in the early life of the individual that make one person better suited for marriage than another. Events that occur early in life are important factors in predicting success in

marriage

_____ .

48. The happiness of the parents' marriage is a factor predictive of marital success. Frank and Margaret both come from families in which the parents were happily married. We can predict that their marriage will be (*more/less*) successful than average.

more

49. The best single predictor of marital happiness is happiness in childhood. Those who recall a *happy childhood* are more likely to have a successful marriage than those whose childhoods were *un_____* .

unhappy

50. Ted had an unhappy childhood. His chances of achieving a happy marriage are (*fewer/greater*) than Jim's, who reports that his childhood was happy.

fewer

51. Another factor that is related to success in marriage is the age of the individuals at the time they marry. Statistics show that the divorce rate is higher for those who marry before they are twenty-one. A certain amount of maturity is necessary for the individual to cope with the demands of married life and parenthood. Consequently, it is not surprising that those who marry in their teens will have a (*higher/lower*) divorce rate than those who marry after the age of twenty.

higher

52. A high school student who hopes to escape from an unhappy home life by marrying will most likely find that his marriage is _____ .

unsuccessful (or unhappy)

53. Productivity in one's life work is an important contributor to one's happiness. As we grow older our abilities change. Performers who depend upon strength, speed, or precision of movement tend to reach their peaks of skill between the ages of twenty-five and twenty-nine. Tennis champions, for example, tend to be (*older/younger*) than thirty.

younger

54. The *peak of productivity* in the arts and sciences occurs later. In most fields the age of maximum productivity is between thirty and forty. Mathematicians and psychologists, for example, reach their peak of _____ before they are forty.

productivity

55. As we grow older we face new problems. There are two main theories of how successful aging is achieved. One is called the *activity* theory, which, as one might guess, accents the importance of _____ in one's life.

activity

56. Because forced retirement curtails the activity of an aging person, the _____ theory stresses the idea that a person who is approaching retirement should make plans to turn to other interests so that he may remain active and view himself as continuing to be significant.

activity

57. Because older people tend to have less energy, this theory suggests that activity be continued on a *part*-time basis—that plans be made for _____*ial* retirement.

partial

58. When a person plans for partial retirement, or plans to continue his activity in a different field after retirement, he is acting in compliance with the _____ theory of successful aging.

activity

59. The second theory of successful aging, the *disengagement* theory, assumes that as a person grows older he views himself differently and thus can make his best adjustment through gradually withdrawing from active participation and responsibility. When one chooses to relieve himself of some responsibility and gradually withdraws from social activity, he favors the

disengagement   _____ theory.

disengagement   **60.** The gradual withdrawal emphasized by the _____ theory is not forced upon the individual but is chosen as a means of adjusting to his new *view* of himself as he grows older. Because the older person has a

view   different self-perception, or _____ of himself, he may choose to withdraw from active participation and responsibility.

61. The theory that stresses the importance of an older person's remaining

activity   *active,* though perhaps at a less intense level, is the _____ theory.

62. A contrasting theory assumes that the older person views himself differently and may choose to gradually withdraw, or *disengage* himself, from responsi-

disengagement   bility. This is called the _____ theory.

63. Both theories of successful aging would appeal to different people because of differing psychological needs and physical requirements. The problems of adjustment to aging are indeed serious when a person who wishes to remain

active   _____ is forcibly retired, or when an ailing person who wishes to

disengage   _____ himself must carry on in business because of financial needs.

self-quiz

Select the alternative that best completes the thought. In some cases several answers are fairly satisfactory; you are to pick the *best* one.

_____ **1.** Changes in the primary sex characteristics refer to
a. changes in the reproductive organs
b. a marked change in voice
c. the growth of a beard
d. an increase in blood pressure and heart rate

_____ **2.** Puberty refers to the period of time
a. before pubescence
b. during pubescence
c. following pubescence
d. that marks the beginning of old age

_____ **3.** The relationship between the age when maturity is reached and adult height reveals that

a. the early maturer tends to grow taller than the late maturer
b. the late maturer ultimately grows taller than the early maturer
c. adult height is more closely related to intelligence
d. very little correlation exists between the two variables

_____ **4.** On the average girls reach puberty during their _____ year.
a. eleventh
b. twelfth
c. thirteenth
d. fourteenth

_____ **5.** Boys who mature early as opposed to those who mature late
a. have poorer self-concepts
b. may find that too much is expected of them

c. are less popular with their class-mates

d. have strong dependency needs

_____ 6. The growth pattern reveals

a. a regular, even rate of growth from infancy

b. that boys mature earlier than girls

c. that the age of maximum growth is the year just before puberty

d. that boys always maintain a height and weight advantage over girls

_____ 7. For most men and women the early adult years are

a. the years of least energy and productivity

b. still filled with adjustment problems carried over from adolescence

c. filled with restrictions imposed by society

d. viewed as the period of greatest happiness

_____ 8. In Western societies the interval between sexual maturity and adult status has

a. decreased because of late maturity

b. decreased because of early marriages

c. increased because of early maturity and the need for extended education

d. increased because of late maturity and early financial independence

_____ 9. Studies have shown that a "democratic family" as opposed to an "authoritarian family" produces an adolescent who is

a. unsure of himself

b. compliant on the surface, but rebellious and impulsive underneath

c. self-indulgent and spoiled

d. self-reliant and effective

_____ 10. A poll designed to study the "parent problem" revealed that

a. there is tremendous parent-child conflict during adolescence

b. four out of five high school students voiced the same specific complaint

c. differences in replies of girls and boys may represent a sex-typing in our culture

d. parent-child conflicts increase over the course of adolescence

_____ 11. Reasons why boys may be more defiant

toward parental authority include all of the following except

a. girls at all ages tend to be more compliant than boys

b. boys are taller and weigh more than girls

c. girls feel less need to rebel in matters concerning sexual behavior

d. in our society boys are expected to be independent and so need to show some defiance to demonstrate this quality

_____ 12. The more important the high school girl *herself* feels an issue to be, the more likely she is to rely on the judgment of

a. her brothers and sisters

b. her parents

c. her clique

d. her teachers

_____ 13. The adolescent girl tends to use the clique

a. to help her in her quest for autonomy

b. to give her support in rebellion against parental authority

c. as a means of finding close personal friendships

d. to form casual group relations

_____ 14. Individual delinquency

a. is usually associated with cultural conflict

b. appears predominantly in "bad" neighborhoods

c. is an attempt by the young person to solve a personal problem

d. usually develops out of social delinquency

_____ 15. Values change with increased education, usually becoming

a. less prejudiced

b. more conservative

c. more ethnocentric

d. less tolerant of diversity

_____ 16. Part of the difference in adjustment between early- and late-maturing boys may be attributed to

a. nursery school experience

b. the type of high school attended

c. the culture in which the boy grows up

d. the number of brothers and sisters the boy has

17. Behavioral distinctions between men and women are based primarily upon
a. biological differences
b. cultural influences
c. differences in ability
d. differences in emotional sensitivity

18. Studies show that the factor most predictive of marital happiness is
a. happiness in childhood
b. the number of brothers and sisters each partner has
c. the background and personality of the wife
d. whether the partners complement rather than replicate each other

19. In the sciences and other fields between one-third and two-thirds of the material contributed is produced by ——————

percent of those active in the respective field.
a. 10
b. 30
c. 50
d. 75

20. There is a sharp increase in suicide rate during
a. adolescence
b. young adulthood
c. middle age
d. later life

key to self-quiz

5. b	10. c	15. a	20. c
4. b	9. d	14. c	19. a
3. d	8. c	13. c	18. a
2. c	7. d	12. b	17. b
1. a	6. c	11. b	16. c

individual exercise

PREDICTING MARITAL SUCCESS

introduction

One of the crucial decisions most young adults make is that of selecting a marital partner. Psychologists have found that men and women do not fall in love as a result of some unfathomable, deep, mysterious force, but rather because each person answers some of the dominant psychological needs of the other.

Because marriage affects the whole course of one's life and has many sweeping social consequences, psychologists and sociologists have designed questionnaires that attempt to measure success in engagement and to predict marital success. The Engagement Success Inventory[1] shown here is both a measure of engagement success and a schedule for predicting marital success. Although intended for use with couples who are engaged, it can be filled out by other persons who would like to know their probability of success in engagement. The value of the results, of course, hinges upon your frankness in answering the questions.

[1] From E. W. Burgess and P. Wallin, *Engagement and marriage.* Copyright, 1953, by J. B. Lippincott Co.

equipment needed

None

procedure

Look over all the alternative answers for each question. Then circle the code letter representing your reply to the question. Read the directions carefully both before and after filling out the questionnaire. Be sure to answer every question. Do not leave a blank to mean a "no" answer. The word fiancé(e) will be used to refer to the person to whom you are engaged or whom you are considering as a possible marriage partner. (*If none, select an acquaintance in order to experience the process of answering such an inventory.*) Do not confer with your fiancé(e) on any of these questions. If you hope to have your fiancé(e) also answer the questions of the inventory, use a separate piece of paper for your answers so that you do not mark this copy. When you have finished the inventory, turn to page 49 for directions for scoring. (*Two columns are provided so that for purposes of comparison, you can enter your fiancé(e)'s responses after you have completed the test.*)

ENGAGEMENT SUCCESS INVENTORY

Questions and possible answers   **Code for answers**

	MAN	WOMAN
1. In leisure time do you prefer:		
Staying at home all or most of the time	a	a
Fifty-fifty reply or equivalent	b	b
Emphasis on staying at home	c	c
To be "on the go" all or most of the time	d	d
Man and woman differ	e	e
2. Do you and your fiancé(e) engage in interests and activities together?		
All of them	a	a
Most of them	b	b
Some of them	c	c
Few or none	d	d
3. Do you confide in your fiancé(e)?		
About everything	a	a
About most things	b	b
About some things	c	c
All other replies	d	d
4. Does your fiancé(e) confide in you?		
About everything	a	a
About most things	b	b
About some things	c	c
All other replies	d	d
5. Frequency of demonstration of affection for fiancé(e):		
Practically all the time	a	a
Very frequent	b	b
Occasional	c	c
All other replies	d	d
6. Are you satisfied with the amount of demonstration of affection?		
Both satisfied	a	a
One satisfied, other desires more	b	b
One satisfied, other desires less	c	c
Both desire more	d	d
One desires less, other more	e	e
Both desire less	f	f

Questions 7 to 17 all relate to the extent of agreement or disagreement between members in a number of areas in their relationship. The answers to these questions are all coded in the same manner. The code is shown below. Record your answers to the questions by circling the appropriate code letter in each question.

	MAN	WOMAN
Code for answers		
Always agree	a	a
Almost always agree	b	b
Occasionally disagree	c	c
Frequently disagree	d	d
Almost always disagree	e	e
Always disagree	f	f

7. Money matters:
  Man: a   b   c   d   e   f
  Woman: a   b   c   d   e   f

8. Recreation:
  Man: a   b   c   d   e   f
  Woman: a   b   c   d   e   f

9. Religion:
  Man: a   b   c   d   e   f
  Woman: a   b   c   d   e   f

10. Demonstration of affection:
  Man: a   b   c   d   e   f
  Woman: a   b   c   d   e   f

11. Friends:
  Man: a   b   c   d   e   f
  Woman: a   b   c   d   e   f

12. Table manners:
  Man: a   b   c   d   e   f
  Woman: a   b   c   d   e   f

13. Matters of conventionality:
  Man: a   b   c   d   e   f
  Woman: a   b   c   d   e   f

14. Philosophy of life:
  Man: a   b   c   d   e   f
  Woman: a   b   c   d   e   f

15. Ways of dealing with your families:
  Man: a   b   c   d   e   f
  Woman: a   b   c   d   e   f

16. Arrangements for marriage:
  Man: a   b   c   d   e   f
  Woman: a   b   c   d   e   f

17. Dates:
  Man: a   b   c   d   e   f
  Woman: a   b   c   d   e   f

18. Do you ever wish you had not become engaged?

	Code for answers	
	MAN	WOMAN
Never	a	a
Once	b	b
Occasionally	c	c
Frequently	d	d

19. Have you ever contemplated breaking your engagement?

Never	a	a
Once	b	b
Occasionally	c	c
Frequently	d	d

20. What things annoy you about your engagement?

None, perfectly satisfied, etc.	a	a
One thing	c	c
Two things	e	e
Three or more	f	f
Its length only	b	b
Being separated only	c	c
Length and one other annoyance	c	c
Separation and one other annoyance	d	d
One annoyance and length and separation	e	e
Two or more annoyances and length and/or separation	f	f

21. What things does fiancé(e) do that you do not like?

None	a	a
One thing	b	b
Two things	c	c
Three or more	d	d

22. Has your relationship ever been broken temporarily?

Never	a	a
Once	b	b
Twice	c	c
Three or more times	d	d

23. If you could, what things would you change in your fiancé(e)?

In physical appearance: _____

_____

_____

In mental, temperamental, or personality characteristics: _____

_____

_____

In ideas: _____

_____

_____

In personal habits: _____

_____

_____

In any other way: _____

_____

_____

24. If you could, what things would you change in yourself? _____

_____

_____

23, 24. The answers to these two questions are coded and scored as if they constituted a single question. Your answer to the two questions combined is simply the total of the number of changes in your fiancé(e) and yourself.

No changes desired	a	a
One change desired	b	b
Two changes desired	c	c
Three changes desired	d	d
Four changes desired	e	e
Five or more desired	f	f

treatment of data

Since this is an individual project, no class summary will be made.

directions for scoring

The code values for the letters of the items of the inventory are as follows:

$$a = 4 \quad c = 2 \quad e = 0$$
$$b = 3 \quad d = 1 \quad f = -1$$

The procedure for scoring the replies is as follows:

Add the scores and enter below.

Number of a's ____ × 4 = ____
Number of b's ____ × 3 = ____
Number of c's ____ × 2 = ____
Number of d's ____ × 1 = ____
Number of e's ____ × 0 = ____
Number of f's ____ × −1 = ____

(Subtract the negative scores from the sum of the positive scores)

interpretation of scores

The individual engagement success score in the Burgess-Wallin Inventory represents the sum of the scores each of you obtained for your responses to all questions in the inventory. Since the more favorable replies to the questions received more points, the higher the total score, the more successful is your engagement relationship. The highest possible score is 92. You may derive your centile score from the following table.

CENTILE NORMS FOR THE ENGAGEMENT ADJUSTMENT SCORE			
Men		Women	
Centile scores	Raw scores	Centile scores	Raw scores
100	92	100	92
95	91	95	91
90	88	90	89
85	85	85	86
80	84	80	85
75	82	75	83
70	81	70	82
65	80	65	81
60	79	60	79
55	78	55	78
50	76	50	77
45	75	45	76
40	74	40	75
35	73	35	74
30	72	30	72
25	70	25	71
20	68	20	70
15	66	15	67
10	62	10	64
5	56	5	59
0	45	0	45

Raw scores between the 25th and 75th centiles are regarded as nonpredictive. Above or below these centiles the possibilities are rather high either for or against marital success, while between them the chances for marital success are about even. Scores above the 75th centile may be regarded provisionally as favorable and scores below the 25th centile as unfavorable to one's general marital success, without considering the characteristics of a specific partner.

how much reliance can be placed on these scores?

Scores of self-inventories have to be interpreted with extreme caution, and they should be used for self-guidance rather than accepted at face value. Burgess and Wallin report correlations between these scores and later marital happiness of $r = .39$ for the men and .36 for the women in their study. These correlations are as high as those obtained between marital happiness and any other premarital factors; such correlations mean that these scores predict less than one-sixth of the total variance in marital happiness. In other words, other factors account for more than five-sixths of whatever determines differences in marital happiness. This interpretation assumes also that the sample population studied was similar to that from which your class is drawn, which may not be the case.

5 sensory processes

programed unit

1. All of man's information about the world comes to him by way of stimuli impinging upon his *sense organs*. Without our eyes, ears, nose, and other

sense
_____ organs, we would know nothing about the people, objects, and events that make up our world.

2. We gain information about the world in which we live by way of our

sense organs
_____ _____ . But a certain *minimum* of sense-organ *stimulation* is required before any sensory experience will be evoked. The minimum physical energy necessary to activate a given sensory system is

absolute
called the *absolute threshold*. To put it another way, the _____ threshold is the intensity at which a stimulus becomes effective.

3. A spot of light in a dark room must reach some measurable intensity before an individual can distinguish it from darkness. In other words, the degree of intensity necessary for it to be seen as a spot of light is its absolute

threshold
_____ for that individual.

4. Likewise, a sound emitted in a soundproof room must reach a certain intensity before it can be heard. The intensity at which it can be heard

absolute
by someone is its _____ threshold.

5. In both of the instances mentioned above, we see that a certain *minimum* of sense-organ stimulation is required before any sensory experience will be

absolute threshold
evoked. This minimum is called the _____ _____ .

6. A pin prick cannot be felt unless the pressure of the pin on the skin reaches a certain intensity. The intensity of pressure necessary for the pin prick to be

absolute threshold
felt is its _____ _____ .

7. We can see from these examples that whether the stimulus is light, sound, or

minimum, stimulation

touch, a certain _____ of sense-organ _____
is required before any sensory experience will be evoked. This minimum is

absolute threshold

called the _____ _____ .

8. There must also be a certain magnitude of difference between two stimuli before one can be distinguished from the other. The minimum amount of difference necessary to tell two stimuli apart is known as the *difference threshold*. Thus two tones must differ to some degree before one is heard as higher than the other. The point at which they can be told apart is the

difference

_____ threshold.

9. The transition between no sensory experience and some sensory experience

absolute

is the _____ threshold; the transition between no difference

difference

and some difference in stimuli is the _____ threshold.

10. Thresholds *vary* from one person to the next and may even *fluctuate* over time within one individual. Therefore, we should think of a threshold measurement as a statistical average. If a psychologist was interested in measur-

difference

ing your *dif*_____ threshold for discriminating between two tones, he would probably not get identical results each time of testing. Likewise, your threshold for discriminating between the two tones would probably not be the same as someone else's threshold.

vary

11. Thresholds not only _____ from one individual to the next but may even *fluctuate* within one individual from time to time.

12. Threshold measurement should be thought of as a statistical average. That is,

fluctuate

for the same person thresholds may _____ from one time

individual (or synonym)

to the next, and thresholds also vary from one _____
to another.

absolute

13. The two kinds of thresholds we have discussed are the _____
threshold, which is the transition between no sensory experience and some

difference

sensory experience, and the _____ threshold, which is
the transition between no difference and some difference in stimuli.

fluctuate

14. Although a person's threshold may _____ from time to time, the changes are not entirely haphazard. One consistent kind of change is called *sensory adaptation*.

adaptation

15. Sensory _____ refers to the reduction in sensitivity as stimulation persists or, conversely, to the increase in sensitivity that occurs with lack of stimulation.

16. If you enter a newly painted room, the smell of fresh paint is strong. After a while, however, you no longer notice the odor. This is an example of sensory

adaptation

_____ .

17. When you plunge into an unheated pool, the water may seem icy. After you have been immersed for a few minutes, your body no longer feels the cold.

sensory adaptation

This is another example of _____ _____ .

reduction **18.** Sensory adaptation refers to the *re*_____ in sensitivity as stimulation persists.

sensitivity **19.** Sensory adaptation also refers to the increase in _____ that occurs with lack of stimulation.

20. When you first enter a darkened theater, you can barely see anything and have trouble groping your way to a seat. After a few minutes in the dark, your eyes become much more sensitive and you begin to see people around

sensory adaptation you. This is an example of _____ _____ .

sensitivity **21.** Sensory adaptation refers both to the reduction in _____

increase as stimulation persists and to the _____ in sensitivity that occurs with lack of stimulation.

22. Sensory adaptation accounts in part for the fact that an individual's absolute

fluctuate threshold may _____ from one moment to the next.

sense **23.** The human eye is one of the most complex _____ organs. Note the drawing of the human eye, and as you proceed consider the location and functions of its different parts. To begin, locate the *cornea*, where light *enters* the eye.

cornea **24.** Light *enters* the eye through the _____ , the amount of light being *regulated* by the size of the *pupil opening*, which is an opening in the *iris*.

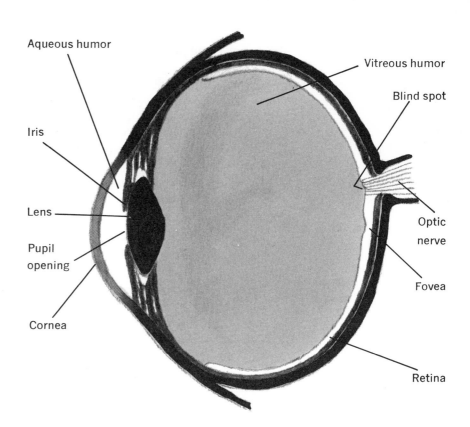

enters pupil	**25.** The cornea is the portion of the eye through which light _____ ; the amount of light entering the eye is regulated by the size of the _____ opening.
cornea pupil opening	**26.** After light has entered the eye through the _____ and its amount has been regulated by the _____ _____ , the *lens* then *focuses* the light on the receptor surface, the *retina*.
cornea pupil, iris	**27.** The parts of the human eye we have identified thus far are the *c*_____ , the *p*_____ , the *i*_____ , and the *lens,* which focuses light on the *retina*.
enters regulated focuses	**28.** Light _____ the eye through the cornea, the amount of light being _____ by the size of the pupil opening, which is an opening in the iris. The lens then _____ the light on the receptor surface, the retina.
lens, retina	**29.** The _____ focuses the light on the receptor surface, the _____ .
vitreous aqueous	**30.** Note that liquids fill the space between the various parts of the eye. The *aqueous humor* fills the space between the cornea and the lens; the *vitreous humor* fills the eye cavity behind the lens. The _____ humor fills a larger cavity than the _____ humor.
aqueous cornea lens	**31.** The vitreous humor fills the eye cavity behind the lens. The _____ humor fills the space between the _____ , where light enters the eye, and the _____ , which focuses light on the retina.
retina	**32.** The lens focuses the light on the _____ , which is made up of a number of specialized cells. Two of these specialized types of cells (*not shown in the drawing*) are of particular interest. These are the rods and cones, which have different functions. (*In the text you will find a diagram showing the rods and cones.*)
retina	**33.** *Rods* and *cones* are specialized cells with *different* functions and are found in the _____ .
different	**34.** Rods and cones, which have _____ functions, are found in the receptor surface, the retina.
rods, cones (either order)	**35.** Two specialized types of cells in the retina are _____ and _____ .
different, retina	**36.** *Cones* are active primarily in *daylight* vision and permit us to see both *achromatic* colors (white, black, and the intermediate grays) and *chromatic* colors (red, green, blue, and so on). The rods and cones are specialized cells with _____ functions and are found in the _____ .
chromatic	**37.** The cones of the retina permit us to see white, black, and the intermediate grays (the achromatic colors), and red, green, blue, and the other _____ colors.

38. The *rods,* in contrast to the cones, enable us to see only *achromatic* colors. The rods function mainly in vision under *reduced* illumination, as in twilight or *night vision.* Cones enable us to see both _____ and _____ colors.

achromatic
chromatic
(either order)

39. The cones function in normal daylight vision, whereas the rods function under _____ illumination, as in night vision.

reduced

40. Rods enable us to see only _____ colors and function in vision under _____ illumination.

achromatic
reduced

41. Cones function in normal _____ vision, whereas the rods function in _____ vision.

daylight
night

42. We noted earlier that when you enter a dark room your eyes gradually become more sensitive to light so that after a while you are able to see more than when you first entered. This is an example of sensory _____ . In this case the experience is known more specifically as *dark adaptation.* Dark _____ is a specific type of _____ _____ .

adaptation

adaptation, sensory

adaptation

43. The experience of dark _____ shows how the rods and cones differ in their functions. When you first enter a dark room the cones in your retina become more sensitive to light. Stated another way, their absolute threshold is (*raised/lowered*).

adaptation

lowered

44. After about five minutes in the dark, the sensitivity of the cones has increased as much as it will. The rods, however, continue to adapt to the dark and become appreciably more sensitive for about a half an hour. You can see better after twenty minutes in the dark than after five minutes because of the functioning of the _____ .

rods

45. The _____ cells no longer increase their sensitivity to light after a few minutes in a dark room because they function best in normal _____ vision. Cones enable us to see both _____ and _____ colors.

cone

daylight
achromatic
chromatic
(either order)

46. The _____ cells function in night vision and enable us to see only _____ colors.

rod
achromatic

47. In the experience of dark adaptation the _____ increase their sensitivity for the first few minutes, but the _____ become increasingly more sensitive over a longer period.

cones
rods

48. The most sensitive portion of the eye in normal *daylight* vision is a small area of the retina called the *fovea,* on which is focused light that comes from the center of the visual field. The *fovea* must contain _____ cells because these function in normal daylight vision.

cone

49. The most sensitive portion of the eye in normal daylight vision is the

fovea

_____ ; it contains *only cone* cells, which are packed closely together

Rod

in a small area. _____ cells are found only *outside* the fovea.

rod

50. The portion of the retina outside the fovea contains *both* _____ and cone cells.

rod, cone (either order)

51. Outside the fovea are _____ and _____ cells. Within the fovea are

cone

only _____ cells, which are closely packed together and function best

daylight

in _____ vision.

52. Not far from the fovea, on the surface of the retina, is an insensitive area, the *blind spot,* where nerve fibers from the retinal cells come together in a bundle to form the *optic nerve,* which carries impulses from the eye to the

nerve

brain. The area where the optic _____ leaves the eye is called the

blind

_____ spot because it contains neither rods nor cones.

53. The most sensitive portion of the eye in normal daylight vision is the

fovea

_____ , which contains only cone cells; the insensitive area is the

blind

_____ spot, where the nerve fibers from the cells of the retina come

optic

together in a bundle to form the _____ nerve.

54. Without looking at the earlier drawing you should be able to label the parts of the eye in the drawing presented here. Check your results with the labeled drawing of the eye. (*Rod and cone cells are not shown, but you should re-*

cone, fovea

member that _____ *cells are concentrated in the* _____ ,

rod, cone

whereas both _____ *and* _____ *cells are found outside the fovea.*)

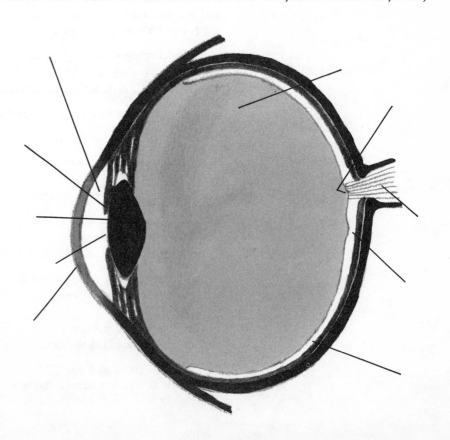

55. Let us now discuss color vision. You recall that red, blue, green, and so on,

chromatic

are _____ colors. We can produce the colors that are familiar to us in a *rainbow* by passing sunlight through a prism, which breaks it into a band of varicolored light.

56. When sunlight is passed through a prism, it breaks into a band of vari-

rainbow

colored light that is familiar to us in the _____ . The colors correspond to *wavelengths,* the *red* end of the rainbow being produced by the *long* light waves, the *violet* end by the *short* light waves.

57. Sunlight sent through a prism produces a rainbow effect. This band of vari-colored light is called a *solar spectrum.* The colors correspond to

wavelengths

_____ , the red end of the spectrum being produced

short

by the long light waves and the violet end by the _____ light waves.

58. The colors of the solar spectrum can be arranged in the form of a *color circle.*

solar

The _____ spectrum is bent back around itself to form a circle as shown below. The break in the color circle between red and violet contains colors that do not appear in the solar spectrum but can be produced by mix-

color

tures of other colors. The colors *opposite* each other on the _____

circle

_____ are called *complementaries.* Note that blue and yellow, red

complementaries

and green are found opposite each other. They are _____ .

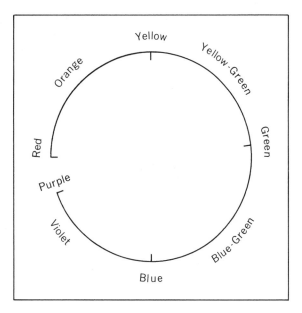

59. Blue and yellow, red and green are complementaries, since they appear

opposite

_____ each other on the color circle. When complementary pairs of colors, such as yellow and blue, red and green, are mixed as *lights* (*not as pigments*), they cancel each other and result in neutral *gray. Spectral colors* (the colors of the solar spectrum) must be opposite each other on the

color circle

_____ _____ in order to be considered complementaries.

spectral

60. The _____ colors resemble a rainbow. When they are op-

complementaries

posite each other on a color circle, they are called _____ .

61. Blue-green and orange are a pair of complementary colors on a color circle. If mixed together as *lights,* the resulting color would be a neutral _____ .

gray

62. Complementaries are spectral colors that are opposite each other on a color circle; when mixed together as _____ , they cancel each other and result in a neutral gray.

lights

63. Some of the colors appear to be more elementary than others; that is, they appear to be composed of a single hue, which is a technical name for the quality of redness, blueness, greenness, and so on, that differentiates one color from another. These elementary colors are called *psychological primaries,* and usually four are named: *red, green, blue,* and *yellow.* Colors such as orange or purple are not psychological _____ , since their components can be recognized—for instance, both red and yellow can be identified in orange.

primaries

64. The _____ primaries are red, green, blue, and yellow.

psychological

65. The psychological primaries are _____ , _____ , _____ , and _____ .

red, green, blue
yellow (any order)

66. Red, green, blue, and yellow appear to be more elementary than other colors and are therefore called _____ primaries. Another set of primaries is called *color-mixture primaries;* these are any three widely spaced colors on the spectrum that can be used to provide all the other colors by *additive mixture.*

psychological

67. Any three widely spaced colors on the spectrum can be used to provide all the other colors by additive mixture. These are called _____-_____ primaries.

color-
mixture

68. Red, green, and blue are widely spaced colors on the spectrum that can be used to provide all the other colors by additive mixture. Therefore we call these colors _____-_____ primaries.

color-mixture

69. The psychological primaries are _____ , _____ , _____ , and _____ . The _____-_____ primaries are any three widely spaced colors on the spectrum that can be used to provide all the other colors by additive _____ .

red, green, blue
yellow (any order);
color-mixture

mixture

70. The *negative afterimage* is an interesting phenomenon in color perception. If you stare at a red circle and then look at a plain gray surface, you will have the experience of seeing a green circle on it; that is, you experience a *negative afterimage.* The afterimage is called "negative" because green is the complementary color of red. You recall that blue and yellow are complementary colors. Were you to stare at a yellow circle and then look at a plain gray surface, you would have the experience of seeing a _____ circle on it.

blue

71. If you stare at a green circle and then look at a plain gray surface, you are

red, negative   likely to see a _____ circle on it; that is, you experience a _____ afterimage.

negative afterimage   **72.** A _____ _____ is so named because, after staring at a particular color, one usually sees its complementary color on a gray surface.

73. Vision is, of course, only one of several human senses. In everyday language

five   most people speak of our having _____ senses: sight, hearing,

taste, smell
(either order)   _____ , _____ , and touch.

74. Students of psychology are expected to be more precise in defining the senses. As you will see shortly, the sense of touch is not one sensation but four. In addition, there are two special senses that provide information about body position and body movement and enable us to keep our balance. There-

senses   fore it is inaccurate to say that man has only five _____ . (*Hearing and the senses dealing with body position and movement and balance are treated in the text.*)

75. Taste, smell, and the skin sensations are important in everyday life, but they do not provide us with the rich patterns and organization that vision and audition do. Vision and audition are spoken of as the "higher senses"; taste,

lower   smell, and the skin sensations are therefore thought of as the " _____ senses."

76. Psychologists have identified four primary taste qualities: *sweet, sour, salt,* and *bitter.* But most taste experience is brought about by a fusion of these qualities with other sense experiences. As you might guess, the "taste" of

smell   strong cheese is considerably affected by our sense of _____ .

taste   **77.** The four primary _____ qualities are *sweet, sour, salt,* and

bitter   _____ . But taste is also affected by other senses. If you were blindfolded and your nostrils were pinched together so that you could not

smell   _____ , you would have trouble distinguishing between the taste of an apple and a raw potato.

sweet, sour, salt   **78.** The four taste qualities are _____ , _____ , _____ ,

bitter (any order); senses   and _____ . Other _____ contribute to taste.

79. The sense of *smell* is from an evolutionary point of view one of the most

senses   primitive and most important of the _____ . Smell has more direct neural pathways to the brain than any other sense.

smell   **80.** The sense of _____ has more direct neural pathways to the brain than any other sense. It plays a more important role in the life of the lower animals than in man.

81. There are four *skin* sensations. That is, the familiar sense of touch is not one sensation but at least four: *touch, pain, warm,* and *cold.* These sensations

skin   are felt through separate *sensitive spots* on the surface of the _____ .

pain

cold (either order)

sensitive

82. Touch is not one sensation but at least four: touch, _____ , warm, and _____ . These sensations are registered through separate _____ spots on the surface of the skin.

touch, pain, warm,
cold (any order)

83. The sensations provided by sensitive spots on the surface of the skin include _____ , _____ , _____ , and _____ .

self-quiz

Select the alternative that best completes the thought. In some cases several answers are fairly satisfactory; you are to pick the *best* one.

_____ **1.** The sense of touch is not one sensation but four:
a. touch, pain, itching, tickling
b. touch, pain, warm, cold
c. pain, itching, tickling, warm
d. pain, itching, tickling, touch

_____ **2.** Rhodopsin is a light-sensitive substance found in the
a. rods
b. cornea
c. bipolar cells
d. cones

_____ **3.** The most sensitive portion of the eye during normal daylight vision is the
a. fovea
b. lens
c. cornea
d. pupil

_____ **4.** The elementary colors, or psychological primaries, are
a. red, yellow, green, blue
b. black, white, gray
c. red, orange, purple
d. orange, yellow, green, blue

_____ **5.** The minimum amount of physical energy necessary to activate a given sensory system is known as
a. stimulus intensity
b. the absolute threshold
c. the psychophysical function
d. sensory adaptation

_____ **6.** When you go from daylight into a darkened theater, at first you have difficulty locating an empty seat. In time, however, dark adaptation takes place and you can see people around you. What part of the eye produces most of the change?
a. the fovea
b. the cones
c. the rods
d. the activated blind spot

_____ **7.** The sense organs for equilibrium are located in the
a. cochlea
b. semicircular canals and vestibular sacs
c. oval window
d. organ of Corti

_____ **8.** The term "solar spectrum" refers to
a. a part of the eye
b. the ultraviolet rays
c. the infrared rays
d. the band of colored lights produced by sunlight passing through a prism

_____ **9.** Damage to the occipital lobe of the right hemisphere will result in blind areas in the
a. right eye
b. left eye
c. right side of both eyes
d. left side of both eyes

_____ **10.** A frequency theory of hearing
a. was suggested by Helmholtz
b. is concerned with where stimulation occurs on the basilar membrane
c. assumes that the cochlea acts like a microphone
d. has been largely discredited

11. The mixture of lights is
a. complementary
b. additive
c. subtractive
d. the same process as mixing pigments

12. The light-sensitive surface at the back of the eye, called the retina, is composed of three main layers:
a. rods and cones, bipolar cells, and the pupil
b. rods and cones, ganglion cells, and the optic nerve
c. bipolar cells, ganglion cells, and the pupil
d. rods and cones, bipolar cells, and ganglion cells

13. If you stare at a red circle and then look at a plain gray surface, you are likely to see a green circle. This phenomenon is termed
a. a negative afterimage
b. a spreading effect
c. simultaneous contrast
d. delayed contrast

14. The minimum amount of stimulation necessary to tell two stimuli apart is known as the
a. absolute threshold
b. psychophysical function
c. difference threshold
d. stimulus intensity

15. If we compare the dimensions of tone with those of color, we find that hue, brightness, and saturation correspond with
a. pitch, loudness, and timbre
b. amplitude, frequency, and timbre
c. pitch, loudness, and overtones
d. pitch, vibrations, and overtones

16. The rods permit us to see
a. in daylight

b. achromatic colors
c. chromatic colors
d. both chromatic and achromatic colors

17. The most common form of color blindness is
a. blue-yellow blindness
b. red-green and blue-yellow blindness
c. red-green blindness
d. black-white blindness

18. If a subject is given a 100-gram weight, his difference threshold is 2 grams. According to Weber's law if we then give him a 400-gram weight, his difference threshold would be
a. 2 grams
b. 8 grams
c. 20 grams
d. 40 grams

19. Hering's theory of color vision
a. is based upon microspectrophotometry
b. proposed three types of cones
c. proposed that color vision is a two-stage process
d. is based upon the color-mixing primaries

20. Ultimately, the most acceptable theory of hearing will probably be
a. the place theory
b. the frequency theory
c. a combination of the place and frequency theories
d. the volley principle

key to self-quiz

20. c	15. a	10. c	5. b
19. b	14. c	9. c	4. a
18. b	13. a	8. d	3. a
17. c	12. d	7. b	2. a
16. b	11. b	6. c	1. b

individual or class exercise

PERIPHERAL COLOR VISION

introduction

Rods and cones are not evenly distributed on the surface of the retina. The periphery contains only rods, with the number of cones increasing as the fovea, or center of the retina, is approached. For this reason, objects that appear on the periphery of one's vision are seen as colorless. As the image of an object approaches the center of the retina, it is possible to distinguish its color. The purpose of this exercise is to determine at what point the color function takes over and whether some colors are perceived more readily than others in peripheral vision. The exercise can be done individually or it can be presented as a class demonstration by the instructor.

equipment needed

A circle of yellow paper and one of red, about two inches in diameter, attached by a thumb tack to the end of a stick or pencil. If colored paper is not available a yellow and a red pencil may be used. Try to obtain yellow and red objects of equal brightness; that is, do not use a bright yellow circle and a dark red one.

procedure

The entire procedure should be read before you start the experiment. Seat the subject and have him cover his left eye with one hand while fixating with his right eye a spot on the wall about six feet in front of him. You might place a thumb tack on the wall for him to fixate on, or any other mark will do. Tell him that you want him to report the color of objects that you will slowly move in from the periphery of his visual field. Remind him not to shift his gaze from the fixation point while he is being tested. Start with the yellow disc about six inches to the side of the subject's right ear; keeping the disc the same distance from his head, gradually move it in an arc from the ear to the center of the visual field. Mark on the appropriate diagram on page 63 (Figure 1) the approximate point at which the subject correctly identified the color. Follow the same procedure with the red disc. Then present each color moving from the subject's left ear to the center of his visual field. Again move the disc in an arc six inches from the subject's head. Repeat the experiment two more times; in all you will need three

estimates for each color from the left side and three from the right. Try to present the colors in a random order; that is, do not consistently alternate red and yellow or present three red followed by three yellow.

Next you want to determine peripheral sensitivity to colors in the vertical plane, that is, as the object is moved from above the subject's head down toward his eye level. Start with the yellow disc six inches above the subject's head and move it slowly forward and down in an arc six inches from his eye. Note the point at which the color can be identified and mark it on the appropriate diagram. Repeat this procedure starting six inches below the subject's chin. Obtain three estimates for each color starting from above and three from below.

treatment of data

Figure 2 on page 63 shows the results from a hypothetical subject. A rough average is made of the three marks on each side and an arc drawn from the average to the center of the visual field. Note, for example, that for this subject, red and yellow are both perceived at about the same spot on the left-hand periphery (line a is approximately the same length for the two colors), but yellow is perceived further out than red on the right-hand periphery (line b is longer for yellow than for red). The bottom diagrams show the hypothetical results for vertical peripheral vision. For this subject, yellow has a greater vertical range of sensitivity than red.

Analyze your subject's results in a similar manner by determining the average points and their distance from the center of vision.

questions for discussion

1. How do your subject's results compare with those of the hypothetical subject?

2. For your subject, which color has the greatest horizontal range of sensitivity? Which has the greatest vertical range?

3. Compare your results with those of several classmates. Do you find individual differences in sensitivity?

4. The usual finding is that yellow is perceived further out on the horizontal periphery than is red. Recalling the discussion of theories of color vision presented in the text, what explanation can you offer for these results?

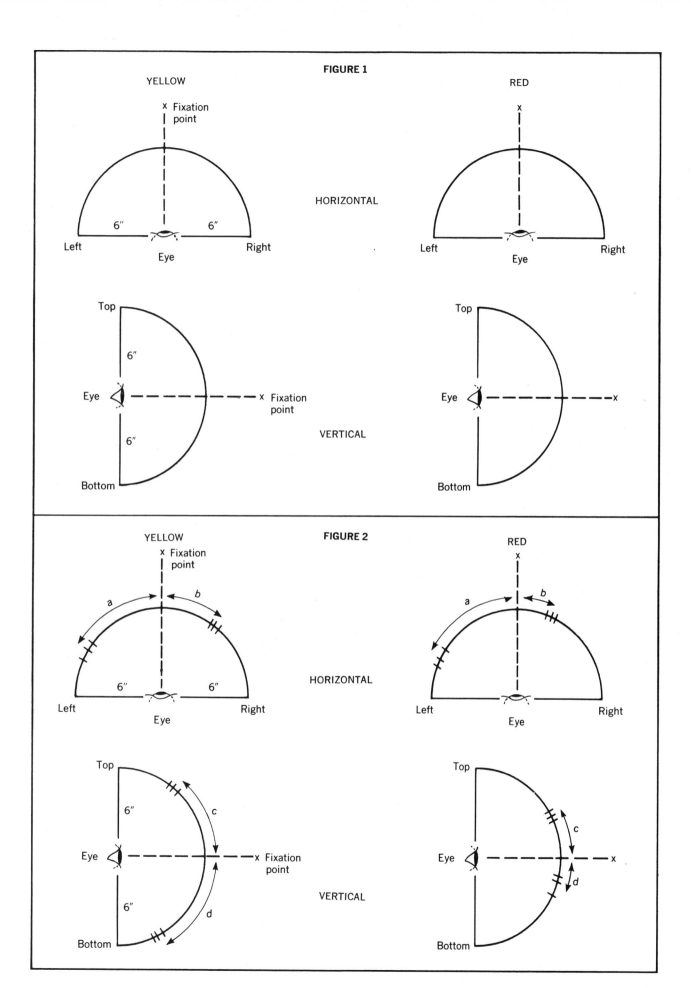

FIGURE 1

YELLOW

x Fixation point

HORIZONTAL

6"   6"

Left   Right

Eye

Top

6"

Eye —— x Fixation point

VERTICAL

6"

Bottom

RED

x

HORIZONTAL

Left   Right

Eye

Top

Eye —— x

VERTICAL

Bottom

FIGURE 2

YELLOW

x Fixation point

a   b

HORIZONTAL

6"   6"

Left   Right

Eye

Top

6"

c

Eye —— x Fixation point

VERTICAL

6"

d

Bottom

RED

x

a   b

HORIZONTAL

Left   Right

Eye

Top

c

Eye —— x

d

VERTICAL

Bottom

6 perception

programed unit

1. In our perception of the world around us, we respond not to isolated stimuli but to *patterns of stimuli* that are organized into a *meaningful whole.* When looking at a painting of a landscape, you perceive not isolated daubs

patterns   of paint but _____ of stimuli that are organized in some meaningful way.

patterns   **2.** In listening to a piece of music, you hear _____ of tones rather than isolated tones. The word "pattern" implies that the tones are or-

meaningful   ganized in some *m_____* way.

3. As you sit at your desk reading this unit, there are many stimuli imping-ing upon your sense organs, but what you actually perceive depends upon

stimuli   your *past experience* with patterns of _____ .

experience   **4.** When we say that perception depends upon past _____ , we imply that at least some aspects of perception must be learned.

5. When you look at a silver dollar held at eye level, the pattern of

stimuli   _____ impinging upon your eyes is quite different from the pat-tern produced by the same coin laying on a table. In both instances, however,

shape   you perceive the shape of the coin as round. In other words, the _____ of the coin is perceived as *constant* regardless of the viewing angle.

6. Similarly, we tend to perceive an object as having a *constant* color regard-less of the degree of illumination upon it. A tennis ball is perceived as white whether it is lying in bright sunlight or in the shade of a tree. That is, the

constant   tennis ball is perceived as having a _____ color.

7. The tendency to perceive objects as the same regardless of changes in the conditions of perception is called *object constancy*. We recognize a tin can as being cylindrical regardless of its position. This is an example of _____ constancy.

object

8. The fact that we perceive an object as being one particular color even when the illumination is changed is another illustration of _____ _____ .

object

constancy

9. A closed door is rectangular in shape, but as it swings open toward you its shape goes through a series of distortions. When the door is partially open it is actually a trapezoid, in terms of the pattern of stimulation on the retina. When it is completely open we see only a vertical line the thickness of the door. Although we can easily distinguish these changes, what we perceive is an unchanging door swinging on its hinges. The fact that you perceive the door as a rectangle regardless of its position is an illustration of _____ _____ .

object

constancy

10. Psychologists distinguish among several kinds of object constancy. For example, the tendency to perceive objects as of standard shape, regardless of the viewing angle, is known as _____ constancy.

shape

11. When we see a person close to us, we may recognize that he is about 6 feet tall. If we perceive this same person at a distance of 100 yards, the image on the retina is much smaller than it was when he was right next to us. Still we perceive him as being approximately the same *size*, 6 feet tall. This is an example of _____ constancy.

size

12. We perceive a tin can as being cylindrical, regardless of its position, because of _____ constancy.

shape

13. We perceive a fence post at the end of the block as being as tall as the one next to us because of _____ _____ .

size constancy

14. The fact that an orange flag is perceived as orange even when the conditions of illumination change is an example of c_____ constancy.

color

15. Another kind of object _____ is *location* constancy. Even though the stimuli impinging upon our senses change rapidly as we move about, we perceive objects as maintaining a fixed location.

constancy

16. The tendency to perceive objects as being in a fixed location, regardless of continual changes in stimulation, is known as _____ _____ .

location

constancy

17. When we speak of object constancy, then, we are speaking about the tendency to perceive objects as _____ regardless of alterations in illumination, viewing angle, distance, or other conditions of perception.

constant

18. The general name given to the tendency to perceive objects as the same regardless of changes in the conditions of perception is _____

object

constancy

_____ .

location

19. We have examined four kinds of object constancy: _____ ,

color, size, shape
(any order)

_____ , _____ , and _____

constancy.

20. The perceptual constancies imply organization within perception. If you look around, you will notice that certain objects seem bolder and better defined than others. Writing upon a blackboard stands out against the background of the blackboard. We call what stands out the *figure* and the background the *ground*. The perceptual organization of figure and ground—in the above

figure

example, white against black—constitutes the _____ *-ground* relationship.

21. When we look at a picture of a person standing on a beach with the ocean

figure

behind him, the person is the _____ and the ocean is the

ground

_____ .

22. An object standing out against a uniform background is an example of a

figure-ground

_____ - _____ relationship.

23. Another example of organization within perception is the tendency, called *perceptual grouping,* to *group* stimuli into some sort of pattern or structure. In the top figure below, you tend to perceive three pairs of straight lines with

right

an extra line on the _____ . In the bottom figure, the addition of extensions to the same lines makes you perceive three broken squares and an

left

extra line on the _____ .

24. The tendency to group stimuli according to a pattern of some sort is called

grouping

perceptual _____ .

figure-
ground
perceptual grouping

25. Two examples of organization within perception are _____ -

_____ relationships and _____ _____ .

26. Many problems in perception are still not well understood. One of these is *visual illusions.* You are probably familiar with geometrical illusions like those below.

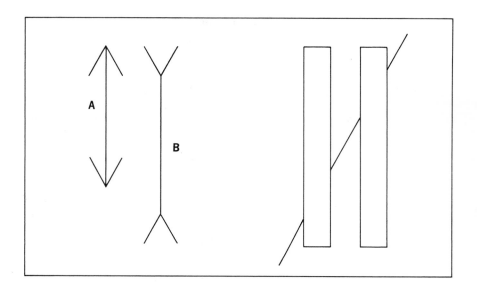

For the figure on the left, line segment B looks longer than line segment A, though both are actually the same length; this is an example of a visual

illusion _____ . For the figure on the right, the line that projects through the two rectangles is actually straight, though it appears staggered.

visual illusion This is another example of a _____ _____ .

27. Another type of illusion is *apparent motion,* the illusion of motion when there is no real movement of the object. If you stare at a fixed spot of light in a dark room, after a few seconds the light will appear to move about in an erratic manner. This phenomenon, called the *autokinetic effect,* is an

motion example of apparent _____ .

illusion **28.** Apparent motion is the _____ of motion when there is no real movement.

29. One example of apparent motion, the movement of a fixed spot of light in a

autokinetic dark room, is the _____ effect.

motion **30.** Another example of apparent _____ , familiar to you as the basis of "motion pictures," is called *stroboscopic motion.* If a series of pictures (each picture slightly different from the preceding one) is presented rapidly enough, the pictures blend into smooth motion.

31. The illusion of motion created when separated stimuli, not in motion, are

stroboscopic presented rapidly in succession is called _____ motion.

motion **32.** Stroboscopic _____ and the autokinetic effect are both examples

apparent of _____ motion. Apparent motion, as you recall, is one form

illusion of visual _____ .

33. The perception of depth is another problem in the study of perception. The

three   surface of the retina has only two dimensions, yet we perceive in _____ dimensions.

three   **34.** The process by which we perceive in _____ dimensions is similar to the effect produced by the old-fashioned stereoscope. The stereoscope is a device by means of which two flat pictures, one presented to each eye, combine to yield an experience of depth. The pictures appear to be identical but are actually photographed from slightly different *angles*.

35. Since our eyes are separated in our head, each views the world from a

angle   slightly different _____ . The combination of these two scenes

depth   provides the experience of _____ .

36. The perception of depth that results from the overlapping visual fields of the two eyes is called *stereoscopic vision*. Stereoscopic vision depends upon the

different   fact that each of our eyes sees a slightly _____ picture.

37. Having two eyes helps us to perceive depth and distance by means of

stereoscopic vision   _____ _____ . But a person with only one eye can still use many cues to determine the distance or depth of an ob-

one (or a single)   ject. Cues that require the use of only _____ eye are called *monocular distance cues*.

38. If one object cuts off the view of another, we assume that the first object is nearer. Since we can make this observation with only one eye, it is a

monocular   _____ distance cue.

39. Another monocular cue is the fact that parallel lines appear to converge in the distance. When you look down a railroad track, the rails appear to come

monocular   together at the horizon. This is a _____ cue to distance.

40. The fact that objects appear to decrease in size with distance is another cue

distance   that a person with only one eye could use to estimate *dis_____* .

41. Thus we see that there are many cues that can be utilized to judge the depth or distance of an object. Some of these require the use of only one eye.

monocular   These are called _____ distance cues. Others require the use of both eyes; these are *binocular* cues.

42. When we judge the distance of an object, we generally depend upon both

monocular, binocular   _____ and _____ cues.
(either order)

binocular   **43.** Stereoscopic vision is a _____ cue, while the fact that objects appear to decrease in size with increasing distance is a

monocular   _____ cue.

44. As adults, we know that we are capable of certain kinds of visual perception. But disagreements remain over whether our abilities to perceive the spatial aspects of our environment are learned or whether we are born with them.

Those who support the role of *learning* are called *empiricists*. Those who maintain that we are born with the ability to perceive the way we do are called *nativists*. If one argues that the perceptual constancies must be learned,

empiricists

he is supporting the viewpoint of the _____ .

empiricists

nativists

45. The _____ feel that we have to learn to perceive the world in the way that we do. The _____ , on the other hand, argue that this ability is innate.

46. Most psychologists today agree that practice and experience play a vital role in determining what we perceive. In other words, they emphasize the im-

learning

portance of _____ in perception. This is the position of the

empiricists

_____ . The question that remains is whether we are born with some ability to perceive the world or whether it is all learned.

47. When by the removal of cataracts vision is given to a person who has been blind all of his life, he cannot distinguish a square from a triangle or tell which of two sticks is longer without feeling them. This evidence supports

learning

the role of _____ in perception.

48. On the other hand, there is evidence for some innate basis for what we per-

nativist

ceive. Thus, the _____ viewpoint is not completely wrong.

49. Perception is selective. We pay attention to only a few of the many stimuli that surround us. The question naturally arises, What determines the stimuli to which we will attend? Some of the variables are internal, such as the *needs* and *expectations* of the individual. Those stimuli that are pertinent to one's

expectations

needs and _____ are those most likely to attract attention.

50. A hungry person is more likely to notice the smell of cooking bacon than one

need

who is not. His attention is determined by his _____ for food. A person awaiting an important letter is more likely to pick out the mailman's step

expectation

amid many other sounds. His _____ influences his attention.

needs, expectations
(either order)

51. Thus, internal variables such as _____ and _____ can influence our perception. The characteristics of stimuli are also im- portant. Intensity, size, contrast, and movement are some of the *physical properties of the stimulus* that help to gain our attention. A large, bright red

more

neon sign that flashes on and off is (*more/less*) likely to attract our attention than a small gray poster.

stimulus

52. Physical characteristics of the _____ are external variables

needs, expectations
(either order)

that affect our perception, while _____ and _____ are internal variables.

53. When something attracts our attention, we usually perform certain body movements to enhance our reception of the stimulation—such as turning our eyes in the direction of a visual stimulus or cupping our hands behind our ears so as to hear a faint sound. These body movements in response to changes in the environment are accompanied by a pattern of physiological

reflex

reactions called the *orienting reflex*. The orienting _____ occurs in response to even slight changes in the environment. It includes such physiological changes as constriction of the peripheral blood vessels and changes in muscle tone, heart rate, and respiration.

orienting

reflex

54. These physiological accompaniments of attention, called the _____

_____ , *facilitate the reception of stimulation* and prepare the organism to respond quickly in case action is needed.

55. A loud tone arouses the orienting reflex in a laboratory subject. He now reports that he can see a light that was too faint to be detected before the tone

facilitates (or synonym)

sounded. This demonstrates the fact that the orienting reflex _____ the reception of stimuli.

56. If the same stimulus is repeated a number of times, the orienting reflex gradually diminishes. A *change* in the stimulus or the introduction of a new stimulus will reactivate the orienting reflex in its original strength. Thus the

changes

orienting reflex is responsive to *ch_____s* in the environment. Such a reflex has important survival value for the organism.

57. When we discuss perception, we are usually speaking of *sensory perception*

senses

or, in other words, perception that takes place through the _____ . It has been suggested that there may be perceptions that do not require any sense-organ stimulation. These phenomena have been called *extrasensory perception* (ESP).

58. Research on extrasensory perception has been carried on for a number of years. Although some psychologists believe that the evidence for the existence

extrasensory

of certain forms of _____ perception is indisputable, most remain unconvinced.

59. There are several classifications of ESP. *Telepathy* means the transference

telepathy

of thought from one person to another. In more familiar terms, _____ is the word for "mind-reading."

60. When a person claims to be able to transmit his thoughts across distance so that another person can tell what he is thinking, he is maintaining that

telepathy

_____ exists. Of course, one who claims to be able to receive such thoughts also supports the existence of this phenomenon.

61. One of the most common kinds of research in ESP is based on experiments in card-guessing. The experimenter may ask the subject to guess the symbol on a card that is in a sealed envelope. No one knows what card it is. The ability of the subject to perceive the card is called *clairvoyance*. The perception of objects or events that are not influencing the senses is

clairvoyance

known as _____ . At times, one may not be sure

telepathy

whether _____ or clairvoyance is at work. If someone else knows, for instance, what the card is, then the subject might be perceiving

clairvoyance

the card directly (_____) or he might be reading

telepathy

the thoughts of the person who knows (_____).

62. Another classification of ESP is that of *precognition,* or the perception of a

precognition
future event. For a man who bets on horse races, _____ would seem to be the most valuable kind of ESP.

63. The phenomena of ESP are discussed under a number of classifications: (1)

telepathy
thought transference from one person to another, or _____ ;

precognition
(2) the perception of a future event, or _____ ; and (3) the perception of an object or event that is not influencing the

clairvoyance
senses, or _____ .

64. A related phenomenon has to do with the influence of a mental operation over a material body or an energy system—for example, the idea that wishing for a given number affects the number that will come up in a throw of dice. This is called *psychokinesis.* If you can move a vase on your desk by merely willing it to move, you are demonstrating the operation of

psychokinesis
_____ .

65. A person who feels that he is a better roulette player than others is (unless

psychokinesis
he is cheating) operating with some belief in _____ .

self-quiz

Select the alternative that best completes the thought. In some cases several answers are fairly satisfactory; you are to pick the *best* one.

_____ **1.** To attain perspective in a picture the artist may
   a. increase the size of an object with distance
   b. place objects that are farther away, lower in the picture
   c. make the "grain" become finer as distance becomes less
   d. blur the detail of a distant object

_____ **2.** Microelectrode recordings from single nerve cells in the visual cortex of the cat show that such cells
   a. respond to large or diffuse spots of light
   b. respond to specific forms of visual stimuli
   c. do not respond to visual stimuli
   d. are organized to perceive form but not motion

_____ **3.** When we view an object at a distance, we judge its size according to
   a. location size

   b. perspective size
   c. object size
   d. a compromise between perspective size and object size

_____ **4.** The idea that we are born with the ability to perceive the way we do is the viewpoint of
   a. nativists
   b. empiricists
   c. Berkeley
   d. Locke

_____ **5.** It appears that attention involves a screening process such that at any given moment only certain sensory impulses reach the brain, while others are filtered out. Recent evidence indicates that the control, or filtering, center is the
   a. limbic system
   b. hypothalamus
   c. reticular formation
   d. thalamus

_____ **6.** Reversible figures such as the Necker cube reveal that
   a. perception is an active search for the

best interpretation of sensory information

b. we should not trust our visual senses
c. it is possible to maintain a steady fixation of only one aspect
d. with practice any figure can be seen in reverse

_____ 7. The process familiar to us as the basis of making films is
a. the autokinetic effect
b. the phi phenomenon
c. the optical illusion
d. stroboscopic motion

_____ 8. When we watch a door swing on its hinges, its shape changes from a rectangle, to a trapezoid, to a thin vertical line. But we perceive an unchanging door because of
a. shape constancy
b. size constancy
c. color constancy
d. location constancy

_____ 9. When vision is given to an adult who has been blind from birth, he is unable to
a. distinguish figure from background
b. fixate and scan figures
c. identify from sight objects that are familiar by touch
d. follow moving figures with his eyes

_____ 10. The fact that snow at night still looks white is an example of
a. set in perceiving
b. perceptual constancy
c. the phi phenomenon
d. stereoscopic vision

_____ 11. A man with vision in only one eye is unable to see
a. colors
b. space relationships including three-dimensional configurations
c. objects with stereoscopic vision
d. forms

_____ 12. When the goggles are removed from the eyes of animals that have worn them since birth, they have difficulty discriminating
a. different colors
b. a moving stimulus from a nonmoving stimulus
c. differences in brightness

d. between a disc with horizontal stripes and one with vertical stripes

_____ 13. The apparent movement of a stationary light in a dark room is called the
a. location constancy
b. phi phenomenon
c. autokinetic effect
d. stroboscopic effect

_____ 14. If a person believes that he can foretell future events, he believes in
a. telepathy
b. clairvoyance
c. precognition
d. psychokinesis

_____ 15. Stratton's experiment with distorting lenses indicates
a. the importance of learning in perception
b. that we are never certain how perceptual processes occur
c. the importance of our innate perceptual processes
d. how we organize our perceptual field

_____ 16. If you view a spot of light within a frame and the frame is moved while the spot remains stationary, you will
a. feel as if you are moving
b. perceive both the spot and frame as moving
c. perceive the spot as moving
d. perceive the frame as moving

_____ 17. Brightness constancy is primarily due to the fact that the brightness of an object
a. is determined by the amount of light it reflects
b. is judged in relation to its surroundings
c. is judged the same regardless of its surroundings
d. depends upon its color

_____ 18. The phenomenon of extrasensory perception does *not* include
a. telepathy
b. clairvoyance
c. precognition
d. psychokinesis

_____ 19. When the mother called her infant from the side of the visual cliff, he
a. crawled on the deep side

b. first patted *the glass with his* hand and then crawled on the deep side
c. remained immobile
d. refused to crawl on the deep side

_____ **20.** Experiments with infants show that size constancy
a. is an innate ability
b. is present to some degree in the early months but improves with age
c. is solely the result of learning
d. never appears before six months

class exercise

EXTRASENSORY PERCEPTION

introduction

Extrasensory perception is a controversial topic in psychology. Many psychologists doubt that it is possible to transfer thoughts from one person to another without any physical intermediary. Others claim that thought transference—a form of ESP known as telepathy—has been adequately demonstrated in the laboratory. This exercise is similar to some laboratory experiments that have been conducted to demonstrate the existence of telepathy. The procedure has been simplified, however, to avoid the necessity of elaborate statistical analysis.

equipment needed

An Indian-head nickel and a screen to shield the "sender" from view of the class.

procedure

The instructor will select from the class someone who feels that he might be a good "sender of thoughts." The sender will sit behind a screen and toss a nickel for 10 separate trials, each time concentrating on the side of the coin that faces up (either buffalo or Indian head) and trying to transfer this image to the class, which will act as subjects. One student will observe the sender and record the results of each toss. It is best if the sender shakes the coin in a glass or cup and then inverts the container to deposit the coin on a flat surface.

The instructor will start each trial by saying the word "now"; the sender will toss the coin and concentrate upon the upturned image; the instructor will say "receive" and each student will try to concentrate upon the image being sent; when the instructor says "record" each student will write by the proper trial number the word "buffalo" or "Indian head," depending upon the image he feels he has received.

treatment of data

On the basis of chance we would expect 5 Indian heads and 5 buffalos from ten coin tosses. And if a subject's guesses were based on chance alone, rather than ESP, we would expect him to be correct on 5 out of his 10 guesses—or 50 percent of the time. With only 10 trials we would expect considerable chance variation from the 50/50 results. Many more trials would be required before chance effects would become insignificant. But our experiment should give us a rough approximation.

The instructor will read the results of the 10 trials so that you can score your guesses. He will then determine by a show of hands the number of students obtaining 1 correct guess, 2 correct guesses, and so on. How many students had results that were below chance level? How many above chance level? How many exactly at chance level? What do you think the results demonstrate concerning the possibility of ESP?

The instructor will now select the three students with the lowest number of correct guesses and the three with the highest number and repeat the experiment with the same sender and these students.

questions for discussion

1. Are the students who were good receivers in the first part of the experiment still scoring above chance for the second ten trials? Are the students who were initially poor receivers still poor?

2. How do these results affect your interpretation of the findings from the first experiment?

3. What additional controls would you want to see enforced to make this a better ESP experiment?

individual exercises

A. THE PHI PHENOMENON

This drawing illustrates the phi phenomenon. Hold the hand in either position and alternately close the right and left eyes. While actually seen in a station-ary position, the finger appears to move. Thus you get a perception of motion without a moving stimulus.

Why does this occur? Can you think of an industry that depends on this same phenomenon?

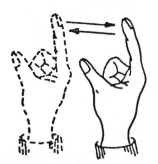 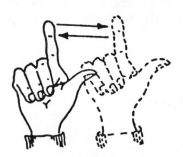

B. THE AFTEREFFECTS OF MOTION

Cut out the spiral disc on page 75 and paste it on a piece of cardboard. Attach it with a thumb tack to the end of a pencil. Spin the disc slowly and stare steadily at it as it moves. Stop the disc and notice what happens. Does it seem to be turning in the opposite direction? If you were turning the disc so that the spiral was expanding, it will seem to contract when stopped, and vice versa. When the spiral is turning steadily, our visual system tends to suppress the perceived motion, apparently by generating some sort of opposing process. When the actual movement stops, the opposing process continues for a while, and you see it as apparent motion in the opposite direction.

Now look at the spiral again as it spins slowly, then turn to look at a blank wall or a picture. The opposing process will even make the wall or picture appear to move in the opposite direction to the direction of the spiral's movement. The process apparently is not limited to spirals but applies to anything in the visual field.[1]

You may have noticed a similar effect in nature. If you look steadily at a waterfall or a flowing river for a while and then transfer your gaze to the rocks beside the falls or the river bank, whatever you are looking at appears to move in the opposite direction from the flow of water.

[1] Courtesy of Dr. Thomas Cornsweet, Stanford Research Institute.

7 states of awareness

programed unit

1. There are various states of awareness, or *consciousness*. Even the familiar, *normal waking consciousness,* in which we can report what is happening around us, is not a simple state. While we are listening to a friend describing a play he attended, we may explain to him why we could not attend and at the same time be thinking of the examination scheduled for the next hour. It is clear that normal waking consciousness is (*simple/complex*).

complex

2. Not all of our waking states are *alert;* we may find ourselves staring blankly into space, neither examining anything nor thinking of anything in partic-

alert

ular. This state in which we are less *a_____* contrasts with a state of mental activity or alertness that is sometimes called *vigilance.*

3. The squirming, pencil-chewing, and finger-tapping one does while studying

vigilance

are methods of keeping oneself alert, or in a state of _____ .

4. As you might expect, studies show that loss of sleep results in poor per-

vigilance (or attention)

formance on tasks that require sustained _____ .

consciousness

5. Besides the normal waking *c_____* , in which we can report accurately what is happening around us, there are other states of waking awareness in which consciousness is altered, such as excessive fatigue, delirium, intoxication, and ecstasy.

6. Some *altered* or *distorted* states of consciousness are caused by disease or

altered (or distorted)

by drugs. An example is *delirium,* a state of _____ consciousness most often associated with alcoholism, but which may accompany high fever. This is a confusional state, a departure from reality, with both *hallucinations* and *delusions.*

delirium

7. *Hallucinations,* which are found in the state of _____ , are *sense-like perceptions* that have a minimum of support from external stimuli. If a person hears his mother reprimanding him when in reality his mother has

hallucinations   been dead for five years, he must be experiencing _____ .

8. False sensory perceptions that have a minimum of support from external

hallucinations   stimuli are called _____ .

9. *Delusions* are *faulty thought systems* in which sense perceptions may be accurate but *events misinterpreted*. For example, a mental patient believes that creatures from another planet are trying to gain control of his thoughts by sending impulses through the electrical outlets in his room. He sees a nurse plug in a lamp and believes that she is in league with his persecutors. The

misinterprets   patient's sense perceptions are accurate, but he *mis*_____

delusions   the events he perceives. He is experiencing _____ .

10. The same patient also sees green spiders crawling out of the electrical outlets when actually there are no spiders in his room. He is experiencing

hallucinations   _____ in addition to his delusions.

11. Both hallucinations and delusions may occur during the altered state of

delirium   waking consciousness that is called _____ .

12. The state that is most commonly contrasted with waking consciousness is

sleep   *sleep*. We might think of _____ as a state of *lessened awareness* and activity.

13. Sleep is *not* altogether unconscious, since we can recall many of our dreams. Sleep does not come about simply because the bodily processes resulting from waking activities require it, since, to a degree, a person can choose either to sleep or to remain awake regardless of the condition of the body. It is *not* entirely quiescent, because some people toss and turn in their sleep and some even sleepwalk. Therefore we think of sleep as a state of lessened

awareness   _____ rather than a state of complete unawareness.

Sleep   **14.** _____ is a state of lessened awareness. Because it differs from the normal conscious state, we think of it as an altered state of consciousness.

15. In recent years scientists have discovered *four stages* of sleep. They have done this by using the *electroencephalogram* (abbreviated *EEG*), a method of studying the electrical action of the brain, and have found changes in the brain waves with deepening of sleep. They have also observed that *rapid eye movements* (abbreviated *REMs*) tend to occur during *dreams*. If subjects are awakened during a period of rapid eye movements, you would

dream   expect them to report that they have just had a _____ .

16. We can measure the electrical action of the brain with the electroencephalo-

EEG   gram (abbreviated _____), and we can tell whether a person is dreaming

REMs   because there will be rapid eye movements (abbreviated _____) accompanying dreaming.

movements   **17.** It is during *Stage 1* sleep that rapid eye _____ (REMs) usually occur. Therefore, _____ must occur more frequently during Stage 1 than during the other stages of sleep.

1, rapid
eye movements

18. Stage _____ of sleeping is often accompanied by REMs, or _____ _____ _____ .

REMs

19. Stage 1, with accompanying rapid eye movements (abbreviated _____), usually occurs in the *last third* of the night. Keep in mind that the four stages of sleep are determined by the nature of the brain waves rather than by the sequence of sleep. It is during the last third of the night, then, that we are

dreams

most likely to have _____ , since rapid eye movements occur then.

20. Do not confuse the various stages of sleep with the sequence of sleep. That is, Stage 1 of sleep is not predominant in the first hour of sleep but instead

third

occurs in the last _____ of the night.

1

21. Dreaming occurs during Stage _____ sleep.

electroencephalogram

rapid eye movement

22. The letters EEG symbolize _____ ;

the letters REM symbolize _____ _____ _____ .

rapid eye movements

1

23. During the period of REMs, or _____ _____ _____ , in Stage _____ of sleep, it is very difficult to arouse the sleeping subject. This dreaming stage is sometimes known as *paradoxical sleep,* because the subject is near to being awake by one criterion, the EEG, but is hard to arouse by another criterion, REMs.

24. The word "paradoxical" refers to a statement seemingly absurd or contradictory, yet in fact true. We can readily understand, then, why the term

paradoxical

_____ sleep is used to describe a phenomenon in which a subject is near to being awake by one criterion, EEG, but hard to arouse by another criterion, REMs.

25. During Stage 1-REM sleep, a subject is very difficult to arouse. This is known

paradoxical sleep

as _____ _____ , because the subject is difficult to arouse but appears to be nearly awake by the EEG criterion.

dream

26. Though the subject is more likely to _____ during Stage 1-REM sleep, occasionally a subject awakened from non-REM (NREM) sleep reports a dream. However, the dreams during NREM sleep are more like the *images* and *thoughts* that sometimes occur in the *initial* onset of sleep.

27. Some subjects report dreams during NREM sleep. However, their dreams

images
thoughts (either order)

more closely resemble the _____ and _____ that occur in the initial onset of sleep.

28. Does everyone dream? If we accept the Stage 1-REM evidence, then it is true that *everyone* dreams, though some people recall very few dreams. Thus

everyone

we can say that (*everyone/not everyone*) dreams.

29. Another interesting question is, "Can the sleeper react to stimuli from the environment without awakening?" During REM sleep, if stimuli such as spoken names are presented while the person is dreaming, the subject is not likely to awaken but instead will *incorporate* the external stimuli into his dreams in some manner. Thus, if John is in Stage 1-REM sleep and he hears the name "Mary" (the name of his girl friend) spoken to him, he is

incorporate

likely to _____ her name into his dream in some manner.

30. The answer to the question "Can the sleeper react to the environment without awakening?" is (*yes/no*).

yes

31. Both *sleeptalking* and *sleepwalking* occur primarily during NREM sleep and

1-REM

probably not in relation to dreaming, which occurs in Stage _____-_____ sleep.

sleepwalking
sleeptalking
(either order)

32. Occurring primarily in NREM sleep are two phenomena, *sleep*_____

and *sleep*_____ .

33. The most influential theory of dreams within the last half-century has been that of Freud. He believed that *unconscious* impulses were responsible for the dream, and that the aim of the dream was the *gratification* of some *drive*. Harry, who has been married two years, dreams that he is single. According

unconscious

to Freud, Harry has a(n) _____ wish that he were single.

unconscious

34. According to Freud, dreams express _____ im-

gratification

pulses and provide the _____ of some drive.

35. According to Freud's analysis, the *remembered* aspects of a dream constitute the *manifest content* of the dream. However, the *real meaning* of the same dream, or the *latent content,* is not directly expressed but is instead dramatized in disguised form; even the dreamer cannot readily discern its hidden meaning. If Bob recalls that he dreamed last night that he was flying over

manifest

the campus grounds, this would be the dream's _____
content, since it is the remembered content of the dream.

36. The real meaning of Bob's dream is incomprehensible to him; it is the

latent

_____ content of the dream.

37. Freud believed that dreams are highly *symbolic* and basically *wish-fulfilling*.

gratification
(or fulfillment)

That is, the dream is directed toward the _____
of some drive, or unconscious wish.

38. Dreams are difficult to interpret, even for the dreamer, because they are

symbolic, unconscious

highly _____ . They express the _____
impulses of the dreamer.

39. Sexual tensions may be reduced by erotic dreams. In this case the dream may

unconscious

satisfy some of the _____ impulses of the dreamer;

wish

thus its function is _____-fulfilling.

40. Freud believed that dreams are the *guardian of sleep*. In dreams unfulfilled

symbolic

guard

impulses appear in disguised or *sym_____* form; thus the dreams prevent the sleeper from being awakened by the disturbing impulses. In this sense dreams serve to *g_____* sleep.

sleep

41. Partial support for Freud's notion that dreams are the guardian of _____ comes from research in which subjects were *deprived* of their normal quota of dreams by being awakened whenever they began to dream; the onset of dreaming was indicated by REMs, which, as you recall, occur during

1

Stage _____ sleep.

42. After being deprived of dreams for several nights, the subjects were allowed to sleep freely; now they dreamed much more than usual. These results

deprived

suggest that dreams are necessary. A person who has been _____ of dreams tends to dream more than usual.

43. If dreams are necessary, perhaps one of their functions, as Freud said, is to

guard

manifest

latent

_____ sleep. According to Freud, the aspects of the dream that are remembered are the _____ content. The real, hidden meaning of the dream is its _____ content.

44. Another altered state of consciousness, which was once believed to be similar to sleep, is *hypnosis*. Evidence indicates, however, that hypnosis differs from sleep; EEG measures taken during hypnosis are like those of

stages

waking rather than any of the four _____ of sleep.

is not

45. We can thus say with assurance that hypnosis (*is/is not*) like ordinary sleep.

46. An individual in a *hypnotic state* does not initiate activity but waits for the hypnotist to tell him what to do. Thus we may say that one characteristic of

hypnotic

the _____ state is a decrease in the *planning function*.

47. Another characteristic of the hypnotic state, in addition to a decrease in the

planning

_____ function, is a *reduction in reality testing*. A hypnotized individual will readily accept reality distortion or hallucinated experiences (for example, petting an imaginary rabbit that he has been told is sitting on his lap). The same person in the normal waking state would usually reject

reality

such a distortion of _____ .

48. The hypnotic state thus differs from the normal waking state in (1) a de-

planning function

reality

crease in the _____ _____ and (2) a reduction in _____ testing.

reality testing

49. Closely related to the reduction in _____ _____ under hypnosis is an increase in *suggestibility*. The hypnotized person will readily accept suggestions. If he is told he is very warm, he may begin to perspire. If told that he is angry, he may show signs of irritability.

suggestibility

50. Another characteristic of the hypnotic state is increased *sug_____* .

is not

51. Let's review. Hypnosis (*is/is not*) similar to sleep. Hypnosis also differs from the normal waking state. A hypnotized person usually shows a decrease

planning function	in the _____ _____ , a reduction in
reality, suggestibility	_____ testing, and increased _____ .
consciousness	**52.** Hypnosis is an altered state of c_____ usually in-
hypnotist	duced by another person, the h_____tist. It is possible, however, for a
state	person to induce an altered _____ of consciousness on his own
	through a kind of *self-hypnosis* or *controlled meditation*.
	53. The Hindu system of *yoga* and *Zen,* which is derived from the Buddhist
controlled	philosophy, both stress a kind of self-hypnosis or _____
	meditation in which one strives to exclude all extraneous thoughts and
	stimuli by concentrating on a single object or thought or by focusing concen-
	tration on one's own breathing.
Zen	**54.** The kind of meditation achieved by those who practice yoga or _____
consciousness	frequently results in an altered state of _____ .
hypnosis	**55.** Two methods for altering waking consciousness are _____
meditation	and controlled _____ . It is also possible to produce
	profound changes in conscious experience by means of drugs.
	56. Drugs that affect man's *behavior* and *conscious experience* are called *psycho-*
	active drugs. *Tranquilizers* reduce anxiety and make a person feel more
psychoactive	serene; they are one class of *psycho*_____ drugs.
	57. *Energizers* are drugs that act as stimulants to help overcome depression and
psychoactive	fatigue. They form a second group of _____ drugs.
tranquilizers	**58.** Two groups of psychoactive drugs are _____
energizers (either order)	and _____ .
behavior	**59.** Psychoactive drugs are drugs that affect man's _____ and
experience	conscious _____ .
	60. A third class of psychoactive drugs is called *psychedelic,* or *"mind-manifest-*
	ing," because these drugs produce profound alterations in one's perceptions
mind-manifesting	and conscious experience. The psychedelic, or *mind-*_____ ,
	drugs include *LSD, marijuana,* and the *amphetamines*.
	61. Marijuana produces a mild feeling of excitement or euphoria. LSD, on the
	other hand, may produce serious distortions of consciousness, including
psychedelic	hallucinations. LSD and marijuana are both *psyche*_____ drugs.
	62. The amphetamines, also psychedelic drugs, are powerful stimulants that pro-
	duce restlessness and irritability and may cause severe psychological dis-
	turbances and brain damage. Since the amphetamines are stimulants, they
energizers	could be classed as *en*_____ . But because they produce
	profound alterations in perception and conscious experience, they are classed
psychedelic	as _____ drugs.

63.

psychoactive
tranquilizers, energizers
(either order)
psychedelic

To recapitulate: drugs that affect man's behavior and conscious experience are called _____ drugs. They include _____ , _____ , and mind-manifesting, or _____ , drugs.

64. In studying the effects of drugs it may be difficult to determine whether the changes observed in the subject's behavior result from the drug or simply from the power of *suggestion*. For example, if a subject is given a drug that he knows is a stimulant, he may expect to feel excited and energetic. Some of his behavior or the feelings he reports may stem from his expectations rather than from the actual physiological effects of the drug. To control for

suggestion

the possible effects of *sug_____* , experimenters use a group of subjects that receives a *placebo,* an *inert substance* that looks and tastes the same as the experimental drug but has no physiological effects.

65. For example, in an experiment to determine the effects of LSD on behavior, one group receives a sugar cube containing a drop of LSD, while the control group is given a plain sugar cube. The plain sugar cube is called a

placebo

_____ .

66. In an experiment to determine the effects of caffeine on memory for sentences, one group is given coffee and the other group Sanka (or some other

placebo

form of decaffeinated coffee). The Sanka is a _____ .

inert
suggestion
(or expectation)

67. A placebo is an _____ substance used in drug studies to control for the effects of _____ .

self-quiz

Select the alternative that best completes the thought. In some cases several answers are fairly satisfactory; you are to pick the *best* one.

_____ **1.** Some of the patterns that emerged in experiments with meditation reveal that the
  a. low responders reported detachment
  b. high responders reported dizziness and fogginess
  c. low responders felt intensification of bodily sensations
  d. high responders felt detachment

_____ **2.** Dreaming is usually associated with
  a. ease of awakening
  b. Stage 3 of sleep
  c. rapid eye movements
  d. a decreased arousal threshold

_____ **3.** Sleeptalking and sleepwalking occur

  a. primarily during REM sleep
  b. in about one-half of the subjects studied
  c. with equal frequency in both sexes
  d. primarily during NREM sleep

_____ **4.** People who are likely to be susceptible to hypnosis are
  a. weak and passive
  b. dependent
  c. troubled, anxious, or withdrawn
  d. normal and outgoing

_____ **5.** Studies of the sleeper's reaction to the environment have shown that
  a. subjects are unable to discriminate auditory signals during sleep
  b. sleep learning is impossible
  c. subjects can be taught to respond to a verbal signal given during REM sleep

d. the state of sleep is a completely inert one

_____ **6.** When the alcoholic believes he has seen a pink elephant, this is considered a(n)
   a. hallucination
   b. delusion
   c. dream
   d. peak experience

_____ **7.** A characteristic of the hypnotic state is that
   a. the planning function of the hypnotized individual remains active
   b. reality testing is increased
   c. the hypnotized subject becomes more suggestible
   d. attention becomes less selective

_____ **8.** We squirm, scratch, tap with our fingers, and so on, to maintain a state of vigilance. Recent physiological studies suggest that we are keeping active the
   a. limbic system
   b. reticular formation
   c. frontal lobes
   d. cerebral cortex

_____ **9.** In a study of the effects of marijuana it was found that
   a. performance on tests of motor skills showed impairment for the experienced subjects
   b. physiological changes for both groups were significant
   c. performances on tests of motor skills showed impairment for the inexperienced subjects
   d. the inexperienced group had many subjective experiences

_____ **10.** Subjects attempting to control the EEG alpha rhythm
   a. did so best when concentrating on mental arithmetic
   b. were able to do so only after several months
   c. were never successful
   d. were able to do so after only a brief period of practice

_____ **11.** Dreaming occurs in which stage of sleep?
   a. Stage 1
   b. Stage 2
   c. Stage 3
   d. Stage 4

_____ **12.** According to Freud's theory of dreams, the real meaning of the dream is called its
   a. latent content
   b. manifest content
   c. day residue
   d. displacement

_____ **13.** Does everyone dream?
   a. after the age of sixty people stop dreaming
   b. yes, everyone dreams
   c. nonrecallers actually do not dream
   d. scientists have been unable to determine whether everyone dreams

_____ **14.** The sugar pill that is given to a patient who thinks it is a helpful medicine is called a(n)
   a. placebo
   b. tranquilizer
   c. psychoactive drug
   d. energizer

_____ **15.** Waking consciousness
   a. is a single, simple state
   b. includes states of fatigue, delirium, intoxication, and ecstasy
   c. reveals our inability to look, listen, talk, and plan all at the same time
   d. only includes states of alertness

_____ **16.** Lysergic acid diethylamide (LSD) has
   a. proved to be harmless in its effects
   b. a standard, predictable effect upon the user
   c. highly individual and unpredictable effects upon the user
   d. been shown to be of little use in treating mild neurotic disturbances

_____ **17.** The amount of time spent in each of the sleep stages
   a. is distributed evenly throughout the night
   b. is the same for everyone
   c. is roughly: Stage 1, 35 percent; Stage 2, 15 percent; Stages 3 and 4, 50 percent
   d. varies from person to person, but for any one person the pattern is consistent

_____ **18.** Hypnotic susceptibility is
   a. a vague, unmeasurable quality
   b. a relatively stable personality characteristic

c. infrequent among college students

d. only a theoretical concept

___ 19. In one study the subject was aroused each time he began to dream. Later allowed to sleep freely, the subject

a. dreamed more than he did before deprivation

b. no longer had any dreams

c. returned to his normal quota of dreams

d. spent less than the average time dreaming

___ 20. The rhythms of sleeping and waking are controlled by

a. the hypothalamus

b. changes in dark and light

c. temperature changes

d. all of the above

key to self-quiz

20. d	15. b	10. d	5. c
19. a	14. a	9. c	4. d
18. b	13. b	8. b	3. d
17. d	12. a	7. c	2. c
16. c	11. a	6. a	1. d

individual or class exercise

BEHAVIOR MODIFICATION WITHOUT AWARENESS

introduction

As you have seen from this chapter, there are varying states of awareness. At times we are perfectly aware of what we are doing and seem to know why we are doing it. At other times we may do something and not know the cause. For example, when we are whistling a tune we do not always know how we came to choose this particular song. Sometimes we find out when we become aware of someone else whistling or humming the same song. This exercise is set up to show that we can be influenced by stimuli and not know that our behavior has been changed, much less what has changed it.

A fair amount of research data indicates that a person's verbal behavior can be influenced through subtle reinforcement. In this exercise the attempt will be made to cause a subject to give one kind of response rather than another kind, while keeping him unaware of the fact that he is being influenced. This type of study demonstrates the fact that some influences on behavior occur below the level of awareness.

equipment needed

A stopwatch or watch with a second hand. Small notebook or pad and pencil.

procedure

This exercise may be done in class, with the instructor supplying the subject. Or you may try it yourself on your own subject. Tell your subject that you are interested in investigating word associations, and that you want him to recite as many different nouns as he can think of and to continue to do so until told to stop. For the first minute the experimenter should do nothing. For the second minute he should say "um-hmm," or "okay," or nod his head after each plural noun but should do nothing after singular nouns. The experimenter should vary the type of reinforcement ("um-hmm," "okay," or nod) in a random order and should make his responses seem as natural as possible. If the experiment is done in class, a third person can be used to unobtrusively record the number of plural nouns given in each of the one-minute intervals. If you are conducting the experiment on your own, you can jot down marks in your notebook as the subject talks, using one kind of symbol for plural nouns (just the letter *P* will do) and a different symbol for singular nouns. The percentage of plural nouns should increase from the first to the second minute due to the reinforcing effect of the experimenter's responses.

Now select a different subject and reverse the sequence, reinforcing plural nouns during the first minute and doing nothing during the second. The percentage of plural nouns should decrease from the first to the second minute. In both instances ask the subject at the end of the procedure what he noticed about the experimenter's behavior and what he thought the procedure was all about. If he comments on the experimenter's responses, ask whether he felt that they had any effect on his behavior. You can also ask him whether he thought the percentage of singular or plural nouns changed as he went on. Usually the subject will not be aware that his verbal behavior has changed, nor will he be aware of the influence of the experimenter's responses.

This experiment can also be done with the subject reciting other parts of speech and can be conducted with groups of subjects. For instance, an experimental and a control group can be set up. The experimental group is given reinforcement after the desired response, while the control group receives no reinforcement.

individual exercises

A. EXPERIMENTAL MEDITATION

There are a number of ways of attaining a sense of detachment or meditation. Try both of the following techniques to see which helps you best in freeing your mind from extraneous thoughts while expanding your awareness. For either procedure you should choose a time when you are not sleepy; sit relaxed in a comfortable chair or on the floor supported by pillows. For the first procedure put an object such as a vase or a bowl on a table about 8 feet in front of you, keeping the background as simple as possible. Now concentrate all your attention on the object, excluding all other thoughts or feelings or body sensations. Do not try to analyze the object or associate ideas with it; simply concentrate on it as it is. After a few minutes you will find that it will be difficult to keep your eyes in proper focus. Do not try to retain a sharp focus; let your eyes unfocus as they will but continue to concentrate on the object for at least five minutes.

How did you feel? Were you able to avoid being distracted by events going on around you? Did you have a feeling of detachment, of being able to step aside and watch your feelings and ideas flow by without getting involved in them? Were there any perceptual distortions of the object being viewed? Did you have a feeling of more intense perception of the object? Was the state a pleasurable one?

Try the second technique and see if you get the same results. Again sit in a comfortable position but do not be so relaxed that you will go to sleep. Breathe naturally and focus your attention on your breathing: the movements of your chest and stomach, not the sensations in your nose and throat. Try to avoid being distracted by extraneous thoughts or stimuli. Keep your attention on your breathing, turning aside all other thoughts.

What are your feelings? Are they similar to or different from those elicited by the first technique? How do the sensations in both cases differ from those you experience while drowsy or in a half-asleep state?

After you have tried these two meditation techniques, reread the section in the text entitled "Meditation and self-induced alterations of consciousness" (Chapter 7, pages 178–80). How do your experiences compare with the findings described in the text?

B. RECORDING DREAMS

Keep a notebook in which you record your dreams as soon as you wake up in the morning. With practice you will find that you remember more of your dreams than you thought possible. Keep a record for several weeks. Are there recurring themes in your dreams? Can you trace events in your dreams to things that happened during the day? Do you dream in color? (Women tend to more than men.) Are your dreams populated by familiar people or by strangers? Do members of the opposite sex appear in your dreams more frequently than members of the same sex? Do you see yourself in your dreams? Do certain strong emotions permeate all your dreams?

The intention of this exercise is not to psychoanalyze yourself by means of dream analysis but to find out as much as you can about your own dreams and what factors you think influence them. It might be interesting to compare your dream experiences with those of a fellow classmate.

8 learning and conditioning

programed unit

1. *Learning* is a *relatively permanent change* in *behavior* that occurs as the

learning

result of *practice*. Not all changes in behavior can be called *l*_____ ; thus the definition must be qualified.

permanent

2. Learning is a relatively _____ change in behavior. This specification excludes changes in behavior resulting from such temporary conditions as fatigue or adaptation.

practice

3. Learning occurs as a result of _____ . By this statement we exclude from the definition of learning behavioral changes due to maturation, disease, or physical injury.

change

4. Therefore we say that learning is a relatively permanent _____ in

behavior, practice

_____ that occurs as the result of _____ .

5. Learning is one of the most basic problems in psychology. There are various explanations of learning, but we shall concentrate on two important inter-

learning

pretations of _____ .

6. Some psychologists interpret learning as *habit formation.* By this they mean that one learns a particular behavior by *associating* a stimulus with a re-

learning

sponse. This process, then, is referred to as associative _____ .

7. Learning to respond with a certain name when we perceive a stimulus object

associative

is an example of _____ learning. For example, we

habit

form the *h*_____ of saying "pen" when we ask for an ink-filled writing instrument.

8. The formation of a *habit* involves associating a *stimulus* with a *response.* If a smoker lights a cigarette whenever he begins to sip a cup of coffee, he has

87

stimulus, response | associated the _____ of coffee-drinking with the _____ of smoking.

9. Some habits consist of the association of several stimuli with a particular response. If a smoker always lights a cigarette when he sees another person smoking (as well as when he begins to sip coffee), then he has connected more than one stimulus with the smoking response through the process of

associative | _____ learning.

10. If habits are acquired by connecting a stimulus with a response and if stimulus-response connections are built up through associative learning, then

associative | we can say that habits are the result of _____ learning.

11. Let us say that whenever a given individual seats himself at his office desk, he leans back and lights a cigarette before opening his mail. We can then say that he has built up a connection between the stimulus of sitting at his office desk and the response of lighting a cigarette. In other words, he has built

habit | up a _____ of smoking in response to particular stimuli through

associative learning | _____ _____ .

12. Some psychologists argue that habit formation cannot adequately explain all learning, especially in humans. They agree that one can learn a poem by learning a connection between each word as a stimulus and the next word as a response, but they say that when one also *understands* the meaning of the poem, he is no longer operating on the basis of associative learning

understanding | alone. They regard *u_____ing* as a significant part of the learning process.

13. This second group of psychologists argues that *cognitive processes,* the processes of *perceiving* and *inferring* the *relationships* among events, are

processes | necessary for many types of learning. By cognitive _____ we refer to the perceptions and inferences that the learner makes about the

relationships | *rel_____* among events in his environment.

14. Thus the two groups of psychologists differ in their interpretations of learning. One thinks of learning in terms of habit formation, or the build-up of

associations | _____ between stimuli and responses. The other feels that often learning is not an associative process but rather a

cognitive | _____ process. Cognitive processes enable the learner to make inferences about events in the world; future behavior is governed by these inferences rather than by an automatic sequence of stimulus-response associations. (We will return to the distinction between associative learning and cognitive processes toward the end of the programed unit.)

15. In the study of associative learning, a particular experimental arrangement has often been used. A dog is placed in a harness and apparatus is set up in such a way that the dog's salivary flow can be accurately measured. Then some meat powder is placed on the dog's tongue, and the dog will secrete a copious amount of saliva. Since this response of salivating will take place even if the dog has never before been exposed to meat powder, it is an *unlearned*

response | *response.* Such a response is called an *unconditioned* _____ .

unconditioned	**16.** We find that blinking an eye to a puff of air aimed at the eye is also an unlearned response. Thus we can call it a(n) _____ response.
unconditioned response	**17.** If putting a bottle into the mouth of a newborn infant gives rise, the first time, to sucking, we would call the sucking a(n) _____ _____ .
response	**18.** Any response to a stimulus that is an unlearned response can be called an unconditioned _____ .
unconditioned	**19.** If a response that is unlearned is called an *unconditioned response,* then it seems logical to call the stimulus that gave rise to that response an _____ *stimulus.*
stimulus	**20.** In the case of the salivation mentioned above, the meat powder that gave rise to the salivation is called an unconditioned _____ .
response	**21.** Suppose now, in the dog experiment mentioned above, we ring a bell just before the meat powder is delivered to the dog. If this is done often enough, the bell will eventually give rise to the _____ of salivation even if the meat powder is not presented.
learned	**22.** The bell becomes the stimulus for the response of salivation. However, since the bell would not elicit salivation before it was associated with the meat powder, the connection between the bell and the salivation had to be *l_____* .
stimulus	**23.** Thus the bell is a learned stimulus, and we call that sound a conditioned _____ .
unconditioned	**24.** A *conditioned stimulus* is a stimulus that would not by itself give rise to the desired response but that gains the power to do so by being associated with an *un_____* stimulus.
conditioned	**25.** If putting a bottle into the mouth of an infant gives rise to sucking, this illustrates an unconditioned stimulus (bottle in mouth) that elicits an unconditioned response (sucking). If, later on, the child begins to suck at the *sight* of the bottle, then this stimulus (sight of bottle) would be called a(n) _____ stimulus.
unconditioned unconditioned	**26.** In the case of a stimulus that gives rise to a response the first time the stimulus is offered, the stimulus is called a(n) _____ stimulus and the response a(n) _____ response.
conditioned	**27.** If we have to associate the stimulus with an unconditioned stimulus before it has the power to evoke the response, the learned stimulus is called a(n) _____ stimulus.
	28. If the response to an unconditioned stimulus is called an unconditioned re-

sponse, then the response to a conditioned stimulus will be called a(n)

conditioned

_____ response.

29. The connection between a conditioned stimulus and a conditioned response

learned

must be _____ .

30. The connection between an unconditioned stimulus and an unconditioned

unlearned (or innate)

response is _____ .

31. *Classical conditioning* is the name given to the method by which organisms acquire (learn) connections between stimuli and responses through associative learning. It can be defined as the formation of an association between a

conditioned

conditioned stimulus and a c_____ response through repeated presentation of the conditioned stimulus in a controlled relationship with the unconditioned stimulus until the conditioned stimulus alone produces the response originally elicited by the unconditioned stimulus.

32. The experiment described above, in which the dog learns to salivate to the

classical

sound of a bell, is an example of _____ conditioning.

33. The more times we present the conditioned stimulus with the unconditioned

conditioned

stimulus, the stronger will be the response to the _____ stimulus.

34. In other words, the more often the conditioned stimulus is associated with the unconditioned stimulus, the better the animal will learn the association.

unconditioned

The pairing of the conditioned stimulus with the u_____ stimulus is called *reinforcement,* because the pairing makes the conditioned response stronger.

35. If we pair the bell (conditioned stimulus) with the meat powder (unconditioned stimulus) twenty times, the salivation to the bell will be stronger than if we only pair them ten times. The association between the bell and the salivation is stronger in the former case because the association has been

reinforced

*re*_____ more often.

36. The paired presentation of the conditioned stimulus and the unconditioned stimulus, which strengthens the conditioned response, is called _____

reinforcement

_____ .

37. However, if we set up in a dog the response of salivating to a bell (the conditioned stimulus) and then continually ring the bell without giving any meat

unconditioned

powder (the _____ stimulus), eventually the dog will stop salivating to the bell.

38. In other words, if we pair the conditioned and unconditioned stimuli until the dog responds with salivation to the conditioned stimulus, and then continually

reinforcement

present only the conditioned stimulus, so that there is no *re*_____ , gradually the dog will stop salivating to the stimulus.

39. Repetition of the conditioned stimulus without reinforcement is called *extinc-*

tion. The association between the bell and the meat powder is weakened by presenting one without the other. In *extinction* we repeatedly present the

conditioned

_____ stimulus without the unconditioned stimulus.

40. When we present the conditioned stimulus without the unconditioned stimulus, the conditioned response is weakened because it is not being

reinforced

*re*_____ .

conditioned
unconditioned

41. Let us suppose that on Monday we present a bell (_____ stimulus), then meat powder (_____ stimulus), and elicit the response of salivation.

42. We continue this procedure until the response occurs to the conditioned

conditioned

stimulus alone. Then on Tuesday we present only the bell (_____

stimulus

_____) and continue presenting only the bell until the animal no longer gives the response of salivation. This process is called

extinction

_____ .

43. We now allow the animal to rest for two days; then on Thursday we present the conditioned stimulus (bell) again without the unconditioned stimulus (meat powder). Usually the animal will respond with salivation. In other words, the response is recovered after extinction and without any more reinforcement. This is called *spontaneous recovery*. It is called "spontaneous"

reinforcement

because the response recovered without any additional _____ .

44. Following extinction the return of the conditioned response without more

spontaneous recovery

reinforcement is called _____ _____ .

45. Suppose we condition a dog to respond with salivation to a touch on the back near the hindquarters. To do this we touch the dog on the back and, a second later, put meat powder on its tongue. Let us call the touch near the hind-

conditioned

quarters (which is the _____ stimulus) stimulus 1 (S_1).

46. Once this conditioning has been established, if we touch the dog on another spot on its back (S_2), we find that the dog will make the response of salivation to this stimulus as well, although it has never been reinforced for this

S_1

stimulus. Therefore S_2 has substituted for _____ .

47. Responding to S_2 with the response that was conditioned to S_1, even though S_2 has not been established as a conditioned stimulus, is called *generalization.* The more similar S_2 is to S_1, the stronger will be the tendency to generalize.

generalization

In _____ the organism makes the *same* response to a new stimulus that it learned to make to an old stimulus; it does so because the new stimulus is similar in some way to the old stimulus.

48. Generalization consists of the following sequence: (1) a stimulus is conditioned to a response; (2) the organism is presented with a new stimulus that is similar to, but not identical with, the conditioned stimulus; (3) the or-

same

ganism responds to the new stimulus as though it were the _____ as the old one.

49. When an organism makes the same response to a stimulus (S_2) that it has learned to make to a different stimulus (S_1), we note the operation of the

generalization

principle of _____ .

50. Let us suppose that, in the experiment described above, every time we touch the dog near the hindquarters (S_1), we put meat powder on its tongue and we never put meat powder on its tongue after touching the dog on the other spot (S_2). Eventually the dog will no longer respond to S_2, although it will

respond

continue to _____ to S_1. The animal has learned to tell the two stimuli apart (to react to them differentially).

51. In the situation just described, the dog has learned to *discriminate* between

same

the two stimuli and thus does not make the _____ response to both of them.

52. When the organism learns *not* to make the same response to both of the stimuli—that is, when it distinguishes between them—we call the process *discrimination*. When there are two stimuli, one of which is *always* reinforced and the

discriminate
(or distinguish)

other *never* reinforced, the organism will in time _____ between them and respond to the former and not to the latter.

53. If we condition a dog to salivate to a tone of 1000 cycles, reinforcing the tone with food, and then present a 500-cycle (lower) tone, the dog will probably salivate in response to both tones. However, if we never reinforce the 500-cycle tone with food but always reinforce the 1000-cycle tone, the dog will eventually stop salivating in response to the 500-cycle tone but will continue to salivate to the 1000-cycle tone. This is an example of the process

discrimination

of _____ .

54. In classical conditioning the stimulus in some way forces the response. Thus

salivation

the meat powder gives rise to _____ as an involuntary

involuntary

response; the air puff gives rise to blinking as a(n) _____ , not as a voluntary, response.

55. There are other kinds of behavior in which the stimulus leads to the response but does not force it. For example, the stimulus of someone's ringing your doorbell will usually lead to your going to the door to open it; however, the

does not

stimulus (*does/does not*) force you to do so.

56. In the example in the preceding frame, if you don't want to open the door, you don't have to. The response of opening the door is called an *operant*

response

response because such a _____ usually "operates" on the environment.

57. If we put a hungry rat in a maze that contains food, it will make certain responses to get to the place where the food is; if we cover the food, the rat

operant

will learn to turn over the cover. These are _____ responses.

58. Whenever an organism acts in order to get something from the environment (when it does something to operate on the environment), we may call this an

operant

_____ response.

59. *Operant conditioning* differs in certain ways from classical conditioning. In the classical-conditioning situations we discussed, the animal was passive; it did not have to do anything in order to receive the unconditioned stimulus (the reinforcement). When we were teaching the animal to salivate to a bell,

unconditioned

we rang the bell and then delivered the meat powder (the _____ stimulus) regardless of what the animal did.

operant

60. In *op*_____ conditioning, however, the animal must make some kind of response in order to get the reinforcement.

61. In classical conditioning the animal can be passive and still be reinforced; in

operant

_____ conditioning the animal must be active in order to be reinforced.

62. Operant conditioning refers to increasing the probability of a response by

reinforcement

following the response with _____ .

63. For example, we want Johnny to develop the habit of working hard in school. To do this we give him extra spending money for each high grade he receives. Since the extra money strengthens the response of working hard in school,

reinforcement

it constitutes a _____ of the response of working hard in school.

64. Jimmy continually runs into the street and his mother fears that he will get hurt. She wants to strengthen a response of avoiding the street whenever the stimulus of the street is perceived, so she spanks Jimmy whenever he goes

reinforcement

into the street. The spanking constitutes a _____ of the response of avoiding the street.

65. We have been assuming that every time an organism did something we would reinforce it. Thus every time a rat ran to the end of the maze, we would give it food. Suppose, however, we gave the rat reinforcement only every other time it performed the act that led to reinforcement. This procedure is called *partial reinforcement*. When we reinforce an organism only part of the time,

partial reinforcement

we are using _____ _____ .

66. Since a child's mother is not always present to reinforce a desired response,

partial

_____ reinforcement is the state of affairs that is most prevalent in everyday life.

67. One of the characteristics of partial reinforcement is that it makes the behavior more resistant to extinction than the behavior that is subject to 100

partially

percent reinforcement. Thus when a child is _____*ly* reinforced for a given behavior, this behavior tends to persist against many nonreinforcements.

68. When Jimmy cleans his room his mother notices his efforts only 40 percent of the time. She rewards him each time that she notices. With this reinforce-

longer than

ment schedule, Jimmy's behavior of cleaning the room will last (*longer than/ not as long as*) it would if 100 percent reinforcement were used.

69. As in classical conditioning, an operant response can be extinguished. If we suddenly stopped giving Johnny extra spending money for making good

reinforcement

grades, we run the risk that Johnny will eventually stop working hard (if money was his only reason for working). We would be producing *extinction* of the response of working hard by withdrawing _____ .

70. If a rat has learned to press a bar to receive food and the delivery of food no longer follows a bar press, we say that the operant response of bar-pressing

extinction

is undergoing _____ .

71. Classical conditioning and operant conditioning are two important but clearly different forms of learning. In classical conditioning, learning depends upon the experimenter's pairing of the unconditioned stimulus with the conditioned

passive

stimulus; in this sense the learning is (*active/passive*), since the organism cannot determine when the pairing will occur. In operant conditioning, the organism acts upon the environment in order to obtain reinforcement. The strength of the organism's response increases whenever the response is fol-

reinforcement

lowed by _____ .

72. So far we have discussed classical and operant conditioning: two simple forms of learning that can be viewed as *habit formation*. When more complex forms of learning are analyzed (such as mastering calculus, finding your way about a new city, or memorizing the lines of a play), it is doubtful that habit formation alone is sufficient to account for what takes place. Learning in

habit

these situations undoubtedly involves more than simple _____

formation

_____ ; it requires perceiving and understanding the relationships among events occurring in the environment. The process of perceiving and, in turn, understanding the relationships among events are what

cognitive processes

earlier we called *cog*_____ _____ .

73. Often we learn to solve a puzzle by *suddenly* perceiving a relationship, previously not seen, between parts of the puzzle. This type of problem-solv-

sudden

ing through _____ perception of a relationship is called *insight* learning.

74. Since insight requires perceiving new relationships among parts of a problem,

cognitive processes

it reflects the operation of _____ _____ rather than simple habit formation.

Note: Much of man's behavior is governed by the laws of classical and operant conditioning. To say that man is a creature of his habits is to describe at least part of his behavior accurately. At the same time, habit formation alone is not enough to account for some of the complex forms of learning and problem-solving that we will encounter in later chapters. In these cases learning depends upon man's ability to perceive and infer relationships among objects and events in his environment. These processes of perception and inference are what psychologists refer to as cognitive processes. They represent a higher form of learning that permits man to be more than an organism that responds automatically to each stimulus input. To understand learning, one needs both to understand the laws that govern classical and operant conditioning and to take account of the role of cognition.

self-quiz

Select the alternative that best completes the thought. In some cases several answers are fairly satisfactory; you are to pick the *best* one.

_____ 1. When Tolman theorizes about how rewards and punishments influence behavior, he distinguishes between
   a. knowledge and learning
   b. learning and performance
   c. behavior and performance
   d. behavior and knowledge

_____ 2. Which of the following is *not* a measure of success of conditioning?
   a. amplitude of CR
   b. latency of CR
   c. number of trials to criterion
   d. amplitude of CS

_____ 3. The response to the ringing of a telephone is considered
   a. operant behavior
   b. respondent behavior
   c. discriminative behavior
   d. conditioned behavior

_____ 4. Mirror drawing, target tracking, and rote memorization are all examples of
   a. sensorimotor skills
   b. multiple-response learning
   c. operant conditioning
   d. classical conditioning

_____ 5. In a study by Köhler, a chimpanzee trying to reach the fruit outside its cage solved the problem by
   a. the trial-and-error method
   b. rote memorization
   c. insight
   d. modeling its behavior after the experimenter

_____ 6. Extinction of a response is likely to occur when
   a. there is only partial or intermittent reinforcement
   b. the conditioned response generalizes to other stimuli
   c. the unconditioned stimulus is presented continually without the conditioned stimulus
   d. the conditioned stimulus is presented continually without the unconditioned stimulus

_____ 7. In operant conditioning, reinforcement
   a. elicits the response
   b. is always positive
   c. follows the response
   d. is always negative

_____ 8. A hungry animal engages in food-seeking behavior; after being fed this behavior disappears. This supports the view that reinforcement is
   a. more a function of the reinforcing activity than of the reinforcing stimuli
   b. not essential for learning to occur
   c. important only in motivating the animal to respond
   d. drive-reducing

_____ 9. Rats were exposed to a bright light while being injected with an overdose of insulin. In time the bright light alone produced a response that was almost indistinguishable from that produced by insulin. The unconditioned stimulus in this experiment was the
   a. bright light
   b. insulin
   c. hypodermic needle
   d. shock reaction

_____ 10. In operant conditioning the rat learns to press the bar only in the presence of a light. The light serves as
   a. a distractor stimulus
   b. a discriminative stimulus
   c. partial reinforcement
   d. the operant stimulus

_____ 11. The term "learning" refers to changes in behavior that result from
   a. the influence of drugs
   b. maturation
   c. temporary conditions like adaptation
   d. practice and are relatively permanent

_____ 12. In the experiment that used operant-conditioning techniques to encourage the withdrawn, shy nursery-school child to talk and join in group activities, the reinforcing stimulus was
   a. candy
   b. ignoring behavior

c. attention

d. verbal disapproval

_____ 13. The sight of the baby's bottle after he has been nourished by it for some time will be likely to cause the hungry baby to start drooling. The *sight* of the bottle is a(n)
a. unconditioned stimulus
b. unconditioned response
c. conditioned stimulus
d. conditioned response

_____ 14. A learning curve for sensorimotor skills usually shows a pattern of
a. decreasing gains
b. decreasing losses
c. increasing gains
d. increasing losses

_____ 15. A feature of secondary reinforcement that has important practical implications is that
a. it has a wide degree of generalization
b. an animal can learn it readily
c. no special laboratory equipment is needed for training
d. it narrows the range of possible conditioning

_____ 16. Which of the following is most difficult to explain in terms of drive-reduction theory?
a. hungry rats are usually very active
b. a rat presses a lever to terminate shock
c. hungry rats will learn to choose the correct path in a maze, even though they are reinforced with a nonnutritive substance
d. hungry rats learn to run a T-maze when milk is injected directly into the stomach as reinforcement

_____ 17. If we could regulate the parameters of reinforcement to produce an optimal learning condition, we would

a. delay the reinforcement and increase its amount
b. delay the reinforcement and decrease its amount
c. give immediate reinforcement and increase its amount
d. give immediate reinforcement and decrease its amount

_____ 18. In Pavlov's experiment with classical conditioning, the dog salivates when a light is turned on, even though food may not follow. In this case the salivation is called a(n)
a. conditioned response
b. unconditioned response
c. conditioned stimulus
d. unconditioned stimulus

_____ 19. Classical conditioning, sometimes called the method of stimulus substitution, fails to account for
a. the acquisition of habits
b. the existence of secondary reinforcement
c. novelty in behavior
d. the amplitude of the conditioned response

_____ 20. Which of the following is *not* true of insight?
a. insight depends upon the arrangement of the problem situation
b. once the solution occurs, it can be repeated promptly
c. the solution achieved with insight can be applied to new situations
d. insight depends upon a gradual process of trial and error

key to self-quiz

20. d	15. a	10. b	5. c
19. c	14. a	9. b	4. b
18. a	13. c	8. d	3. a
17. c	12. c	7. c	2. d
16. c	11. d	6. d	1. b

class exercise

THE PROCESS OF LEARNING

introduction

Learning so pervades human activity that any curiosity about the nature of man and his behavior sooner or later leads to inquiry about how his habits are formed, how his skills are acquired, how his preferences and tastes develop, how his knowledge is obtained and put to use. But what exactly is "learning"? Although there are many varied definitions of this process, it might be defined as the modification of behavior through experience. This exercise will enable you to study the process of learning that goes on in modifying previously acquired behavior.

equipment needed

Red pencil or pen with red ink. A stopwatch or watch with a second hand.

procedure

Tear out page 99, which you are to use for this experiment. When the instructor says "Go," write the letters of the alphabet backward in a vertical column from top to bottom. *Do not sacrifice accuracy for speed.* Your instructor will allow you twenty seconds to write as many letters as you can for each trial. If you complete the alphabet, start over again. As soon as he says "Stop," fold the paper along the vertical line for each trial. This procedure will be continued for fifteen trials. Start with Trial 1 when the signal is given.

treatment of data

1. At the end of the fifteenth trial, count the number of correct letters on each trial and record these numbers at the bottom of page 99 in the space provided.

2. Copy the number of correct letters for each trial under "Score" in the following table.

Trial	Score	Trial	Score	Trial	Score
1		6		11	
2		7		12	
3		8		13	
4		9		14	
5		10		15	

3. Your instructor will ask you to record on a slip of paper the number of letters you got correct on each trial so that the average number of correct letters per trial for the class as a whole can be ascertained. When your instructor reads these group averages for each trial aloud, enter them in the space in the following table.

Trial	Group average	Trial	Group average	Trial	Group average
1		6		11	
2		7		12	
3		8		13	
4		9		14	
5		10		15	

4. Now plot your learning curve and the learning curve of the class as a whole on the graph on page 98. Use a pencil for your curve, and a red pencil or red ink for the class curve.

questions for discussion

1. Are there differences between the shape of your learning curve and that of the class? How do you account for the difference?

2. Does your progress from trial to trial indicate gradual learning?

3. Were there variables in this particular learning experiment that were uncontrolled?

4. How would you test for the permanence of learning to write the alphabet backward?

LEARNING CURVE

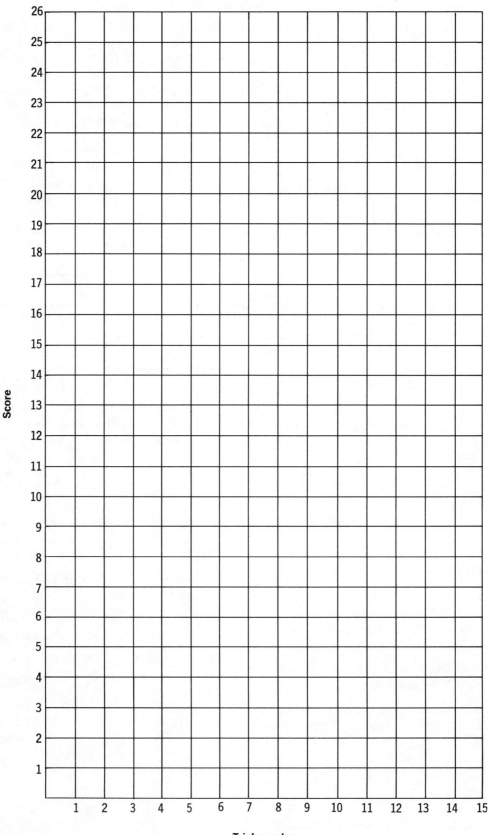

Score

Trial number

Trials

1	2	3	4	5	6	7	8	9	10	11	12	13	14	15

NUMBER
CORRECT

Trial
number

| 1 | 2 | 3 | 4 | 5 | 6 | 7 | 8 | 9 | 10 | 11 | 12 | 13 | 14 | 15 |

9 memory

programed unit

1. There are several ways in which we can show that we remember something. One kind of *remembering* is called *redintegration,* which refers to remembering the *whole* of an earlier experience on the basis of *partial cues.* Redintegration is one of several kinds of _____ .

remembering

2. To redintegrate means to reestablish an earlier experience on the basis of partial _____ . In sorting through a box of souvenirs you discover a seashell you picked up on the beach while vacationing with friends several years ago. The shell brings back vivid memories of the spot where you found it and the people you were with. This kind of remembering is called _____ .

cues

redintegration

3. In this example of redintegration, the seashell that evokes other memories is a _____ cue.

partial

4. While cleaning out a desk drawer Mrs. M. comes across the theater program of a play she and her husband attended the night they became engaged. The program, which evokes happy memories of that evening, is a partial cue for the process of _____ .

redintegration

5. When partial cues reestablish an earlier experience, we speak of redintegrative _____ . This kind of memory is distinguished from other kinds of remembering because it reconstructs the experience with its setting in time and place.

memory (or remembering)

6. Another kind of remembering is *recall,* which differs from redintegration in that you may not remember the circumstances under which learning took

recall

place. For instance, you may _____ a poem by reciting it, even though you may not be able to remember when you learned it or who taught it to you.

7. You can sing many songs you learned as a youngster even though you may *not* remember the circumstances under which you learned them. This kind

recall

of remembering is known as _____ .

remembering (or synonym)

8. Recall is an easier kind of _____ to measure than redintegration of earlier experiences and is therefore the kind of remembering commonly studied in the laboratory.

9. When we ask a laboratory subject to memorize a series of letters, and then

recall

to reproduce them, we are measuring _____ . The percentage correct is the recall score. This kind of remembering is easier to study than

redintegration

_____ , which involves the reestablishment of a past event and its surrounding circumstances.

recall

10. Of the two kinds of remembering mentioned thus far, _____ is the kind more likely to be studied in the laboratory.

11. Still another kind of remembering is *recognition*. Two other ways of remem-

recall, redintegration (either order)

bering are _____ and _____ .

12. *Recognition* merely requires the acknowledgement of something or someone as *familiar*. To measure recognition we might have a subject look through a series of cards containing words (or pictures). We then mix this series with an equal number of new words (or pictures) and ask the subject to indicate which ones he has seen before and which are new. Since the subject is asked merely to pick out the items that look familiar to him, this would be a test of

recognition

_____ .

recognition

13. Police use the kind of remembering called _____ for the identification of suspected criminals. The suspect is sandwiched in among a group of others, and a witness is asked to pick out the suspect merely on the basis of familiarity.

14. Recognition is one kind of remembering; it differs from recall and redintegration in requiring only that something or someone be recognized as

familiar

_____ .

15. Another way to show that something is remembered from past experience is to measure *relearning*. Material that you think you have completely forgotten may be easier to relearn a second time because it was once learned in the past. For example, suppose in high school you memorized Lincoln's Gettysburg Address so that you could recite it without an error. It took you one hour to accomplish one perfect recitation. In college, not having seen or practiced the speech in the meantime, you are sure you have forgotten it completely. But you find that you can now learn the speech to the same *criterion of mastery* in less than a quarter of an hour. Something must have been remembered from the original learning that was evidenced by the test

relearning of *re*_____ .

16. To test for relearning in the laboratory, we have the subject learn a list of word pairs well enough to achieve a certain standard of performance or

mastery criterion of _____ . Being able to go through the list once with-

criterion out any errors would be one _____ of mastery.

17. Four months later the subject relearns the same list to the same criterion of

mastery _____ . If the second learning requires fewer trials than the first, then we assume that there has been some *saving* due to the prior

saving learning. *Retention* of earlier learning is measured by the *s*_____ in relearning.

18. Study the formula given below, which expresses the saving due to prior

learning _____ in the form of a *percentage*.

$$\text{Saving score} = \left[\frac{\text{Original trials} - \text{Relearning trials}}{\text{Original trials}} \right] \times 100$$

saving 19. The _____ score is expressed in the form of a percentage.

20. If a subject initially required twenty trials to learn a list of word pairs and four months later required twenty trials to relearn the same list, his saving

0, no score would be _____ . In this case there is (*good/no*) evidence of retention.

21. If initially you required twenty trials to learn a list and four months later required ten trials to learn the same list, your saving score would be

50 _____ percent.

22. Tom learned a list of 100 Russian words in fifty trials. A year later he

60 learned the same list in twenty trials. His saving score would be _____ percent.

23. To obtain a saving score you subtract the number of relearning trials from the

original original trials, divide by the number of (*original/relearning*) trials, and then

multiply _____ by 100.

24. A saving score is an indication of how well the subject *retains* the learned material. The effects of intervals of *no* practice after initial learning, as shown by tests introduced at set periods following learning, can be plotted on a curve called a *retention curve*. Retention of learning, expressed as a

percentage saving score *p*_____ , is plotted against the intervals of time since initial learning.

25. Study the curve in the graph on the following page. As the label on the

retention vertical axis indicates, it is a _____ curve.

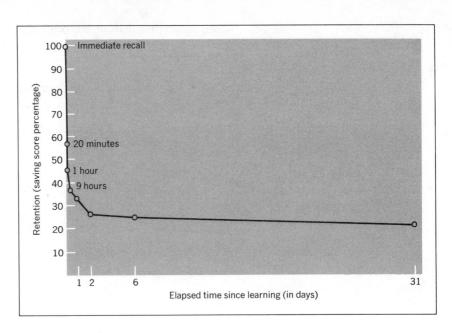

A saving score is an indication of how well the subject retains the material. The effects of time on retention of learning can be plotted on a

26. A saving score is an indication of how well the subject retains the material. The effects of time on retention of learning can be plotted on a

retention curve

_____ _____ . Note that a typical retention curve falls *rapidly* at first and then gradually tapers off.

rapidly

27. Though the curve of retention generally falls _____ at first and then gradually tapers off, the rate at which forgetting occurs will vary greatly with the materials used and with the circumstances under which learning takes place.

28. Let's review. We have discussed four kinds of remembering. These are

redintegration, recall, recognition
relearning (any order)

_____ , _____ , _____ , and _____ .

29. Of these kinds of memory only three can be readily studied in the laboratory.

recognition, recall

relearning (any order)

These three are _____ , _____ , and _____ .

30. Sometimes you may not be able to recall a certain piece of information but can show by recognition or ease in relearning that you have some memory of it. Thus, recognition and relearning are more sensitive measures of memory

recall

than _____ .

31. There are three traditional theories of *forgetting*. One of them, the theory of *decay* through disuse, assumes that learning leaves a "trace" in the brain; this *memory trace* involves some sort of physical change that was not present prior to learning. Some theorists believe that forgetting occurs because the

memory

_____ traces fade or decay with the passage of time, so that traces of material once learned gradually disintegrate and eventually disappear altogether.

32. As you look at a picture, it may reveal a wealth of detail, but after a period of time you forget many of the details of the picture. This lends credence to

decay

the view that forgetting is due to de_____ of the memory trace.

decay, memory

33. One theory, then, attributes forgetting to _____ of the _____ trace.

34. There are arguments, however, against the theory that the memory trace decays with the passage of time. Some old people can vividly recall events of their youth whereas they can barely remember the events of the day. This

decay

fact suggests that memories do not simply _____ .

35. A second theory assumes that it is not the passage of time that determines the course of forgetting but what we do in the interval between learning and recall. New learning may *interfere* with material that we have previously

interference

learned. Thus *inter*_____ rather than decay is the crucial factor.

36. The interference theory attributes forgetting to *retroactive* and *proactive inhibition*. *Retroactive inhibition* emphasizes that *new* learning interferes with *old* learning and thus causes forgetting of what was learned earlier. Assume that two hours ago you learned a list of twenty words. Now you learn a new

old

list of twenty words. The *new* learning should interfere with the _____

retroactive

list you learned two hours ago. Forgetting in this instance is caused by _____ inhibition.

37. The theory that new learning may interfere with the retention of the old is

inhibition

known as retroactive _____ .

38. An experimental group learns list A, then learns list B, and after an interval tries to recall list A. The control group learns list A, rests, and then tries to recall list A. If the control group does much better in recalling list A than the

retroactive

experimental group, we attribute the difference to _____

inhibition

_____ .

39.

Experimental group	Learn A	Learn B	Recall A
Control group	Learn A	Rest	Recall A

retroactive

The above is an arrangement for testing _____ inhibition.

40. A certain amount of retroactive inhibition occurs as the result of *normal waking activity*. Two groups of subjects learn a list of words. The subjects in one group go about their usual activities for three hours and are then tested for recall of the word list. The other group is tested at the same time but spent the intervening three hours sleeping. The latter group shows better retention of the word list. We conclude that some amount of retroactive in-

waking

hibition occurs as the result of normal _____ activity.

41. The notion that studying for an exam just before going to bed yields a better test performance than studying earlier in the day for the same amount of

retroactive

time, is based on the theory of _____

inhibition

_____ .

42. A companion interference theory, based on the same principles as retroactive inhibition and known as *proactive inhibition,* maintains that *prior* learning can also interfere with the learning and recall of *new* material. Note how the experimental arrangement below differs from that for testing retroactive

inhibition   inhibition. It is a method for testing *proactive* _____ .

| Experimental group | Learn A | Learn B | Recall B |
| Control group | Rest | Learn B | Recall B |

43. When *prior* learning interferes with the learning and recall of *new* material,

proactive   _____ inhibition is demonstrated.

new   44. Retroactive inhibition emphasizes that _____ learning interferes with

old   _____ learning. Proactive inhibition, on the other hand, emphasizes

prior (or synonym)   that _____ learning interferes with _____ learning.
new

45.
| Experimental group | Learn A | Learn B | Recall A |
| Control group | Learn A | Rest | Recall A |

retroactive   The above arrangement is for testing _____ inhibition.

| Experimental group | Learn A | Learn B | Recall B |
| Control group | Rest | Learn B | Recall B |

proactive   The above arrangement is for testing _____ inhibition.

forgetting   46. The theories of _____ discussed above emphasize the *decay* of memory traces through *disuse,* and the *interference* that *new* learning and *prior* learning exert on retention.

47. Thus far we have discussed two theories of forgetting. The first emphasizes

decay, disuse   the _____ of memory traces through _____ ; the second

prior (or synonym)   emphasizes the interference that new learning and _____ learning exert on retention.

48. A third theory of forgetting is that of *motivated forgetting.* That is, some memories are forgotten and cannot be recalled because their recall would in some way be unacceptable to the person because of the shame, anxiety, or

motivated   guilt they might activate. Amnesia is a dramatic example of _____ forgetting, since in amnesia certain personal memories are inaccessible to recall but impersonal memories remain intact.

49. The concept of *motivated forgetting* is based on the principle of *repression.* In repression, individuals forget certain memories because of the way they relate to personal problems; their recall would produce shame, anxiety, or guilt. If an individual cannot consciously remember an act of which he is

repressed   ashamed, many psychologists would say that the memory is _____*ed.*

motivated   50. A third theory of forgetting is that of _____ forgetting, whereby a person cannot consciously recall certain memories that would produce too much guilt, shame, or anxiety if recalled. Through the process

repression   of _____ these unacceptable memories are denied conscious expression.

51. If you committed an act that made you feel very guilty, ashamed, or anxious, the memory of that act may become inaccessible to conscious awareness

repression

motivated

through the process of _____ . When repression accounts for the loss of certain memories, we speak of _____ forgetting.

52. Motivated forgetting refers to the fact that memories are sometimes repressed from conscious awareness if recalling them would activate a person's feelings

*guilt, anxiety
(either order)*

of shame, _____ , or _____ .

53. The theory of motivated forgetting proposes that repressed memories are *not permanently lost,* they are just inaccessible to awareness. The fact that a person may become aware of repressed memories during psychotherapy or while

permanently

lost

under hypnosis indicates that such memories are not _____

_____ .

memory

trace

54. The theory that attributes forgetting to decay of the _____

_____ , however, implies that memories are permanently lost.

55. We have discussed three traditional theories of forgetting. The interference theory postulates two kinds of interference with learned material,

retroactive
proactive (either order)
decay

motivated

_____ and _____ inhibition. Of the remaining two theories, one stresses _____ of the memory trace through disuse, while the other considers _____ forgetting, based on the principle of repression.

56. Because no single one of these theories gives an adequate account of forgetting, a number of theorists have argued for a *two-process* theory. They propose that one type of storage mechanism is involved in remembering events just recently perceived and a different type is involved in the recall of

two-process

material that has been repeatedly practiced. A _____-_____ theory, then, postulates that there are two different storage mechanisms, one for *short*-term memory (*STM*) and the other for *long*-term memory (*LTM*).

57. A two-process theory of memory postulates that there are different storage

LTM

mechanisms for STM and for _____ .

58. Your own telephone number, which you have used repeatedly, is a relatively permanent memory and would be stored in LTM. The telephone number that you have just looked up in the directory will remain with you only

STM

momentarily in _____ . Unless you make a conscious effort to focus attention on the new number by repeating, or *rehearsing,* it to yourself, it is quickly lost from memory.

59. Incoming material enters the STM mechanism and, while there, can be recalled as long as it is *rehearsed.* If the information is not rehearsed, it will

rehearsed

fade rapidly. Once an item ceases to be _____ , its trace in STM begins to decay.

STM

60. Information can be maintained in _____ as long as it is rehearsed, but only a limited number of items of information can be rehearsed at the same time. The set of items being maintained in STM at any one time is called the *rehearsal buffer*.

61. The rehearsal _____ is the set of items, or memory traces, being

buffer

STM

maintained in _____ at any point in time.

62. The rehearsal buffer has a limited capacity because only a certain number of

rehearsed

items can be _____ at the same time. When new information enters STM the person must decide whether to include this item among those currently being rehearsed or permit it to decay.

63. Information remains in the rehearsal buffer until new, incoming information replaces it or until it is coded and transferred to LTM. If an item in the rehearsal buffer is replaced by new information before it is transferred to

LTM

_____ , it decays and is permanently lost.

64. In contrast to STM, the LTM mechanism has a virtually unlimited storage

LTM

capacity. Theoretically, once material is transferred to _____ , it should never be forgotten.

65. Actually, we know that this is not true. There are cases in which material we knew very well is not available to us. Forgetting may occur because the *cues* needed to retrieve the material are incomplete. For instance, an exam question may not contain the relevant cues to allow the retrieval of the ap-

cues

propriate information. If the _____ needed to retrieve the material are not complete, it will appear that the material has been forgotten.

66. It is also possible that initially only part of the desired information was

STM

coded into LTM and the rest decayed and was lost from _____ . In this case complete retrieval would not be possible—the information would not be available.

67. Forgetting may also occur when memories stored in LTM would make us feel ashamed or anxious. Repressed memories are permanently stored but

motivated

are inaccessible for retrieval. This is an example of _____ forgetting.

two-process

68. A _____-_____ theory of memory postulates two storage

short

mechanisms. One deals with _____-term memory and one with

long (either order)

_____-term memory.

69. Incoming material enters STM and is maintained there for a brief period in

rehearsal buffer

the _____ _____ . Rehearsal prevents the mem-

decaying

ory trace from _____ . Information in the rehearsal buffer

LTM

may be coded and transferred to _____ . Information not transferred to

decay

LTM will rapidly _____ . Information that is transferred will be stored permanently in LTM, from which it may be retrieved unless the

cues

_____ needed for retrieval are incomplete.

70.   Now that we have discussed the theories of forgetting, a logical question is, How can we improve recall? One useful technique in memorizing a poem or a series of words is to form a *mental image* of the items. For example, to memorize a set of chemicals that forms a certain compound one might visualize the chemicals as they appeared in labeled beakers upon a table. This

recall   mental picture would facilitate re_____ of the chemicals.

71.   If one learned a series of unrelated word pairs, such as *dog-bicycle* or *bird-sweater,* by visualizing a dog wearing a silly hat riding on a bicycle or a

mental   shivering bird dressed in a sweater, he would be using _____ images to facilitate recall.

72.   The *organization* of material in some meaningful fashion is another technique to improve memory. Thus a long list of minerals could be remembered more readily if the items were organized into categories (such as precious and nonprecious stones, rare and common metals) than if they were simply

Organization   learned in random order. *Org*_____ aids memory.

73.   If one wanted to remember the names of the original thirteen colonies, it

organize   would help to _____ them according to geographic location

image   or to form a mental _____ of them as portrayed on a map.

74.   A third technique to aid in memorizing is *self-recitation*. Studies have shown

reciting   that re_____ material to yourself increases retention better than simply reading and rereading the material. If you have two hours to devote to the study of an assignment that you can read in thirty minutes, you could reread the assignment four times or you could read it once and spend three-fourths of your time asking yourself questions about the material you have

self-recitation   read. Active recall, or *self*-_____ , would be the better of the two methods.

75.   The three techniques to improve recall that we have mentioned so far are

mental images,   forming _____ _____ , _____ ,
organization
self-recitation   and _____-_____ .

76.   If you wish to retain something over a long period of time, should you learn it to the point of bare recall or should you *overlearn* it? By *overlearning* we mean learning something well beyond the point of bare recall. Experimental evidence shows that a moderate amount of overlearning aids retention. Therefore, if you wish to retain new learning over a considerable period of

overlearn   time, you would be wise to _____ the material *beyond bare mastery* of it.

overlearning   77.   A moderate amount of _____ aids retention. Therefore, you learn something you wish to retain for an extended period of

bare   time beyond _____ mastery of it.

78.   Let's review. There are three traditional theories of forgetting. These are (1)

trace   decay of the memory _____ through disuse; (2) the

interference   _____ of new learning with old learning, which is

retroactive

proactive

motivated

repression

known as _____ inhibition, or of prior learning with new learning, which is known as _____ inhibition; and, finally, (3) _____ forgetting, which utilizes the process of _____ , whereby unacceptable memories become inaccessible to conscious awareness.

two-process

short, long (either order)

79. Since no one of these theories can adequately explain forgetting, some psychologists have proposed a _____-_____ theory of forgetting, which distinguishes between _____-term and _____-term memory.

images, organize

recitation

overlearn

80. We can improve our memories in several ways. We can make use of mental _____ to help in recall; we can _____ the material in some meaningful fashion; and we can make use of self-_____ to increase retention. It is also desirable to _____ material beyond the point of bare mastery.

self-quiz

Select the alternative that best completes the thought. In some cases several answers are fairly satisfactory; you are to pick the *best* one.

_____ **1.** When you reconstruct a past occasion with its setting in time and place, you are said to _____ the event.
  a. redintegrate
  b. recall
  c. recognize
  d. relearn

_____ **2.** Which of the following is the least likely to be helpful in improving learning and memory?
  a. sleeping ten minutes between periods of study
  b. forming mental images of what you wish to memorize
  c. carefully organizing what you wish to learn
  d. reciting to yourself during study

_____ **3.** The term "rehearsal buffer" refers to
  a. the practice time necessary for material to enter STM
  b. the set of traces being maintained in STM at any one time

  c. the set of traces being maintained in LTM at any one time
  d. the area surrounding LTM, which prevents decay of the memory trace

_____ **4.** A subject learns list A and then learns list B. After an interval he attempts to recall list A. This is a test of
  a. retroactive inhibition
  b. proactive inhibition
  c. motivated forgetting
  d. intentional recall

_____ **5.** The type of curve showing the amount of material retained as a function of time is called a
  a. saving curve
  b. relearning curve
  c. retention curve
  d. repetition curve

_____ **6.** Sometimes we can recite a poem from memory but cannot remember the circumstances under which we learned it. This kind of remembering is called
  a. recognition
  b. recall
  c. relearning
  d. redintegration

_____ **7.** Trace-dependent forgetting
   a. occurs when the information is stored in memory, but we are unable to retrieve it
   b. is caused by the actual decay of the memory trace
   c. is most clearly illustrated in the TOT state
   d. is supported by the theory of motivated forgetting

_____ **8.** The more lists a subject has previously learned
   a. the better his retention of the newly learned list
   b. the better his retention of the initial lists
   c. the poorer his retention of the newly learned list
   d. the poorer his retention of the initial lists

_____ **9.** An individual who, following brain surgery, is unable to transfer new information from STM to LTM would most likely
   a. forget his name
   b. fail to recognize someone he met a few minutes ago
   c. fail to recognize members of his family
   d. be unable to carry out mental arithmetic

_____ **10.** In cases of repression, forgetting is usually due to
   a. decay of the memory trace
   b. retroactive inhibition
   c. proactive inhibition
   d. personal factors that make the memory unacceptable

_____ **11.** The long-term memory system
   a. makes complete retrieval possible
   b. is a rapidly decaying system
   c. is characterized by trace-dependent forgetting
   d. provides an unlimited place for permanent storage

_____ **12.** Proactive and retroactive inhibition are examples of which theory of forgetting?
   a. decay through disuse
   b. interference effects
   c. motivated forgetting
   d. amnesia

_____ **13.** The kind of remembering most easily tested in the laboratory is
   a. redintegration
   b. recall
   c. recognition
   d. relearning

_____ **14.** Short-term memory is the storage place for
   a. your own name
   b. addition and multiplication tables
   c. the name of the person you just met
   d. the words and grammar of your language

_____ **15.** If recall is tested after an interval of rest
   a. no forgetting occurs
   b. just as much forgetting occurs as when the subject is active
   c. more forgetting occurs than when the subject is active
   d. less forgetting occurs than when the subject is active

_____ **16.** When rehearsal is prevented, items remain in STM
   a. permanently
   b. only after they have been transferred to LTM
   c. less than a half a minute
   d. only a minute

_____ **17.** Failure to recall immediately a word that is familiar has been called
   a. passive decay
   b. an all-or-none process
   c. _déjà vu_
   d. the TOT state

_____ **18.** If a student required 90 trials to learn a long list of Russian words and a year later required 30 trials to learn the same list of words, his saving score would be approximately
   a. 30 percent
   b. 50 percent
   c. 66 percent
   d. 90 percent

_____ **19.** In cases of amnesia, the person is usually unable to
   a. speak his native tongue
   b. read magazines and newspapers
   c. remember the multiplication tables
   d. none of the above

_____ **20.** A subject cannot recall the target word *symposium*. If he is in the TOT state, he is most likely to guess
    a. conference
    b. simple
    c. moratorium
    d. symbidium

key to self-quiz

20. d	15. d	10. d	5. c
19. d	14. c	9. b	4. a
18. c	13. b	8. c	3. b
17. d	12. b	7. b	2. a
16. c	11. d	6. b	1. a

individual or class exercise

IMAGERY VERSUS REHEARSAL IN MEMORIZING

introduction

The purpose of this exercise is to determine the effectiveness of two different techniques for memorizing a list of word pairs (called paired-associates). One technique is simply to repeat the two words several times; this is the sort of procedure one might use in memorizing the vocabulary of a foreign language. The other technique involves associating the two words by means of some kind of mental image.

equipment needed

Stopwatch or watch with a second hand.

procedure

Find a willing subject and read him the following instructions.

> The purpose of this experiment is to investigate two different techniques for memorizing word pairs. I will read a list of 20 paired nouns, one at a time. Your task is to learn the pairs so that later, when I give you the first word of a pair, you will be able to tell me the word that goes with it. There are two memory techniques I want you to use. For some pairs you are to repeat the two words aloud four times. For other pairs you are to remain silent while forming a mental image or picture in which the words are associated or interacting in some way—the more vivid or unusual the image the better. For example, if I give you the word pair "dog-bicycle," you might picture a dog dressed in a clown suit riding on a bicycle. Just before I give you each word pair, I will tell you which method of memorizing to use by saying either "repeat" or "image." For the pairs you are to rehearse aloud four times, try to avoid forming any mental images.
>
> After you have been given all 20 pairs, I will say "count" and you are to count backward from 99 until I tell you to stop. I will then test your memory by saying the first word in each pair, and you are to tell me the word that goes with it.
>
> Do you have any questions?

Answer any questions by repeating the appropriate part of the instructions. Start with the first paired-associate in the study list on page 113; give the appropriate instruction and then say the pair aloud. Continue in the same way until the list is completed. Time the presentation, allowing approximately 10 seconds for the study of each pair. You should practice the procedure at least once before trying it out on your subject.

After all 20 paired-associates have been presented, ask your subject to count backward from 99 for approximately 30 seconds. This task will prevent him from rehearsing the last few paired-associates. Now test his memory by reading aloud the words in the first column of the test list (S_1) and recording his responses in the second column (S_2) (see page 113). After you have completed the list check his responses for errors and tabulate the number of correct responses for repetition pairs and the number correct for imagery pairs. Record these numbers in the appropriate space. Bring your results to class so that your instructor can tabulate the results for the entire class.

questions for discussion

1. Which learning technique was most effective for your subject?

2. How did his results compare with those from the entire class?

3. Were there individual differences in the total number of words recalled? In the effectiveness of the two memory techniques?

4. Why does the test list present the paired-associates in a different order from the study list?

5. Why does the study list present the repetition and imagery pairs in a random order rather than some fixed order, such as alternating repetition and imagery pairs?

6. How might the results of this study be applied to memorization tasks you encounter?

7. A properly controlled study would include one

group of subjects who learn the list as given and a second group for whom the repetition and imagery paired-associates are switched; that is, word pairs the first group memorized by repeti- tion would be learned by the second group through imagery, and vice versa. What variables that might have influenced the present exercise would be controlled by this procedure?

PAIRED-ASSOCIATE STUDY LIST

Instruction	Paired-associates
repeat	1. rabbit—house
repeat	2. boy—rope
image	3. shoe—mountain
repeat	4. table—skull
image	5. doctor—flag
image	6. book—fish
repeat	7. slave—party
image	8. lamp—bird
image	9. heart—water
repeat	10. ladder—baby
repeat	11. teacher—pudding
image	12. mule—dress
repeat	13. kettle—fox
image	14. snake—fire
image	15. tree—queen
repeat	16. flower—money
image	17. harp—elephant
repeat	18. bear—candle
repeat	19. clock—moon
image	20. horse—potato

PAIRED-ASSOCIATE TEST LIST

S_1	S_2
1. clock	
2. table	
3. snake*	
4. shoe*	
5. flower	
6. lamp*	
7. boy	
8. horse*	
9. book*	
10. rabbit	
11. harp*	
12. slave	
13. mule*	
14. heart*	
15. bear	
16. ladder	
17. doctor*	
18. kettle	
19. teacher	
20. tree*	

* imagery pair

Total correct (repetition) _____

Total correct (imagery) _____

10

optimizing learning

programed unit

1. One of the newest methods of organizing material to be learned, based on the principles of learning theory, is called *programed learning*. You should be familiar with this method, since much of this study guide is presented in the

programed   form of _____ learning.

2. In programed learning, the material is arranged so that the student can learn it on his own with a minimum number of errors. Each item, called a *frame*,

frame   builds on the preceding *fr*_____ in such a way that there is little conceptual distance between them.

3. In other words, each frame tries to convey only a small amount of new in-

step   formation—the *steps* between frames are very small. The size of a *s*_____ is important; the smaller the step size, the fewer will be the *errors* made.

errors   **4.** Small steps are necessary to ensure a minimum number of _____ . The idea is for the student to make a correct response to each frame and

incorrect   rarely, if ever, make an _____ response.

5. Because programed material is set up so that the student can learn on his own without a teacher or tutor, he can proceed at his *own rate*. Some students can go through a program twice as rapidly as others and still learn as

rate   much. Their _____ of learning is rapid.

6. If we start 100 students on a given set of programed material, some will finish in a week while others may take two weeks or more. This is possible

own rate   because each student can proceed at his _____ _____ .

7. If a student must make an *active response* to some kind of stimulus (for example, writing his response to a frame), his learning is likely to be better than if he merely sits and listens to the same material given in lecture form. Since in making a response the student is *active* in some way, we call this

active   _____ learning.

8. There is evidence that active learning is more efficient than passive learning. Thus, in programing, the fact that the student must make an active

response   _____ to the material is considered an advantage over merely listening to a lecture.

9. In programed learning the student finds out whether he is right or wrong *immediately* after he makes his response. This type of *feedback* permits immediate correction of an error, and the knowledge that his answer is correct

response   serves as immediate *reinforcement* of the correct _____ .

feedback   The student gets immediate *fe*_____ of results, which aids efficient learning.

10. In programed learning, then, immediate feedback of results leads to imme-

reinforcement   diate _____ of the correct response. Also, the learner

active   cannot be passive in the learning process; he must be _____ .

11. Once you had written your response in the previous frame, you were able to get immediate feedback of results. If you responded with the words "rein-

reinforcement   forcement" and "active," you received immediate _____

correct (or right)   by learning that your response was _____ .

12. To recapitulate: In programed learning the material is arranged in small

steps, own rate   _____ so that the student can proceed at his _____ _____ without the aid of a teacher or the limitations of a class schedule.

responses   **13.** Also, the student must make active _____ , which are

feedback   then reinforced by immediate _____ of results.

14. Some instructional programs follow a straight sequence of questions and answers; each time the student answers an item he moves on to the next regardless of whether his response was correct. These are called *linear programs.*

programs   Linear _____ can be presented in book form, as in this study guide.

15. More complicated programs, called *branching programs,* provide alternative answers from which the student can select. If he chooses a wrong answer, his error is pointed out to him, and he may be *branched* to additional material

branching   that will help him avoid that error again. A *br*_____ program

linear   thus provides a more *individualized* type of instruction than a _____ program.

16. In a branching program a student who has done well on a number of questions may be given a chance to jump ahead to more complicated material.

individualized (or   Branching programs thus provide more _____ instruc-
individual)   tion than linear programs.

17. Either type of program allows the student to proceed at his own _____ . rate

But only a _____ program permits him to skip ahead or go back for additional remedial material. branching

18. Branching programs are usually too complicated to present in textbook form and must be presented by means of a *computer*. Programed material presented by a _____ is called *computer-assisted instruction* (CAI). computer

19. In computer-_____ instruction the computer keeps track of the student's progress and decides from one moment to the next what material to present. Computer-assisted instruction thus provides a highly _____ type of instruction. assisted / individualized

20. Let's review. When a student progresses from one frame to the next regardless of whether his response was correct, he is using a _____ program. linear

21. If the student is given alternative answers from which to select and the frame that is presented next depends upon the answer chosen, he is using a _____ program. branching

22. Linear programs (*do/do not*) need to be presented by a computer. Programs that may require computer assistance are called _____ programs. do not / branching

23. The most highly individualized type of instruction is provided by a _____ program presented by a _____ . branching, computer

24. An important problem in the efficiency of learning procedures is the extent to which the learning of one thing helps in the learning of something else. A boy who has learned to shoot at a target with an air rifle may find it *easier* to hit the target when he begins to practice with a 22-caliber rifle than if he had had no practice at all. His learning with the air rifle has made it _____ to learn to handle the 22-caliber rifle. easier

25. The air-rifle learning makes the 22-caliber learning easier because the handling of both rifles requires similar skills. Psychologists believe that in such situations aspects of the earlier _____ are *transferred* to the new learning. learning

26. In learning to shoot an air rifle, a boy should learn, among other things, to hold the gun steady, to line up the front and rear sights on the target, and to squeeze the trigger slowly rather than with a quick jerk. All of these acquired skills can usefully be _____ when he learns to shoot the 22-caliber rifle, thus making the new learning easier. We call this *positive transfer*. transferred

27. When having learned one thing makes it easier to learn something else, we say that the learning has been transferred. We call this _____ transfer. positive

28. John learns bookkeeping in a job in a firm that has its books set up in a manner that John has never seen. Yet, because of his previous training, it is easier for him to master this new system than it would have been had he not

positive   had the previous training. This is an example of _____ transfer.

29. Sometimes having learned one task makes it more *difficult* to learn a new task. For example, if you learn to drive using a car with an automatic shift, it may be more difficult to learn to shift gears in a car with a stick shift than it would be if you had never learned to drive at all. This example illustrates

transfer   *negative tr_____* .

30. If having learned task A makes the learning of task B more difficult than it

negative   would have been if task A had not been learned, _____ transfer is taking place.

31. If, on the other hand, having learned task A makes the learning of task B easier than it would have been if task A had not been learned, there has

positive   been _____ transfer of learning.

32. *Transfer of learning* refers to the effect of past learning on subsequent learn-

easier   ing. In other words, if previous learning makes it either _____ or

harder (either order)   _____ to learn something else, transfer has occurred.

harder   **33.** Negative transfer occurs when having learned task A makes it (*easier/harder*) to learn task B. Positive transfer occurs when having learned task A makes it

easier   (*easier/harder*) to learn task B.

34. We do not approach each new task in life as if it were completely new. We can carry over skills learned in the past to the new situation. We can do this

transfer of learning   because of _____ _____ _____ .

35. Besides transfer of learning, another matter of interest to those concerned with efficient learning procedures is the spacing of learning trials or practice sessions. *Massed practice* refers to practice sessions that are crowded together, with no intervals of rest; that is, the person continues from one trial

rest   to the next without any _____ periods in between.

36. If we instruct a person to learn a list of paired-associate items (a common experiment in learning) and tell him to continue with the next *trial,* or run through the list, each time he gets to the end of the list, without resting in

massed   between, we have instructed him to use _____ practice.

trials   **37.** *Spaced practice,* on the other hand, implies rest periods between _____ or sessions.

38. If we ask the person who is learning paired-associate items to rest for one

spaced   minute between each trial, we are using _____ practice.

39. It has been found in many experiments that a rest period between trials

spaced   seems to improve the efficiency of learning. In general, the _____ practice method leads to the most rapid learning.

40. One explanation for the superiority of _____ practice proposes that the changes produced in the nervous system by learning need time to *consolidate,* or set, in order to be stored in memory.

spaced

41. Spaced practice would provide a better opportunity for these changes to *con*_____ than would _____ practice.

consolidate, massed

42. It is obvious that another important factor influencing the efficiency with which a person learns is his motivation. If a student works through a program in algebra for the pleasure of acquiring knowledge, he has *intrinsic motivation,* since he desires to learn something without expecting any reward other than a feeling of inner satisfaction. Similarly, a boy who wants very much to learn to drive a car needs no reward as an incentive; he eagerly learns to drive, spurred on by _____ motivation.

intrinsic

43. *Extrinsic motivation* refers to performing a task for the sake of a reward that is artificially established and not inherent in the task itself. Teachers use grades as an incentive to make students study and learn. Because the student may learn simply to achieve a grade of A or B instead of to acquire new knowledge, we say that his motivation is _____ rather than intrinsic.

extrinsic

44. Jane enjoys music. She plays the violin in a string quartet composed of friends and spends hours practicing to improve her technique. Her motivation is _____ because she requires no reward other than the enjoyment inherent in playing the instrument. Her brother, Dave, on the other hand, dislikes music and practices the piano only because his mother pays him a dollar for each hour of practice. His motivation is _____ because he needs a reward to encourage him to perform.

intrinsic

extrinsic

45. The most genuine satisfaction in learning comes from tasks that have been initiated through _____ motivation. But when an individual has to be spurred on to some activity for an arbitrary reward, such as money or a grade, his motivation is _____ .

intrinsic

extrinsic

46. The distinction between intrinsic and _____ motivation is not clear-cut, and most learning situations involve both types of motivation. John may learn to dance because he thinks that the skill will improve his social life; in this case the motivation is _____ . He may also fear the derision of his classmates if he is inept and awkward on the dance floor; so part of his motivation may be _____ .

extrinsic

intrinsic

extrinsic

47. In general, learning is more satisfying and more efficient if the motivation involved is primarily _____ .

intrinsic

48. If we wish an organism to learn some desired behavior, we must *reinforce* it in some way. We may choose to reinforce it either by *reward* or *punishment.* In more technical terms, we may choose between (1) positive reinforcement, or reward for the desired behavior, and (2) negative reinforcement, or _____ for incorrect responses.

punishment

49. Since we may use either reward or punishment to bring about desired behavior, we must consider which is more effective. There is evidence that in most instances positive reinforcement, or ＿＿＿＿＿ , is more effective.

reward

50. One of the reasons that reward is generally more effective than punishment in the control of behavior is that the reward emphasizes that the organism is responding correctly. Reward ＿＿＿＿＿＿＿＿ the desired response.

reinforces (or strengthens)

51. On the other hand, punishment only tells the organism that it is wrong, without guiding it toward an alternative, correct response that may then be *rewarded*. Therefore, ＿＿＿＿＿ tells the organism what the desired response is and punishment does not.

reward

52. Furthermore, punished behavior may be temporarily suppressed but not weakened, and will reappear when the ＿＿＿＿＿＿＿ ceases.

punishment

53. In those instances in which punishment is effective in changing behavior, it usually accomplishes its purpose by forcing the individual to select an alternative response that may then be ＿＿＿＿＿ .

rewarded

54. The above are some of the reasons that psychologists feel that ＿＿＿＿＿ is generally more effective than ＿＿＿＿＿＿ in the control of behavior.

reward
punishment

55. Another factor that has an important influence on learning is the degree of *anxiety* connected with the task to be learned. If a student is very anxious to do well on an exam, will he perform better than a student who is less ＿＿＿＿＿ ?

anxious

56. Subjects who are rated as *high-anxious* perform better on simple tasks involving a single response than subjects who are rated as *low-anxious*. For example, in a classical-conditioning study in which an eye-blink response (elicited by a puff of air) is conditioned to a bell, high-anxious subjects condition more rapidly than ＿＿＿＿-＿＿＿＿＿ subjects.

low-anxious

57. High-anxious subjects perform (*better/worse*) than low-anxious subjects on simple conditioning tasks involving a single response.

better

58. On more complex tasks, however, low-anxious subjects usually perform better. On complex tasks a high state of ＿＿＿＿＿ generally has a detrimental effect upon performance.

anxiety

59. Bob is very anxious about his grade on a math test. He is apt to perform (*better/worse*) than Steve, who is not so concerned.

worse

60. One reason that anxiety is *det*＿＿＿＿＿ to performance is that anxiety arouses a number of responses that may *interfere* with learning. Worry and concern about doing well may ＿＿＿＿＿ with concentration on the task at hand.

detrimental

interfere

61. On simple tasks involving only a single response the best performance is

high-anxious

low-anxious

given by _____-_____ subjects. On more complex tasks _____-_____ subjects perform better.

62. When stress is introduced into a learning situation by telling the subject that he is doing poorly or emphasizing the importance of "doing well," the performance of high-anxious subjects becomes worse while that of low-anxious subjects usually improves. Thus, stress has a detrimental effect upon the

high-anxious

low-anxious

performance of _____-_____ subjects, but it usually improves the performance of _____-_____ subjects.

63. For low-anxious subjects, stress serves to focus attention on the task; for high-anxious subjects, stress may arouse a number of responses that

interfere

_____ with learning.

self-quiz

Select the alternative that best completes the thought. In some cases several answers are fairly satisfactory; you are to pick the *best* one.

_____ **1.** Transfer of learning depends largely upon
   a. the doctrine of formal discipline
   b. formal mental training
   c. the transfer of specific skills or principles from one task to another
   d. the extinction of inappropriate conditioned responses

_____ **2.** The body of material presented by a teaching machine is called a
   a. text
   b. workbook
   c. program
   d. lesson

_____ **3.** When CAI is used to teach reading in the first grade
   a. boys progress through the curriculum more slowly than the girls
   b. girls progress through the curriculum more slowly than the boys
   c. both the boys and the girls progress more slowly than the control group
   d. boys progress through the curriculum as rapidly as the girls

_____ **4.** Learning to make an old response to a new stimulus generally
   a. is harder than learning a new response to a new stimulus
   b. results in negative transfer
   c. results in positive transfer
   d. results in conflicting response tendencies

_____ **5.** Pressure may result in improved performance for
   a. high-anxious subjects
   b. low-anxious subjects
   c. subjects who have achieved a learning set
   d. all of the above

_____ **6.**

	PHASE 1	PHASE 2
Experimental group	Learn task A	Learn task B
Control group	Unrelated activity	Learn task B

This design is used to study
   a. transfer of learning
   b. knowledge of results
   c. consolidation
   d. massed versus spaced practice

_____ **7.** The program in which the student moves from frame to frame regardless of whether his response was correct is called a
   a. branching program
   b. linear program

c. progressive program

d. horizontal program

_____ 8. Programed instruction makes use of all but one of these learning principles. Which does *not* belong?
a. active participation
b. knowledge of results
c. progress at the individual's own rate
d. delayed reinforcement

_____ 9. An advantage of a branching program is that
a. the student progresses along a single track from one frame to the next
b. where the student goes next depends upon the answer he gives
c. the student moves along at a prepro-gramed rate
d. errors are not pointed out, so that the effects of punishment are avoided

_____ 10. When practice sessions or trials are spaced close together so that a subject continues with one trial after the other without rest periods in between,
a. learning is generally more efficient
b. massed practice is being used
c. the subject is learning a motor skill
d. spaced practice is being used

_____ 11. The basic unit of a teaching program is called a
a. problem
b. question blank
c. sentence
d. frame

_____ 12. When the learning of a new response to an old stimulus is facilitated by the presence of a previously learned inter-vening response, this is called
a. mediated transfer
b. learning to learn
c. learning set
d. stimulus transfer

_____ 13. Spaced practice usually leads to more rapid learning, but seldom does it result in
a. consolidation
b. better retention
c. better learning sets
d. better generalization

_____ 14. Whenever possible, it is advantageous

to use goals that are _____ related to the learning task.
a. extrinsically
b. intrinsically
c. not
d. tangentially

_____ 15. In many instances punishment is less effective than reward because
a. rewards are competitive
b. punishment leads to docility and deference to authority
c. punishment temporarily suppresses a response but does not weaken it
d. punishment establishes strong avoid-ance responses

_____ 16. When a monkey has formed a learning set for a particular class of problems, it
a. can proceed on the basis of "insight"
b. must proceed on the basis of trial and error
c. must pay attention to positional cues
d. becomes fixated and has trouble with additional problems

_____ 17. The most effective type of punishment is
a. severe and delayed
b. inconsistent
c. consistent and delayed
d. prompt and consistent

_____ 18. A learner finds that it is much more difficult to learn task B because of what he learned in task A. We may conclude that
a. the learner is not properly motivated to learn task B
b. there is no mediated transfer
c. there is negative transfer
d. the learner has learned how to learn

_____ 19. Results from studies about anxiety in testing situations reveal that in general
a. high-anxious subjects do better than low-anxious subjects
b. anxiety level has no effect upon per-formance
c. low-anxious subjects do better than high-anxious subjects
d. low-anxious subjects are more in-telligent than high-anxious subjects

_____ 20. According to the research by McGaugh

and Hostetter, which of the following experimental arrangements results in the highest percentage of saving in relearning?

a. learn, waking activity, sleep, relearn
b. learn, waking activity, relearn
c. learn, sleep, waking activity, relearn
d. sleep, waking activity, learn, relearn

individual exercise

ORGANIZATION AS AN AID TO LEARNING

introduction

Organization of material to be learned is one factor that aids retention. This exercise will demonstrate that it is easier to remember a list of related words (words than can be grouped into categories) than a list of words that has no such organization. It will also demonstrate the primacy and recency effects—that is, the tendency to recall more items at the beginning and end of a list than in the middle.

equipment needed

Stopwatch or watch with a second hand.

procedure

Select a subject and tell him that you want him to memorize a list of 20 words. Explain that you will read each word aloud until you have completed the list (on page 123). (Time your reading of the list, allowing approximately 3 seconds per word. You should practice reading and timing the list before trying it out on your subject.) Immediately upon completion of the list, hand the subject paper and pencil and ask him to write in a single column as many words as he can recall, in any order. Give him exactly one minute to write the words he can recall.

Repeat this procedure with a second subject.

treatment of data

You will notice that 10 of the words have no obvious relationship to one another, 5 belong to the category of "furniture," and 5 can be classed as "parts of the body." Check each subject's list and record in the table below the number of words recalled that are categorized words (that is, belong to the categories "furniture" and "body parts") and the number that do not belong to a category. Also note any intrusions (words that are not in the original list) and mark whether they are related to either of the two categories.

	Category words	Non-category words	Intrusions
Subject 1	___	___	___
Subject 2	___	___	___
Total	___	___	___

To demonstrate the primacy and recency effects it is necessary to construct a serial position curve for your two subjects. First go through each subject's recall list and mark each word with the number at which it appears in the original list. In the table below tabulate for the first subject how many of the first four words in the study list he recalled correctly, how many of the second four words, and so on for each of the five segments. Do the same for the second sub-

	Presentation order in word list				
	1–4	5–8	9–12	13–16	17–20
Subject 1					
Subject 2					
Total					

ject, add the results for both subjects in the row marked "total," and plot these numbers on the graph provided on page 124. Connect the data points by a line to show the serial position curve.

There are eight possible correct responses for each point on the curve. In our hypothetical curve the subjects recalled most of the words in the first four positions. This tendency to remember the first words in a list is known as the *primacy effect*. Note that the curve is depressed for words in the middle of the list but rises again toward the end. The tendency to recall words toward the end of the list is called the *recency effect*.

questions for discussion

1. Were more categorized words recalled than words that do not fall into a category? If so, what are the implications for learning?

2. Did the subject's responses tend to cluster in categories? That is, when he recalled one word in the furniture category did it tend to be followed by another word in the same category?

3. Judging from the responses of your two subjects, are there individual differences in the total number of words recalled? In the type of words recalled?

4. Were the intrusion words, if any, related to either of the two categories?

5. What does your serial position curve indicate? Is it similar to the hypothetical one? Do your subjects show a primacy effect? A recency effect? Which is greater?

WORD LIST

* 1. ear	11. flower
2. rabbit	** 12. cabinet
** 3. table	** 13. bed
4. fire	14. paper
5. teacher	15. mountain
** 6. lamp	* 16. shoulder
* 7. arm	** 17. chair
8. ruby	18. bicycle
* 9. finger	19. ring
10. house	* 20. heart

* category of "body parts"
** category of "furniture"

HYPOTHETICAL SERIAL POSITION CURVE

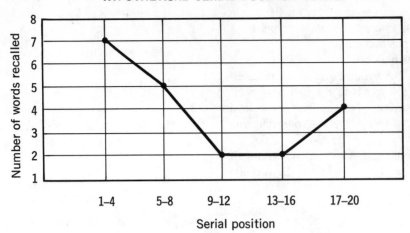

OBTAINED SERIAL POSITION CURVE

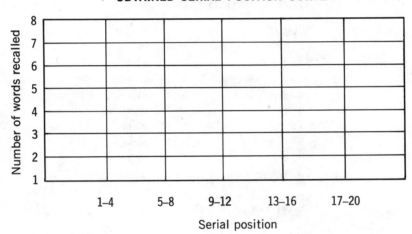

language
and
thought

programed unit

1. Thinking is a cognitive process characterized by the use of *symbolic representations* of objects and events. For instance, when a student uses such symbols as numbers and dollars to estimate how much it will cost him each semester to remain in school, he is engaging in behavior called

thinking
_____ .

representations
2. In thinking, we use symbolic _____ of objects and events.

process
3. Thinking is a cognitive _____ characterized by the

symbolic
use of _____ representations of objects and events.

4. *Symbols* represent, or stand for, something, and they convey *meaning* through some reference beyond themselves. The word "book," for instance,

symbol
is a _____ that represents a collection of printed pages within a firm cover.

meaning
5. Symbols convey _____ ; that is, they provide information about some object or event to which they refer.

6. Because they convey meaning, symbols often suggest appropriate action to the person who perceives them. For instance, the sign POISON is a

symbol
_____ that alerts a person to danger though the danger is not in the sign itself.

symbols
7. We think in _____ . Language itself is a rich symbolic process and therefore much thinking goes on in terms of language.

8. We sometimes use symbols to refer to other symbols. For instance, the

money
symbol $ stands for, or represents, some amount of _____ , another symbol.

meaning	**9.** An important characteristic of symbols is that they convey _____ . When Joan says, "I see red every time my roommates begin to chatter while I am trying to study," the word "red" in our culture conveys a certain
meaning	_____ that we understand.
symbol, meaning	**10.** Likewise, if someone says, "He's an icicle, if I ever met one," the _____ "icicle" conveys a certain _____ to us.
denotative	**11.** Meanings may be *denotative*. That is, they may specify something to which one can point, and all who comprehend the meaning can agree on it. For instance, if a person says, "Please let me use *that* pen," the meaning is _____ , since a specific pen is stipulated.
denotative	**12.** Denotative meanings are *fixed* and *specific*. If a sign reads DETOUR, it is specific. If a sign reads NO TRESPASSING, it, too, is specific. Such meanings are called _____ .
Denotative	**13.** _____ meanings refer to specific things or actions, such as names of objects or specific directions.
connotative	**14.** *Connotative* meanings accompany the denotative meanings of many words. Connotations are emotional, usually expressing some kind of evaluation or preference, and vary from one person to another. When someone says, "He's a radical," the term "radical" has _____ meaning; it may mean different things to different people.
connotative	**15.** In addition to denotative meanings, words may have _____ meanings, which are emotional and usually express some kind of evaluation or preference.
connotative	**16.** "He's a square." The word "square" in this instance has a _____ meaning, since it expresses a personal evaluation.
connotative denotative	**17.** "If Fred were not 'chicken,' he would swim across the river." In this sentence the word "chicken" has a _____ meaning, whereas the word "river" has a _____ meaning.
semantic	**18.** A method has been developed to measure the *connotative* meanings of words. This method of measurement is called the *semantic differential*. *Semantics* refers to meanings words convey, and *differential* refers to the fact that many words mean different things to different people. For instance, we could find what connotative meaning the word "mountain" has for several people by using the _____ *differential* method.
	19. Judging from the way Jim responded on a test measuring the connotative meaning of "mountain," the word evidently has an unpleasant connotative meaning for him. On the other hand, judging from the way Don responded, "mountain" has a pleasant connotative meaning for him. It happened that Jim was cold and hungry when lost during a mountain-climbing expedition—therefore, the word has an unpleasant connotation for him. Don, on the other hand, fishes for trout in mountain streams and has often admired the beauty of the mountains. For him, the word has a pleasant connotation. The

method used to measure this connotative meaning is known as the semantic

differential

_____ .

connotative

20. A method designed to measure the _____ meanings

semantic differential

of words is the _____ _____ .

21. If you wished to know the connotative meanings conveyed by such words as "love," "peace," and "war" to a group of men and women in order to learn whether there are sex differences in what the words mean, you could use the

semantic differential

_____ _____ method.

22. When a symbol stands for a class of objects or events with *common properties,* we say that it refers to a *concept.* For example, the word "man"

concept

refers to a _____ because it stands for a class of objects that have common properties.

23. Words and other symbols, such as signs, stand for concepts of varying degrees of *generality.* The concept "higher education" is more general than the concept "university," which in turn is more general than the concept "Harvard." A symbol that stands for a *class* of objects or events with

concept

common properties is a _____ .

24. A concept is a symbol that stands for a class of objects or events with

common (or synonym)

_____ properties.

class

25. A _____ of objects or events with common properties is represented by a concept.

26. The concept "mammal" is more *general* than the concept "woman," which in turn is more *general* than the concept "mother." Words and signs may

generality

stand for concepts of varying degrees of _____ .

27. "Man," "bat," and "whale" are designated as mammals. Because "mammal" is a concept, man, bat, and whale must have some properties in

common

_____ .

general

28. The concept "art" is more _____ than the concept "painting,"

general

which in turn is more _____ than the concept "water color."

generality

Thus, concepts possess varying degrees of _____ , but they must have some common properties.

29. Concepts that refer to *objects* are usually more easily understood than concepts involving *higher abstractions.* The concept "pencil" refers to a class of

objects

_____ and is easily understood. However, "democracy," "liberty,"

abstraction

and "freedom" are concepts involving a higher level of _____ and are more difficult to understand.

objects

30. Usually concepts that refer to _____ are more easily understood

abstractions

than concepts involving higher _____ .

abstract (or general)	**31.** "Peace" and "happiness" are concepts that are more _____ than "typewriter" and "envelope." Therefore "typewriter" and "envelope"
more	are (*more/less*) easily understood than "peace" and "happiness."
symbols	**32.** As we have said, language is a rich symbolic process; it provides us with verbal _____ with which to communicate with one another, think about events, and manipulate concepts. Language can be analyzed at a number of levels. At the simplest level we can analyze a language in terms of its *elementary sounds,* or *phonemes.*
phonemes elementary varies	**33.** All languages are based on a certain number of elementary sounds, or _____ . The English language is composed of about forty-five phonemes, or _____ sounds, which correspond roughly to the different ways we pronounce the vowels and consonants of our alphabet. If you know a foreign language, you realize that the number of phonemes (*varies/is identical*) from one language to the next.
Phonemes	**34.** _____ are the elementary sounds of a language, and they may vary in number from one language to the next.
phonemes	**35.** Each language has *rules* that specify how the elementary sounds, or _____ , may be combined or sequenced to form a word. For example, in English we have words that start with *str* or *spl* but none beginning with *zb* or *vg* as is common in some Slavic languages.
rules	**36.** Not all phonemes can be used in all combinations. Each language has _____ that specify how phonemes may be sequenced.
phoneme	**37.** The smallest *meaningful* units in the structure of a language are called *morphemes.* Do not confuse the word "morpheme" with _____ , which refers to the elementary sounds of a language.
meaningful	**38.** Morphemes are the smallest _____ units in the structure of a language. Morphemes may be root words, prefixes, or suffixes, and may consist of from two to six phonemes.
meaningful	**39.** The words "banana," "god," and "sweet" are single morphemes. That is, they are the smallest _____ units.
morphemes	**40.** Some words consist of two or more morphemes. The word "sweetness" consists of two _____ , "sweet" and "ness," since both have meaning (the suffix "-ness" implies "being" or "having the quality of").
two	**41.** The word "sincere" consists of a single morpheme. However, if we add the prefix "in-" (which means "without") to form "insincere," we have _____ (*number*) morpheme(s).
one two meaning	**42.** The word "god" consists of _____ (*number*) morpheme. If we add the suffix "-ly" (which means "like") to form the word "godly," we have _____ (*number*) morpheme(s). The word "god" and the suffix "-ly" both have _____ .

43. The smallest meaningful units in the structure of a language are called

morphemes

_____ . One word, however, may combine several morphemes and have several units of sound, or phonemes.

44. Because prefixes and suffixes are also meaningful units, they are also called

morphemes

_____ . The prefix "in-" added to the word "secure"

meaning

changes its _____ . Similarly, if we add the suffix "-less" to "gut," the word conveys a different meaning.

one

45. The word "bath" consists of two phonemes and _____ (_number_) mor-

two

pheme(s). The word "unclear" consists of _____ (_number_) morpheme(s)

prefix

because the word "clear" and the p_____ "un-" both have meaning.

phonemes

46. In addition to analysis in terms of elementary sounds (_____)

morphemes

and meaningful units (_____), a sentence can be analyzed according to the organization of its _phrases_. Such an analysis is called the _phrase structure_ of the sentence.

47. The diagram below shows how a sentence may be analyzed according to its

structure

phrase _____ .

48. The phrase structure of a sentence shows how the words are related to one another and what role each plays in the sentence. If we want to know what role each word plays in a sentence, we can analyze the sentence according to

phrase structure

its _____ _____ .

phonemes

49. Language can be analyzed in terms of elementary sounds (_____),

morphemes

meaningful units (_____), and organization of phrases

phrase structure

(_____ _____). The phrase structure of a sentence, like the sequencing of phonemes and the formation of words, is governed by certain grammatical rules.

50. A psychologist studying the development of language is concerned with how a child first produces sounds, later attaches meaning to them, and eventually learns to generate and comprehend phrases and sentences. Acquiring language is a complicated psychological process that we are only now beginning to understand. At about six months of age infants begin to produce and repeat an immense variety of sounds. This repetition of elementary speech

phonemes   sounds, or _____ , is called *babbling*.

51. The infant lying in his crib repeating "da-da-da" or "guh-guh-guh" to him-

babbling   self is _____ .

babbling   **52.** During the early stage of _____ the infant produces all the

phonemes   sounds, or _____ , that form the basis of any language. The babbling of a Chinese baby at this stage cannot be distinguished from the

babbling   _____ of a Russian or English infant.

53. Gradually, however, babies begin to restrict their babbling to the speech

phonemes   sounds, or _____ , that occur in their native language.

54. Parents tend to *reinforce* those phonemes that occur in their language. If the

reinforce   infant babbles "da-da," the enthusiastic father is likely to _____ the production of this sound by giving his baby smiles and attention.

55. We could say that the infant's vocalizations are "shaped" by the reinforcement provided by the parents. When the child produces a sound that is similar

reinforcement   to a word, the parents are usually quick to provide _____ .

56. In addition to learning how to produce speech sounds, the young child must also learn to *associate* speech sounds with meaning. The principle of reinforcement is crucial here. When a word is paired with a familiar object, as when the mother repeats "spoon" every time she hands the child a spoon, an association is established between the word and the object. The child learns

associate   to _____ the word with the object, and in this way the word acquires meaning.

babbling   **57.** If the child during his *b*_____ says "muk" and the mother, thinking that he has said "milk," hastens to provide his bottle, there is a greater probability that the child will say something similar to "muk" the next time he is hungry. The appearance of the bottle serves as

reinforcement   *rein*_____ for the word uttered by the child; gradually the

meaning   word "milk" acquires _____ .

reinforcement   **58.** It is clear that the principle of _____ plays an important role in language development.

associate   **59.** Learning to produce speech sounds and to _____ these sounds with objects and events is only a small part of learning a language. The child must master the more difficult task of putting words together in sentences. He must learn to produce and comprehend long and complicated sentences using the proper grammatical sequences.

60. Learning to produce and understand sentences appears to involve more than

associating   simply _____ one word with the next. The child learns *rules* for generating acceptable sequences of words. The text discusses

rules   the way in which the child develops grammatical _____ and how he modifies them with experience.

associate

rules

61. Language learning depends upon learning to _____ words with objects and events as well as learning _____ that specify how to comprehend and generate sentences.

62. A child's ability to deal with concepts and abstract relationships is closely related to his ability to use language. For example, in a task designed to teach the concept "smaller" a child is presented with a series of pairs of boxes that vary in size; he is rewarded only when he picks the smaller of the two boxes in each pair. The child who can say to himself "the smaller one is always right" will select the correct box much more often than the child who is not able to verbalize the problem. Thus, the ability to deal with concepts

language

is closely related to the development of _____ ability.

concepts

63. Our ability to deal with _____ and abstract relationships is related to our ability to use language.

64. Thought is closely related to language. One proposal, called the *linguistic-relativity hypothesis,* assumes that *thought* is relative to the *language* in which it is conducted and that the way in which a person conceives the world is *relative* to the structure of his language. If in a particular culture the word "democracy" does not exist, such a concept may be very difficult for people

think

in this culture to understand because they cannot *th*_____ in terms of what the word "democracy" means to others.

relativity

relative

65. The linguistic-_____ hypothesis proposes that one's

thinking is _____ to the language one uses. To the extent that this hypothesis has been supported by experiments, it seems clear that the way a person conceives the world is relative to the structure of his

language

_____ .

66. If in a particular culture there were no verbs to indicate past tense or past action, it is conceivable that this culture's thinking in historical terms would be strongly affected. Were this true, it would lend support to the

linguistic-relativity

_____-_____ hypothesis.

67. Man achieves his most complex use of language and concepts when he tries to solve a problem. The thought processes involved in solving a

problem

_____ have many similarities to the way information is processed by a computer.

68. In the same sense that a computer processes incoming data to solve a problem, man can be viewed as an *information-processing* system. Some psychologists have formulated *models* of human thinking based on the methods of storing, retrieving, and operating on information used in computers. Such

models

models are called *information-processing m*_____ .

processing

69. Information-_____ models of thinking are based on the methods and procedures that characterize the operation of a computer. Such models postulate sophisticated schemes for storing information in memory, and procedures for operating on the stored information to generate "new" information. The text discusses several information-processing models that have been developed to account for complex forms of human thinking and problem-solving.

self-quiz

Select the alternative that best completes the thought. In some cases several answers are fairly satisfactory; you are to pick the *best* one.

_____ 1. The surface structure of a sentence refers to
   a. the intended meaning of a sentence
   b. the actual sound sequence of a sentence
   c. the unintentional meaning of a sentence
   d. only the nouns and verbs in the sentence

_____ 2. Connotative meanings usually
   a. express evaluation or preference
   b. specify something to which one can point
   c. are unemotional
   d. are the same to all who can comprehend them

_____ 3. In the early speech of children a pivot word may be used
   a. with another pivot word
   b. by itself
   c. with words from the open class
   d. only as the first word in the sentence

_____ 4. Studies examining the ease with which concepts are learned found that the easiest concepts to learn were
   a. spatial concepts
   b. number concepts
   c. object concepts
   d. color concepts

_____ 5. A heuristic is
   a. synonymous with the Logic Theorist
   b. a brute-force technique of searching through logical operations to find a solution
   c. a strategy that limits the search for a solution
   d. an information-processing model

_____ 6. The connotative meaning of most words can be expressed in terms of the following three basic dimensions:
   a. potency, evaluative, activity
   b. shape, potency, activity
   c. intellectual, evaluative, potency
   d. ideal, evaluative, activity

_____ 7. Older children perform better than younger children in choosing the remote pair in a transposition task largely because
   a. they can express in words the principle of choice
   b. they have had more experience with the objects that are used in the experiment
   c. remoteness is a concept learned early in childhood
   d. the near pair provides more confusing information

_____ 8. Thinking always involves
   a. insight
   b. autisms
   c. imagery
   d. symbols

_____ 9. Research on concept-attainment by animals indicates that
   a. animals higher up on the phylogenetic scale can learn concepts; those lower on the scale cannot
   b. animals can learn concepts even though they do not have the ability to use language
   c. it is impossible to learn concepts without the use of language
   d. animals think and communicate with language

_____ 10. Evidence suggests that the human information-processing system
   a. is serial in its operation
   b. processes many symbols at a time
   c. holds the symbols to be processed in long-term memory
   d. is aided because of the time needed to transfer information from STM to LTM

_____ 11. The babbling of an infant
   a. is determined by the language of his environment
   b. is the repetition of sounds that form the basis of any language
   c. depends upon his sex
   d. reaches its peak at one year

_____ 12. When information-processing systems are used to imitate the cognitive activity of human beings, they are called

a. simulation models
b. logic theorists
c. thinking systems
d. heuristic strategies

___ **13.** When a symbol stands for a class of objects or events with common properties, it refers to a(n)
a. idea
b. complex
c. thought
d. concept

___ **14.** Grammatical learning by a child
a. can be accounted for by the operant conditioning of words
b. involves learning the rules used for generating sentences
c. only occurs after the child goes to school
d. is governed by simple learning principles

___ **15.** A method for measuring the connotative meaning of words is
a. an opinion inventory
b. a nonsense-syllable test
c. the semantic differential
d. an attitude test

___ **16.** The development of language in children depends upon
a. maturation
b. learning
c. the ability of the child
d. both maturation and learning

___ **17.** To analyze a problem and break it down into its component parts the computer programer constructs a

a. decision block
b. key chart
c. numerical script
d. flow chart

___ **18.** Symbols referring only to specific things or actions have _____ meaning.
a. connotative
b. denotative
c. implicit
d. extrinsic

___ **19.** The smallest meaningful units in the structure of language are called
a. phonemes
b. morphemes
c. syllables
d. phrases

___ **20.** Whorf's linguistic-relativity hypothesis proposes that
a. thought is relative to the language in which it is conducted
b. thought is determined by language
c. language is determined by thought
d. the world is conceived the same by those whose languages differ considerably in structure

key to self-quiz

20. a	15. c	10. a	5. c
19. b	14. b	9. b	4. c
18. b	13. d	8. d	3. c
17. d	12. a	7. a	2. a
16. d	11. b	6. a	1. b

class exercise

THE SEMANTIC DIFFERENTIAL

introduction

Language makes possible the creation and transmission of man's social heritage. Without language, man could not think in terms of such abstract concepts as freedom, justice, democracy, and equality. But language is not an unmitigated blessing. Some words cause no difficulty because they refer to specific things; these words are said to have denotative meanings. Other words have connotative meanings as well as denotative meanings; they generally express some kind of evaluation or preference. Many misunderstandings arise in communication because words have different connotations for different persons.

In order to derive more precisely the connotative meanings of words, Dr. Charles Osgood developed a method of measurement called the *semantic differential*—"semantic" because it has to do with meaning and "differential" because it provides several different dimensions of meaning. This exercise illustrates that certain words may connote various meanings to various students.

equipment needed

Red and blue pencils or pens.

procedure

On page 135 rate each of the words in the left column using the rating scale in the right column. Rate each word according to your first impression or reaction and regardless of how unrelated the word and scale appear. There are no right or wrong answers. Work rapidly. Do not struggle over particular items. There are seven spaces or steps in the scale, and each word should be rated by a check in one of the spaces. An example follows:

ARITHMETIC   easy__:__:__:__:__:__:__hard

If your first impression is that arithmetic is very hard, you should check the space at the extreme right toward "hard." If your first impression is that arithmetic is fairly easy, you should check one of the spaces toward "easy." If your first impression is that arithmetic is neither hard nor easy, you should mark the middle of the scale.

treatment of data

Your instructor will collect your ratings so that the profiles can be plotted on the scales shown opposite. Median responses for the entire group can be shown

by a heavy black line. Median responses for males and females, to find out whether there are sex differences in the connotative meanings of the words, can be shown by a red line (males) and a blue line (females).

LOVE

good__:__:__:__:__:__:__bad

tense__:__:__:__:__:__:__relaxed

strong__:__:__:__:__:__:__weak

dirty__:__:__:__:__:__:__beautiful

deep__:__:__:__:__:__:__shallow

MOTHER

shallow__:__:__:__:__:__:__deep

bad__:__:__:__:__:__:__good

relaxed__:__:__:__:__:__:__tense

strong__:__:__:__:__:__:__weak

dirty__:__:__:__:__:__:__beautiful

SEX

relaxed__:__:__:__:__:__:__tense

beautiful__:__:__:__:__:__:__dirty

good__:__:__:__:__:__:__bad

deep__:__:__:__:__:__:__shallow

weak__:__:__:__:__:__:__strong

FATHER

dirty__:__:__:__:__:__:__beautiful

weak__:__:__:__:__:__:__strong

tense__:__:__:__:__:__:__relaxed

good__:__:__:__:__:__:__bad

deep__:__:__:__:__:__:__shallow

LOVE	good	___:___:___:___:___:___:	bad
MOTHER	shallow	___:___:___:___:___:___:	deep
SEX	relaxed	___:___:___:___:___:___:	tense
FATHER	dirty	___:___:___:___:___:___:	beautiful
PEACE	strong	___:___:___:___:___:___:	weak
LOVE	tense	___:___:___:___:___:___:	relaxed
MOTHER	bad	___:___:___:___:___:___:	good
SEX	beautiful	___:___:___:___:___:___:	dirty
FATHER	weak	___:___:___:___:___:___:	strong
PEACE	deep	___:___:___:___:___:___:	shallow
LOVE	strong	___:___:___:___:___:___:	weak
MOTHER	relaxed	___:___:___:___:___:___:	tense
SEX	good	___:___:___:___:___:___:	bad
FATHER	tense	___:___:___:___:___:___:	relaxed
PEACE	tense	___:___:___:___:___:___:	relaxed
LOVE	dirty	___:___:___:___:___:___:	beautiful
MOTHER	strong	___:___:___:___:___:___:	weak
SEX	deep	___:___:___:___:___:___:	shallow
FATHER	good	___:___:___:___:___:___:	bad
PEACE	beautiful	___:___:___:___:___:___:	dirty
LOVE	deep	___:___:___:___:___:___:	shallow
MOTHER	dirty	___:___:___:___:___:___:	beautiful
SEX	weak	___:___:___:___:___:___:	strong
FATHER	deep	___:___:___:___:___:___:	shallow
PEACE	bad	___:___:___:___:___:___:	good

PEACE

strong___:___:___:___:___:___weak

deep___:___:___:___:___:___shallow

tense___:___:___:___:___:___relaxed

beautiful___:___:___:___:___:___dirty

bad___:___:___:___:___:___good

questions for discussion

1. Does your rating on certain words differ considerably from that of the group? Why?

2. The order of some of the evaluative words was rearranged. Why?

3. Are there sex differences in the connotative meanings of some of the words?

4. What other connotative words might have been used?

individual exercise

RULE-LEARNING IN PROBLEM-SOLVING

introduction

This exercise will enable you to analyze the thought processes involved in finding a rule to solve a problem.

equipment needed

None

procedure

Read slowly down the column on the next page, studying each item one at a time and trying to discover the relationship between the numbers and the letters. To make sure that you are not tempted to look ahead, cover the items with a sheet of paper and expose one line at a time. Try to analyze your mental processes as you proceed. At the point where you entertain your first hypothesis, record it in the space to the right of the item. Record each new hypothesis as it occurs to you until you arrive at the solution. If you cannot discover the rule, it is given on page 280 in the Appendix. Try the experiment on a friend.

questions for discussion

1. How many items did you read before you got your first hypothesis? Was it correct?

2. How many more hypotheses did you try before getting the correct rule?

3. Did you verbalize to yourself as you went along? If so, why was it useful?

4. When you found the correct solution did you have an "Aha!" experience?

5. How is this task related to insight? To concept formation?

6. If you tried the experiment on a friend, how did his approach differ from yours?

Record of hypotheses

372 A	
232 A	
961 B	
563 B	
445 B	
319 A	
858 A	
985 B	
467 B	
834 A	
144 B	
946 B	
393 A	
439 A	
145 B	
928 B	
425 B	
579 A	
958 A	
844 B	
519 A	
598 A	
965 B	
621 B	
414 A	
779 A	
889 B	
593 A	
161 B	
214 A	

12
physiological background of motivation

programed unit

motive

1. By a *motive* we mean something that incites the organism to *action*. Hunger can incite an organism to action; therefore hunger can act as a _____ .

motivated

2. When an organism is quiescent, we say that it is *not* motivated; when it is incited to action, we say that it is _____ .

direction

3. Motivated behavior is also characterized by *direction*. When an organism is incited to action by hunger, it does not simply act at random; its action (or behavior) is in the _____ of food.

action

4. Motivation has to do with two variables: _____ and direction.

direction

5. An animal motivated by thirst will go in the _____ of water.

motivated

6. Any behavior, then, that is characterized by action and direction is called _____ behavior.

physiological

7. This chapter examines those motives that are based on bodily needs; these are called *physiological* motives. Hunger is a function of certain bodily needs that result from lack of food. Hunger is thus classed as a _____ motive.

physiological

8. Thirst results from dryness of the throat and mouth plus other specific bodily needs that occur from lack of water. Thirst is thus a _____ motive.

need

9. In discussing physiological motives a distinction is made between the terms *need* and *drive*. A *need* is defined as a *bodily deficit*. If we lack food, we have a *need* for food. If we lack water, we have a _____ for water.

deficit **10.** A lack of food creates a bodily _____ ; we call this lack a need.

11. Any bodily deficit, or state of deprivation (such as lack of oxygen, food, or
need water), can be defined as a _____ .

12. The need for food is physiological, not psychological, but a state of physiological need has *psychological consequences*. The psychological consequences
drive of a need are called a *drive*. The need for food leads to the hunger *dr*_____ .
While need and drive are related, they are not the same. For example, drive
does not necessarily get stronger as need gets stronger. Men who have fasted
for a long time report that their feelings of hunger come and go, although
their need for food persists. The need persists but the psychological conse-
hunger quences of the need, the _____ drive, fluctuate.

psychological **13.** Drive, then, refers to the _____ consequences
of a need.

14. The *strength* of a drive may be measured in several ways. One measure of
strength drive _____ is *general activity* level. A hungry animal is active. Thus one measure of the strength of the hunger drive would be general
activity _____ level.

drive **15.** Activity level is one measure of the strength of a _____ . Another
measure is the *rate of performing* learned acts. Rats can be trained to press
a bar to obtain a food pellet. A hungry rat will press the bar at a more rapid
rate than one that is not hungry. Thus a measure of the strength of the
rate hunger drive would be _____ of bar-pressing.

activity level **16.** Two measures of drive are general _____ _____ and
rate the _____ of performing learned acts.

17. A third way of measuring drive strength is the *obstruction method*. An
animal that is extremely thirsty will exert more effort to overcome an obstruction to obtain water than an animal that is only mildly thirsty. If an
electrically charged grid is placed between an animal and water, a thirsty
animal will cross the grid to obtain water more often than an animal that is
not very thirsty. Thus the degree to which an animal will overcome an ob-
drive struction to obtain water is a measure of the thirst _____ .

level **18.** Three methods for measuring drive strength are general activity _____ ,
performing, obstruction the rate of _____ learned acts, and the_____
method.

measuring **19.** A fourth method for _____ drive is the *choice method*. If
two drives are active at the same time, and we let the organism choose between either of two appropriate goal-objects, its *choice* should indicate which
of the two drives is stronger.

20. A rat has been trained to obtain food in the right-hand goal box of a
T-maze and to obtain water in the left-hand goal box. We now deprive the
rat of food and water so that it is both hungry and thirsty and note to which
goal box it runs. If the rat runs to the goal box containing water, we assume

stronger (or synonym)	that the thirst drive is _____ than the hunger drive. The comparative strengths of the drives are indicated by the animal's choice;
choice	hence this procedure for measuring drive strength is called the _____ method.
activity level, performing	**21.** We have discussed four methods of measuring drive strength. They are general _____ _____ , rate of _____
method, choice	learned acts, the obstruction _____ , and the _____ method.
need	**22.** We defined drive as the psychological consequences of a _____ . More specifically, a drive is a state of uncomfortable tension that spurs activity until a goal-object or incentive is reached. By satisfying the need to a certain extent, the goal-object will tend to *reduce* the drive. An animal that is deprived of food will develop a need for food. The psychological consequences
need	of the _____ , the hunger drive, will motivate the animal to action.
reduction	**23.** The hungry animal will search for food to reduce the hunger drive. Eating is thus an example of drive _____*tion*.
reduce	**24.** If we are very thirsty, we attempt to move in the direction of water. We do this in order to _____ the thirst drive.
need	**25.** Thirst is a drive based on *deprivation*. If we are deprived of water, the deficit of water in our bodies sets up a _____ for water, and the psychological
drive	consequences of this need become the thirst _____ . The source of
deprivation	stimulation for the thirst drive is water _____ .
deprivation	**26.** An animal that is deprived of food will be motivated to seek it. Hunger is another drive based on _____ .
motivate	**27.** But deprivation is not the only source of drive. Stimuli that are *noxious* also m_____ the organism to action. The drive in this case is a tendency toward action that will remove the painful or noxious stimulus.
noxious	**28.** If we accidentally place our hand on a hot stove, we quickly withdraw it to remove the source of painful stimulation. Thus deprivation and _____ stimuli both serve to motivate the organism.
deprivation stimuli	**29.** Two sources of drive are _____ and noxious _____ .
reducing	**30.** In a state of drive, the organism's behavior is in the direction of removing or reducing the source of stimulation. Motivated behavior can thus be described as *drive-*_____ .
noxious	**31.** The full pattern of motivated activity that we have been discussing has been called the *need-drive-incentive* theory of motivation. Deprivation or _____ stimuli set up a state of need. The psychological consequences of this need produce a state of tension and goal-directed behavior

drive	known as _____ . The drive initiates behavior that is *goal-seeking* or *goal-directed*. This goal-directed behavior leads the organism to an object
reduce	in the environment called a *positive incentive,* which can _____ the drive by satisfying the conditions of need.
incentives	**32.** Reinforcement and reward are terms that refer to positive _____ .
positive	**33.** Food is a _____ incentive that reduces the hunger drive.
incentive, thirst	**34.** Water is a positive _____ that reduces the _____ drive.
consummatory	**35.** The incentive arouses *consummatory* behavior. The organism drinks the water or eats the food. These are examples of con_____ behavior,
drive	which reduces the _____ and ends the motivated behavior sequence.
drive	**36.** Positive incentives reduce a _____ by satisfying a need. But not all positive incentives satisfy a physiological need. Music, which attracts behavior
incentive	toward itself, is a positive _____ , but music-listening, so far as we know, does not satisfy any physiological need.
	37. Hungry rats will run a maze to obtain saccharin, a non-nutritive substance that does not satisfy the need for food. Saccharin is apparently a
positive incentive	_____ _____ even though it does not satisfy a physiological need.
drives	**38.** All objects or circumstances that satisfy needs and thereby reduce _____ are positive incentives, but not all positive incentives satisfy physiological needs.
	39. The need-drive-incentive theory of motivation focuses upon positive incen-
positive	tives. The organism seeks a _____ incentive in order to reduce the drive through satisfying the need upon which the drive is based. But there are some incentives that direct behavior *away* from themselves. These are called *negative incentives*.
incentive	**40.** A negative _____ is any object or circumstance that when
away	perceived or anticipated directs behavior _____ from itself.
	41. A child might be frightened by the sight of a snake and wish to move away
negative	from it. For the child, the snake is a _____ incentive because his behavior is directed away from it.
	42. A rat presses a lever and receives a severe electric shock. After this painful experience there is a strong probability that the rat's behavior will be directed
negative	away from the lever. For the rat, the lever has become a _____ incentive.
positive	**43.** When an object satisfies a need and reduces a drive, it is a _____ incentive; when an object is perceived and anticipated as noxious, it directs
negative	behavior away from itself and it thus is a _____ incentive.

44. A negative incentive exists in the environment as something to be *avoided,* not as a drive within the organism. If you have a pain that is a continuing source of annoyance, such as a headache, it acts as a drive. You are tense and restless and are motivated to seek some means of reducing the pain. A negative incentive is different from a pain drive. It is something to be

avoided

a_____ because of the pain it *might* cause.

45. Negative incentives are thus not easily explained in terms of the need-drive-incentive theory of motivation. They exist in the environment as something

drive

to be avoided and not as a _____ within the organism.

46. There are other motives, not physiological in origin, that are also difficult to explain by a need-drive-incentive formulation. For example, monkeys enjoy *manipulating* various mechanical devices without any evident reward other than the pleasure of "monkeying" with gadgets. This type of behavior can-

drive

not be explained in terms of _____ reduction or bodily needs. It ap-

manipulation

pears, therefore, that *man*_____ is a motive in its own right, since such behavior cannot be explained in terms of drive reduction.

47. Likewise, it seems to be the nature of animals to enjoy activity for its own sake, and to be curious about investigating their environment. Both *activity*

manipulation

and *investigation* as well as _____ cannot be explained in terms of the need-drive-incentive theory because such behavior is not governed by drive reduction based upon known physiological needs.

48. Three motives that do not have physiological correlates and cannot be ex-

activity
investigation,
manipulation
(any order)

plained in terms of the need-drive-incentive theory are _____ , _____ , and _____ .

49. Behavior that is motivated by a bodily need of some sort and that has a

physiological

definite _____ basis can be explained in terms of the need-drive-incentive formulation. However, some behavior, such as

activity, investigation

_____ , _____ , and

manipulation
(any order)

_____ , has no known physiological basis.

50. To summarize: Motivation has to do with both the activating of behavior

directing (or direction)

and the *dir*_____ of behavior. One theory proposes that motiva-

need, drive

tion begins with a _____ , which gives rise to a _____ or state of tension, which leads to behavior.

51. The goal of motivated behavior, according to this theory, is the

incentive, drive

_____ , which is capable of reducing the _____ .

needs

Objects or circumstances that satisfy _____ and reduce drives are

positive

_____ incentives. But it is important to remember that not all positive incentives satisfy physiological needs. People like to listen to music even though such behavior does not satisfy a physiological need based upon deprivation. Likewise, not all behavior can be explained in terms of the need-drive-incentive theory because some behavior, such as

activity, investigation

_____ , _____ , and

manipulation
(any order)

negative

action

direction

, has no known physiological correlates.

52. It is also important to recall that some incentives do not reduce drives but serve to direct behavior away from themselves; these are called _____ incentives.

53. The text describes several theories of motivation in addition to the need-drive-incentive formulation. Theories of motivation seek to explain why an organism is incited to _____ and why its behavior goes in one _____ rather than in another.

self-quiz

Select the alternative that best completes the thought. In some cases several answers are fairly satisfactory; you are to pick the *best* one.

_____ 1. Motivated behavior has two main aspects:
a. activating and energizing
b. searching and activating
c. searching and directional
d. activating and directional

_____ 2. The psychological consequence of a need is called a(n)
a. motive
b. drive
c. goal
d. impulse

_____ 3. Which of the following could be least adequately explained by the need-drive-incentive formulation?
a. hunger, thirst
b. sexual activity
c. pain avoidance, manipulation
d. curiosity, manipulation

_____ 4. A state of deprivation in an organism is called a(n)
a. motive
b. drive
c. incentive
d. need

_____ 5. Water intake in a dog is regulated by
a. dryness in the mouth
b. dryness in the throat
c. the amount of water its body needs
d. the size of its water dish

_____ 6. The concepts of need and drive are parallel but they are not identical because
a. as need gets stronger so does drive
b. as drive gets stronger so does need
c. drive does not necessarily get stronger as need gets stronger
d. they maintain equal strength

_____ 7. Rats whose stomachs were removed for experimental purposes
a. showed hunger behavior much like that of normal rats
b. did not experience hunger contractions and consequently starved to death though food was available
c. manifested specific hungers as compensating behavior
d. provided dramatic evidence that hunger can be explained in terms of stomach contractions

_____ 8. The odor of a female rat in heat will cause a male rat to make intense approach reactions. This illustrates the fact that sexual motivation is largely
a. incentive-related
b. need-related
c. determined by hormone level
d. a function of deprivation

_____ 9. Rats learned to run a maze for bran mash but began to make errors when sunflower seeds were substituted. This is an example of the fact that
a. positive incentives may enhance drives
b. drive-incentive relationships may become channelized

c. drive-incentive relationships follow a cyclical pattern
d. random activity may become learned goal-seeking activity

_____ 10. The behavior-primacy theory of motivation
a. supports the need-primacy theory
b. is based upon deprivation and aversive stimulation
c. accounts for curiosity and for play
d. is based upon the idea that organisms are motivated by a desire for competence

_____ 11. If mechanical devices are placed in a monkey's cage, the monkey will repeatedly take them apart and put them together again. This supports the idea that
a. monkeys are very intelligent
b. monkeys are highly skilled with their hands
c. monkeys should not be kept in cages
d. manipulation is a motive in its own right

_____ 12. Adult men who have been castrated
a. show a rise in sexual activity
b. may show no impairment in sexual functioning
c. show a rapid decline in sexual capacity
d. become homosexual

_____ 13. The need-drive-incentive formulation holds that
a. drives are reduced through consummatory behavior
b. needs are established through positive stimulation
c. motives without specified physiological correlates are primary
d. there are no positive incentives for pain

_____ 14. Any object or circumstance that when perceived or anticipated directs behavior away from itself is termed a(n)
a. minus value
b. negative incentive
c. aversive drive
d. negative motivation

_____ 15. Rats that have been given a fat-free diet
a. show a marked preference for fat

b. show hunger for any kind of food
c. demand only a minimum number of calories
d. provide evidence that food preferences are distorted by learning

_____ 16. Rats sought electrical stimulation of certain brain areas through repeated bar-pressing. This behavior supports the theory that
a. satisfaction is achieved through drive reduction
b. certain goal-activity may be pleasurable apart from conditions of need
c. satisfaction is achieved through need reduction
d. operant conditioning is necessary to attain goal-objects

_____ 17. Measures of general activity level and the rate of performing learned acts help psychologists determine
a. deprivation rates
b. the state of a need
c. drive level
d. stimulation differences

_____ 18. A forced choice among incentives, either positive or negative, induces
a. appetitive behavior
b. aversive behavior
c. approach behavior
d. conflict behavior

_____ 19. Sometimes the physiological basis of a drive is acquired. An example is
a. sex
b. manipulation
c. investigation
d. drug addiction

_____ 20. Pain differs from thirst in that it
a. tends to be cyclical
b. cannot be classified as a drive
c. is episodic
d. is the result of deprivation

key to self-quiz

5. c	10. c	15. a	20. c
4. d	9. b	14. b	19. d
3. d	8. a	13. a	18. d
2. b	7. a	12. b	17. c
1. d	6. c	11. d	16. b

individual exercise

MEASURING MOTIVATION

introduction

Psychologists study motivation in many ways. In laboratory studies precise instruments that measure physiological responses in motivated behavior can be used. However, for classroom purposes it is difficult to make the necessary arrangements to measure physiological changes. For that reason the sentence-completion test that follows has been chosen. Many psychologists feel that it has clinical value in the study of personal adjustment.

equipment needed

None

procedure

Below are fifty incomplete sentences. You will have about thirty minutes to complete all the sentences. Try not to omit any item. Be sure to express your real feeling toward each item. The results will be more valuable if you write down thoughts that occur to you spontaneously, as soon as you see the first word or words of each item. You will be the only person to score the test and to see the results. Therefore, try to be frank and honest by writing the first thought that comes to mind.

After completing the test, score your sentences according to the directions given on page 280 of the Appendix.

1. Boys _____.
2. College _____.
3. I need _____.
4. My nerves _____.
5. Secretly, I _____.
6. My father _____.
7. I wish _____.
8. I'm afraid _____.
9. People _____.
10. The future _____.
11. I worry about _____.
12. I know _____.
13. At night _____.
14. Marriage _____.
15. My mother _____.
16. If I could _____.
17. My studies _____.
18. My friends _____.
19. I get annoyed _____.
20. I daydream about _____.
21. There are times when _____.
22. My feelings _____.
23. My goal _____.

24. I find it difficult _____.

25. Most of my friends _____.

26. I know it is silly but _____.

27. When I was a youngster _____.

28. When I marry _____.

29. My father thinks my mother _____.

30. My family _____.

31. I would do anything to forget _____.

32. A real friend _____.

33. Most of my friends don't know _____.

34. I think a mother _____.

35. I could be happy if _____.

36. Ten years from now _____.

37. Most of all, I _____.

38. Sex _____.

39. Compared with others, I _____.

40. I can't understand _____.

41. My father and I _____.

42. Dating _____.

43. My mother thinks my father _____.

44. The opposite sex _____.

45. What I want most _____.

46. My mother and I _____.

47. My biggest fault _____.

48. Sometimes I _____.

49. My dreams _____.

50. My appearance _____.

questions for discussion

1. Does your score place you above or below the median? What does this mean?

2. Which items were most difficult for you to complete? Why?

3. Does your score correspond to your own evaluation of your adjustment?

4. Does the test reveal some of your current difficulties? Why or why not?

5. How might a clinical psychologist find your responses helpful in diagnosing your difficulties?

6. What are some of the cautions that should be observed in interpreting the results?

13 human motivation

programed unit

1. *Why* men behave as they do has fascinated thinkers from earliest times. Because of the variety and richness of *human motivation,* we often find it difficult to explain "what makes a person tick," which is current jargon for what

motivation   we mean by human _____ .

2. You recall from the preceding chapter that any behavior that is characterized

motivated   by action and/or direction is called _____ behavior.

3. Obviously, not all of the possible motives a person has are expressed at the same time. A motive that is not being expressed is called a *motivational disposition.* At times you may like solitude and quiet contemplation, while at other times you may prefer the boisterous activity of a group of friends. If at present you are enjoying yourself at a party, then your tendency toward

motivational disposition   solitude is a _____ _____ .

4. A latent motive is called a _____ disposition. A

motivational   motive that is active is called an *aroused* motive. In the foregoing example, the tendency toward gregarious activity, which is activated at that given time,

aroused   is a(n) _____ motive.

5. When we speak of an aroused motive, we mean one that is _____

active   at a given time.

6. We all carry with us many tendencies that can lead to incitement to action or to the guidance of the direction of behavior. The particular tendency that is

aroused   active at a given time is called a(n) _____ motive, while other

motivational   tendencies, which are latent at the time, are called _____ dispositions.

7. It is often difficult to infer a person's motives directly from his behavior. This is true for a variety of reasons. First, any *single* act may express *several* motives. For instance, why does Mrs. Angel attend church services at least once a week? Perhaps it is because she enjoys the minister's sermon, or because she enjoys seeing her friends there, or because she enjoys singing in the choir, or because it gives her a feeling of being in close communion with God, or because she wishes to be proper, or because she is trying to atone for her past misdeeds. Her single act of attending church may express all or

motives   most of the _____ we have mentioned.

8. We can never directly observe a person's motive any more than we can directly observe a person's intelligence. We always have to *infer* motives from the behavior the person displays, just as we *infer* intelligence from how well a person performs certain tasks that comprise an intelligence test. If we know that a person is very hungry and we observe him going into a res-

infer   taurant, we can _____ that this behavior is motivated by his hunger drive.

several   **9.** Because a single act of behavior may express _____ motives at any one time, as in the example of Mrs. Angel's church attendance, we can

infer   readily see that it is often difficult to _____ precisely what causes a person to act in a certain way.

10. Sometimes *different* motives may be expressed through the *same* behavior. Stewart is studying architecture to please his father. Tim, on the other hand, is studying architecture to defy his father, who wishes him to major in

same   medicine. Here we see the _____ behavior, majoring in architecture, expressing two different motives, to please and to defy. This illustrates again

infer   how difficult it is to _____ a person's motivation by merely observing what he does.

11. Bill joins the Peace Corps because he feels it important to help people in underdeveloped countries. Steve joins because he wants to escape from living at home under the domination of his parents. Here again we see the same behavior, joining the Peace Corps, serving two quite dissimilar, or

different   _____ , motives.

12. The *same* motive may be manifested through *different* kinds of behavior. Both Alex and Ben wish to express anger toward their fathers. Alex expresses his motive by criticizing his father. Ben, on the other hand, expresses his motive by giving his father the silent treatment. Here we see the same

different   goal being reached through _____ kinds of behavior.

13. Sue and Jean both wish to express their affection to their mother. Sue gives her mother a box of candy; Jean gives her mother an unexpected kiss on

same   the cheek. Again, we see the _____ motive expressed through different forms of behavior.

infer   **14.** Another reason it is often difficult to _____ directly what motivates behavior is that the expression of human motives *differs* from culture to culture and from person to person within a culture. In some cultures, aggression is expressed through singing nasty songs about the person who is the object of aggression; in other cultures, aggression is expressed through fist-fights. This makes it difficult to infer motivation, because the expression of

differ

motives in behavior may ＿＿＿＿＿＿ from one culture to the next or from one person to the next within the same culture.

infer
different
several (or many)
same

person

15. It is often very difficult to ＿＿＿＿＿ a motive directly from behavior. Sometimes the *same* motive is expressed through ＿＿＿＿＿＿＿＿＿ behavior; sometimes a single act may express ＿＿＿＿＿＿ motives; sometimes *different* motives may be expressed through the ＿＿＿＿ kinds of behavior. Then, too, the *expression* of motives may vary from culture to culture and from ＿＿＿＿＿＿ to person within a particular culture.

16. Many theories have been formulated to explain human motivation, but we will discuss only three as representative. These are *psychoanalytic theory, behavior theory,* and *cognitive theory. Psychoanalytic theory,* as proposed by Freud, emphasizes unconscious motivation and stresses *sex* and *aggression*

motives

as the basic *m*＿＿＿＿＿＿ underlying behavior.

psychoanalytic,
aggression

17. Much of our behavior has unconscious components, according to the ＿＿＿＿＿＿＿＿＿＿＿＿＿ theory. Sex and ＿＿＿＿＿＿＿＿＿ are basic motives underlying human behavior.

18. When a person engages in behavior but is *not* aware of the real reason for his behavior, he is directed by *unconscious* motivation. If you meet a stranger

unconscious

and dislike him at first sight, there are probably ＿＿＿＿＿＿＿＿＿＿ motives operating, especially if you are unaware of why you do not like him.

19. If a person is not aware of the real reason for his behavior, we say that his

unconscious

motivation is ＿＿＿＿＿＿＿＿＿＿＿ .

20. Unconscious motives may reveal themselves in several ways. In his dreams the dreamer often expresses desires of which he is unaware. *Dreams,* then,

unconscious

are one way in which ＿＿＿＿＿＿＿＿＿＿＿ motives may be expressed.

21. *Slips of speech* often reveal unconscious motives. John says to his ailing sister, "I regret that you will soon be well" when what he meant to say was "I hope that you will soon be well." His speech slip may express

unconscious

＿＿＿＿＿＿＿＿＿＿＿ hostile feelings toward her.

slips

22. Dreams and ＿＿＿＿＿ of speech are two ways in which hidden or un-

motives

conscious ＿＿＿＿＿＿＿＿ may be expressed.

23. The *sex* drive has a clear physiological basis, but sex can also be a source of unconscious motivation. If a married couple's prolonged sexual difficulties

unconscious

do not stem from organic conditions, they may stem from ＿＿＿＿＿＿＿＿ feelings of hostility, guilt, or fear.

24. A wife who unconsciously wants her husband to take a fatherly role toward her may resist or frequently refuse sexual relations with him because it might stir up feelings of guilt, since she perceives him as a father. Here we

unconscious

see _____ motivation interfering with an activity that should be pleasurable to both mates.

25. Since our culture places certain taboos on the expression of *aggression,* suppressed aggressive feelings may also serve as a source of unconscious

motivation

_____ .

26. A man resents the time and attention his wife devotes to their young son. His resentment leads to aggressive feelings toward the child. But since it is not considered acceptable to feel or express aggression toward one's offspring,

unconscious

these feelings are largely *un*_____ . The father seeks frequent opportunities to restrict and discipline the boy, presumably for "his own good"; he is probably motivated by unconscious feelings of

aggression

_____ .

27. According to psychoanalytic theory the two most important sources of

sex, aggression (either order)

motivation are _____ and _____ .

28. A second theory of human motivation, *behavior theory,* emphasizes stimulus-response relationships and learning in accounting for much of human motivation. One group of behavior theorists has proposed that we classify adult behavior into a few *behavior systems,* such as the *oral, anal,* and *sexual systems, dependency,* and *aggression.* The motive that defines each of these

systems

behavior _____ can be identified in early childhood, and much of adult behavior is predictable from the way in which the individual learns to satisfy these motives.

oral

29. Each behavior system—the _____ , anal, and sexual systems, dependency, and aggression—is thought to consist of a set of habits or customs motivated by a common innate or early-acquired motive. Let us assume that in culture X the infants' *oral needs* are readily gratified and little, if any, feeding or weaning frustration is experienced. In culture Y the infants' oral needs are severely frustrated—feeding is unpredictable and weaning occurs very early, since the mothers must work in the fields. What sort of behavior will be manifested by these infants when they become adults? Will the differences in feeding practices between the two cultures have consequences in

behavior

later life? These kinds of questions interest proponents of _____ systems.

30. A child learns many things from his mother. We can trace the habits that are learned during the early years—in situations, for example, that gratify

needs

or frustrate the child's oral _____ —by studying cultures with contrasting practices to see what the consequences are in later behavior.

31. Some cultures are permissive and some cultures are harsh in toilet-training

system

procedures. If we wished to trace the *anal behavior* _____ from infancy to adulthood, we might learn the consequences of two contrasting procedures of toilet training.

32. Some cultures are permissive and some are very restrictive toward *sexual* behavior. In some cultures, genital play by children would be ignored by

adults; in other cultures, genital play by children would elicit severe punishment. The sexual is another _____ _____ we might trace from infancy to adulthood.

behavior system

33. Cultures also differ in how they handle *aggression* and *dependency*—two more _____ _____ in which we might trace development from infancy to adulthood.

behavior systems

34. The five behavior systems that have been studied by _____ theorists, who focus on stimulus-response relationships and learning, are the _____ , _____ , and _____ systems, _____ , and _____ .

behavior

oral, anal, sexual

dependency, aggression
(any order)

35. The mother's special role in feeding and handling may make the relationship to the mother of special importance to the infant in the development of the *dependency* motive. In other words, the consequences of feeding, or the _____ behavior system, may relate to later *dependent* behavior.

oral

36. Paradoxically, research shows that infants whose oral needs are indulged show *less dependent* behavior than infants who are fed on a strict schedule. Apparently _____ *frustration* is a variable that results in later *dependent* behavior.

oral (or feeding)

37. You would expect, then, that a helpless, hungry infant who has to cry for long intervals of time before he is fed would show (*more/less*) dependent behavior than one whose oral needs are promptly satisfied.

more

38. Feeding frustration, in which the child's oral needs are not satisfied in a consistent manner, seems to result in _____ behavior in later life.

dependent

39. A third theory, the *cognitive theory* of motivation, emphasizes man's ability to plan and to achieve goals. This does not mean that the unconscious and irrational impulses noted by _____ theory or the development of behavior _____ in childhood as emphasized by _____ theory are denied. It is simply another way of looking at some of the facts of human motivation.

psychoanalytic

systems

behavior

40. When a person makes plans, calculates the risks involved, and moves with determination toward a goal, he is motivated by his *cognitions* (a word with the root meaning of "to know"). Concern with plans and setting goals is the basis of a *cog*_____ theory of motivation.

cognitive

41. Our lives are guided by some *long-range* goals as well as many *short-range* ones. Going to college, getting a law degree, winning a place on the Olympic ski team are examples of fairly _____-_____ goals. Losing five pounds by next week or getting an A on the history term paper are examples of short-range _____ .

long-range

goals

42. A fairly immediate, short-range goal is sometimes referred to as a person's *level of aspiration*. When you first entered this course, you may have aspired

aspiration

to achieve an A. This would constitute your level of _____ , since you felt it was something you could attain.

43. Most of us set our goals so that we can succeed. A student who realizes he has relatively poor study habits and a deficient vocabulary may set a lower

level

_____ of aspiration for himself and hope to attain a C in the course.

44. Most of us set our level of aspiration within a "range of challenge"—not so *high* that success is impossible nor so *low* that success brings no satisfaction. If you were a B+ or an A student in high school, you would probably not set

level, aspiration

your _____ of _____ so low that all you hoped to attain was a C average in your college courses.

45. Most people set their goals within the "range of challenge"—that is, not so

high, low

_____ that failure is inevitable and not so _____ that no satisfaction or feeling of success is experienced.

46. When an individual becomes involved in a task and estimates his own level of achievement—that is, sets his own goals—he is *cognizant* of what he is doing. Thus, level-of-aspiration experiments are of keen interest to those

cognitive

psychologists interested in _____ motivation.

47. Some individuals have strong *achievement* motivation. That is, some people have a tendency to define their goals according to some standard of perfection or excellence in the product or performance attained. The college student

achievement

who aspires to an A average certainly has high _____ motivation.

48. There are both conscious and _____ motivational

unconscious

factors operative in achievement motivation. Dick drives himself mercilessly to be the top performer in his class but he does *not* understand why he needs

unconsciously

to be the "best" student. His behavior is _____ motivated.

49. Some people are motivated to achieve by *pleasure in success;* others are motivated to achieve by *fear of failure*. Generally, students with a history of success tend to set *realistic goals* for themselves, while those with a history of failure set *unrealistic goals*. If Mike has a history of success in attaining goals

realistic

he has set for himself, we would expect him to set a(n) _____ level of aspiration for most tasks.

50. Clare has a long history of failure in achieving goals. We would expect her

unrealistic

to have a(n) _____ level of aspiration.

success

51. Some people are motivated to achieve by pleasure in _____ ;

failure

other people are motivated to achieve by fear of _____ .

unrealistic

52. Individuals with a history of failure set _____ goals for themselves. That is, their goals are set either *very high* or *very low*.

53. If a person has a history of failure and sets his goals very *low,* he may avoid the repeated experience of defeat. If he sets his goals very *high,* he would *not* necessarily feel degraded by failure because he aspired to something that is impossible for him to achieve. One can readily see why a person with a his-

high, low (either order)   tory of failure sets his goals very _____ or very _____ . Either way, his self-esteem is protected.

54. Many motives can be understood in relation to the person's *self-image.* An important part of one's self-image is the belief that one's attitudes, beliefs, and behavior are *consistent.* We like to think that our attitudes, beliefs, and

image   related behavior form a consistent pattern or self-_____ . An inconsistency that is detected results in a sense of imbalance, or dissonance, which we then seek to correct.

55. *Cognitive dissonance* refers to a lack of harmony between what we *believe* and what we *do.* We can reduce incongruities, or dissonance, between what

believe   we _____ and what we do by changing either our beliefs or our behavior.

56. When what we do is incongruous, or dissonant, with our beliefs, we experi-

dissonance   ence cognitive _____ .

57. We all have certain assumptions about ourselves, other people, and the world in general. When we uncover information that contradicts our existing

dissonance   assumptions, we may experience cognitive _____ .

58. Frank has always perceived himself as a very honest person. Yet he cheated on an important examination. He would undoubtedly experience some

cognitive   _____ dissonance, since his belief in the sort of person he is is incongruent, or dissonant, with what he did.

59. To reduce his cognitive dissonance, Frank has to change either his

beliefs (or assumptions)   _____ about himself or his behavior.

60. If Frank admitted to himself that he was not as honest as he always thought

dissonance   he was, he would reduce his cognitive _____ . Or, if he could admit to his instructor that he had cheated and feels he should be

cognitive   penalized for cheating, this would also reduce his _____

dissonance   _____ .

61. If a person who smokes regularly reads about the relation between smoking and lung cancer, the new information conflicts with his smoking habit and

dissonance   creates a state of cognitive _____ . He can reduce the dissonance by stopping smoking. If he continues to smoke, he must resolve the dissonance by giving less credibility to the data relating smoking and lung cancer.

62. The fact that heavy smokers profess less belief in the linkage between smoking and lung cancer than nonsmokers or light smokers lends support to the

cognitive dissonance   theory of _____ _____ .

63. We see how the tendency to be consistent influences our behavior. We cling to certain perceptions of ourselves, and when we do something that is incon-

cognitive

dissonance

sistent or incongruent with our self-image, we experience _____

_____ .

64. Some psychologists criticize the types of motivational theories discussed above as being too narrow, since these theories are concerned with brief episodes of choice and behavior rather than with the more profound aspects of human hopes and aspirations. They use the term *self-actualization* to describe a more pervasive motivation whereby the individual seeks to develop his *potential-*

self-actualization

ities to their full capacity. *Self-_____* means the development of one's potentialities to their full capacity.

65. Maslow has proposed that our needs can be arranged in a hierarchy, ranging from the most basic physiological needs to the higher-level motives. Self-actualization would represent fulfillment of motives at the highest level, since

potentialities

to achieve self-actualization is to develop one's _____ to their full capacity.

66. Maslow calls the lower-level motives in this hierarchy *deficiency motives*. Thirst, hunger, and the need for shelter would be examples of deficiency

motives

_____ . Motives that are aroused through deficiencies in the environment are urgent determiners of behavior. If you are continually hungry, the hunger drive will take precedence over other motives.

deficiency

67. The lower-level motives are called _____ motives. Maslow calls the higher-level motives *being motives*. Being motives are concerned with the need for self-esteem and self-actualization.

68. Deficiency motives must be satisfied before one can devote his energies to

being

the higher-level, or _____ , motives.

69. A self-actualizing person is one who is free to devote his energies to the

being

deficiency

higher-level, or _____ , motives. He cannot do this unless his _____ motives are satisfied.

70. If a person's deficiency motives are satisfied, he can devote more energy to

being, self-actualizing

the _____ motives and realize his potentialities as a *self-_____* individual.

self-quiz

Select the alternative that best completes the thought. In some cases several answers are fairly satisfactory; you are to pick the *best* one.

_____ **1.** The psychoanalytic theory of motivation emphasizes two basic drives:
a. dependency and aggression

b. dominance and affiliation
c. achievement and affiliation
d. sex and aggression

_____ **2.** According to behavior theory a "behavior system"
a. develops out of frustration

b. develops from physiological motivation

c. has its origins in adolescence

d. consists of a set of habits motivated by an innate or early-acquired motive

3. Man's awareness of what is going on, his capacity to plan and to anticipate the future, is the basis of

a. psychoanalytic theory

b. frustration-aggression theory

c. behavior theory

d. cognitive theory

4. Children with a history of success tend to set goals that are

a. very low and therefore guarantee further success

b. realistic so that they have a chance of reaching them

c. very high so that they do not feel degraded by failure

d. regulated by a fear of failure

5. Highly motivated boys tend to have

a. cold and unappreciative parents

b. mothers who make few demands upon them

c. parents who set low goals for them

d. supportive parents who set high goals for them

6. Sadism is

a. the tendency to be always melancholy

b. the motive to inflict pain upon oneself

c. the motive to inflict pain upon others

d. synonymous with masochism

7. Infants on a self-demand feeding schedule, as compared to those strictly scheduled, showed in adult life

a. less dependent behavior

b. more dependent behavior

c. aggressive behavior

d. more frustration

8. Whiting and Child selected five behavior systems to investigate. Which of the following do *not* have an evident physiological basis?

a. sex and elimination

b. hunger and sex

c. sex and dependency

d. dependency and aggression

9. Behavior that leads to a goal is called

a. goal motivation

b. achievement orientation

c. instrumental activity

d. motivational arousal

10. Unconscious motives may be expressed through

a. dreams

b. slips of speech

c. symptoms of neurotic illness

d. all of the above

11. A motivational disposition is a(n)

_____ motive.

a. aroused

b. latent

c. inferred

d. ambivalent

12. Schachter found that those who showed the higher tendencies toward affiliation under threat of pain were

a. the youngest children in two-child families

b. the middle children in a family

c. only and first-born children

d. children who had highly nurturant mothers

13. Not taking too many cups of coffee before retiring, or determining to leave a card game in order to have enough sleep the night before an exam are examples of

a. short-term plans

b. long-term plans

c. stop-plans

d. safety-plans

14. The term used by Maslow to describe the development of full individuality, with all facets of the personality in harmony, is called

a. sense of competence

b. self-actualization

c. productive orientation

d. creative becoming

15. Aroused motives

a. are enduring personality characteristics

b. are those motives being expressed at the moment

c. can always be inferred from behavior

d. are independent of motivational tendencies

_____ 16. If an individual's score is interpreted as below that of a group to which he feels superior, he is likely to

a. increase his level of aspiration

b. lower his level of aspiration

c. maintain the same level of aspiration

d. no longer aspire

_____ 17. The expression of human motives

a. differs from culture to culture and from person to person

b. is instinctive in nature

c. is more or less the same in all known cultures

d. defies any sort of rough classification or analysis at present

_____ 18. In one study of aggression the more punitive the mother, the

a. less aggressive were the boys in doll play

b. less aggressive were the girls in doll play

c. more aggressive were both boys and girls in doll play

d. more submissive were both boys and girls in doll play

_____ 19. The fact that the same goal may be reached by different kinds of behavior reveals that

a. behavioral differences are culturally determined

b. it is not always possible to infer motives from behavior

c. different goals may be reached by the same instrumental behavior

d. any simple set of instrumental activities may serve several goals at once

_____ 20. When a person detects a lack of consistency between what he believes and what he does, he experiences

a. cognitive dissonance

b. a diminished level of aspiration

c. functional autonomy

d. an increased drive toward self-actualization

key to self-quiz

20. a	15. b	10. d	5. d
19. b	14. b	9. c	4. b
18. c	13. c	8. d	3. d
17. a	12. c	7. a	2. d
16. a	11. b	6. c	1. d

class exercise

MOTIVES IN ADVERTISING

introduction

Advertising experts realize that their advertisements must appeal to consumers' motives. Some advertising appeals to physiological motives, and some to social or status motives. Often the motive appealed to is quite different from the motive or need that would actually be satisfied by the product.

This exercise is intended to make you more aware of (1) the various needs appealed to in much of the advertising found in magazines and (2) the frequent discrepancy between the "appealed to need" and the "need satisfied."

equipment needed

Ten advertisements from popular magazines, such as *Life, Glamour, Esquire, Playboy,* or *Time.*

procedure

Bring to class any ten advertisements from popular magazines. Examine each advertisement carefully with the intention of analyzing the drives and motive appealed to in each instance. In the first column of the table on page 158 list the name of the product advertised. In the next column list the motive appealed to. Try to decide the nature of the motive, whether it is primarily physiological or primarily social. Mark a *P* or an *S* beside the motive to denote its basic appeal. In the next column indicate the motive that would actually be satisfied if the product were used. In the last column make a check mark if there is a discrepancy between the "appealed to motive" and the "motive satisfied." In the space below the chart total the number of advertisements appealing to each kind of motive.

	Product advertised	Motive appealed to	Motive satisfied	Discrepancy
1.				
2.				
3.				
4.				
5.				
6.				
7.				
8.				
9.				
10.				

Motive appealed to   **Total**

Physiological   _____

Social   _____

questions for discussion

1. Which kind of motivation is most frequently appealed to in the advertising you analyzed? How do you explain this?

2. How often is there a discrepancy between the motive appealed to and the motive satisfied?

3. Do you think advertisers have a good understanding of human motivation?

14 affect and emotion

programed unit

1. *Affective states* range from the *mild* feelings of pleasantness and unpleasantness that accompany much of our behavior to the more *intense* states usually identified as *emotions*. John feels mildly happy today, whereas Bill feels intensely angry. The feelings of these two men differ greatly, but both would

affective

be considered _____ states.

states
2. Affective _____ include a wide range of feelings. When we find the touch of velvet pleasant and that of sandpaper unpleasant, these are

mild

(*mild/intense*) affective states; fierce anger or joyful exaltation constitute

affective

more intense _____ states, or emotions.

3. Affective states include feelings that are *mild* or *intense, pleasant* or *un-*

mild

pleasant. Whether experiences are pleasant or unpleasant, _____ or

affective

intense, they are called _____ states.

4. There are many intermediate states between the mild experiences of pleasant-

unpleasantness

ness and _____ and the more violent and intense feelings that are usually called *emotions*. It is difficult, therefore, to say where *feelings* leave off and *emotions* begin. Instead we shall be con-

affective

cerned with the whole range of _____ states.

mild
5. Affective states, then, include experiences that are _____ or intense,

unpleasant

pleasant or _____ .

affective
6. Emotions or _____ states can thus be classified as those

pleasant

that are _____ (such as joy and love) and those that are

unpleasant

_____ (such as anger and grief).

159

7. In addition to the classification into pleasant and unpleasant states, emotions can be scaled according to the *intensity* of the experience. **Rage and panic** would be classified as intensely *un*_____ affective states; ecstasy and joy as _____ pleasant emotions.

unpleasant

intensely

8. Intense _____ states are accompanied by widespread *bodily changes*. Some of these changes, such as muscular tension, grimacing, and moaning, are controlled by the *central nervous system;* others, such as accelerated heart rate, the flow of tears, and "butterflies" in the stomach, are under the control of the *autonomic nervous system*. Some changes, such as altered rate of breathing, are controlled by both the central _____ _____ and the _____ nervous system.

affective

nervous

system, autonomic

9. The tears Mary sheds after learning that her fiancé has been seriously injured in an accident are controlled by the _____ nervous system; her moans and other sounds of distress are under the control of the _____ _____ _____ .

autonomic

central nervous system

10. Because emotions are accompanied by widespread _____ changes, one way to classify emotions might be according to the bodily responses involved. If a person always became red-faced and breathed rapidly when angry and became pale and breathed slowly when afraid, these differences in bodily _____ might prove a useful means of distinguishing between anger and _____ .

bodily

changes (or responses)

fear

11. Unfortunately, the attempt to differentiate emotions on the basis of _____ changes has not proved very successful. The physiological symptoms of the different emotions vary from one individual to the next, and there is too much overlap between the symptoms. The face may flush during fear as readily as during anger. Hence redness of the face (*would/would not*) be a useful measure for distinguishing between the two emotions.

bodily

would not

12. The problem of distinguishing among emotional states is further complicated because the *situation* in which the bodily _____ of emotion occur will often influence how the person *labels* the emotion.

changes

13. For example, if a subject is given a drug that produces profound bodily changes, he will tend to label his emotional state in accordance with the behavior of those around him. If his fellow subjects are acting in a gay and euphoric manner, the person will tend to label his emotional state as euphoria; if his fellow subjects are expressing angry feelings, he will tend to _____ his emotion as anger.

label

14. The label that a person attaches to the bodily changes of emotion depends to some extent upon the *s*_____ in which these changes occur. Situational factors influence how a person will _____ his emotional state.

situation

label

15. One of the earliest theories of emotion was the *James-Lange theory,* which proposed that what we feel as emotion is the *feedback* from the bodily

James | changes. According to the _____-Lange theory, we see a wildcat, start to run, and then experience the emotion we call fear.

James-Lange | **16.** The notion that the feeling of sorrow results from the tears that flow when a person hears tragic news is a statement of the _____-_____ theory of emotion.

bodily | **17.** The James-Lange theory maintains that emotion is defined by _____ responses that are perceived and labeled after they occur. The experience of

feedback | emotion is *fe*_____ from the bodily changes.

Lange | **18.** More recent modifications of the James-_____ theory stress the role of *perception* in emotion. A person's emotional response to a situation de-

feedback | pends not only upon *fe*_____ from bodily changes but also upon how he *perceives* the situation *before* the bodily changes occur.

19. You see a wildcat and start to run, but you run only because you perceive

perception | the wildcat as dangerous. Thus your *p*_____ of the situation influences your emotion.

20. According to the James-Lange theory, emotions are perceived and labeled

after | (*before/after*) they occur.

21. Theories that stress the role of perception in emotion maintain that one's

perception | initial _____ of the situation influences the emotional response.

22. Some of the ways in which we express emotions are *innate,* appearing at birth or developing through *maturation*. As soon as he is born the infant can cry. Crying is thus an innate expression of emotion. When he is about six months old the infant will laugh when his mother smiles or makes funny

innate | faces. Laughing is thus an inborn, or _____ , expression of emo-

maturation | tion. But it requires a period of *mat*_____ before it appears.

23. Although the infant is born with the capacity to cry and develops the capacity

maturation | to laugh through _____ , most aspects of emotional behavior are acquired through *learning*.

24. As he grows older the child learns the *occasions* when it is appropriate to cry and when it is appropriate to laugh. He also learns the *form* of emotional

learns | expression that is proper in his culture; for example, he _____ to express anger verbally rather than by hitting.

25. In our society women express sorrow by crying; men usually inhibit their

learning | tears. This is an example of the influence of *l*_____ on emotional expression.

26. To recapitulate: Some expressions of emotion are innate; they appear at

maturation | birth or develop through _____ . Crying and laughing

innate | are examples of _____ emotional expressions. However, learning

occasions	is important in determining the o_____ when certain emo-
form	tions are appropriate and in shaping the f_____ of expression acceptable within the culture.

27. Emotion is closely related to motivation. The emotion of fear, for example, acts much like an *aversive drive*. Whatever behavior acts to reduce the fear is likely to be learned. If an animal is repeatedly shocked in a small compartment, it will quickly develop a conditioned fear response to the compartment. It will learn to press a lever or turn a wheel in order to escape from the compartment in which it experienced shock to another compartment that is "safe"; the animal will continue these responses for many trials even though it no longer receives shock. In this case fear has acquired the prop-

reducing
erties of a *drive*. Behavior that *reduces* the fear, or is *drive-_____* , will be learned.

reduction
28. The emotion of fear and the impulse toward fear *re_____* are

hunger
not unlike the hunger drive and the impulse to reduce _____ pangs.

drive
29. Some emotions thus can act as a _____ to motivate behavior. Emotional experiences can also be sought as *goals*. We go to a comedy to enjoy

goal
a good laugh. The emotion in this case is a _____ .

30. John recklessly rides his motorcycle because he enjoys the thrill of possible

goal
danger. Emotion in this case is a _____ .

drives, goals
(either order)
31. Thus, we see that emotions can serve as _____ or as _____ .

32. Fear as an emotion usually has a specific object. Fear motivates the individual to escape from the feared object and to avoid contact with it. Usually the fear is realistic, but sometimes it may be extreme and inappropriate, in which case it is known as a *phobia*. A phobia is *extreme fear* in the *absence of real danger*. A boy who is excessively fearful of harmless spiders probably

phobia
has a _____ , since there is no real danger.

33. Bill is extremely fearful of closed spaces although they present no real

phobia, fear
danger. He has a _____ . Most people have a _____ of rattlesnakes because they constitute a real danger.

34. Fear usually has a realistic object. A phobia, on the other hand, is

extreme, real danger
_____ fear in the absence of _____ _____ .

35. Closely related to fear is *anxiety,* which is a state of apprehension or uneasiness that, too, may act as a drive. Usually the object of anxiety is less specific than the object of fear. For instance, a person who generally feels that something terrible is going to happen, even though there are no real

anxiety
reasons for feeling this way, is experiencing _____ .

does not
36. Fear usually has a specific object; anxiety usually (*does/does not*) have a specific object.

37. Psychologists use the word *"anxiety"* in different ways, but it most commonly refers to a condition in which the person feels a *vague fear* or apprehension for no clearly specified reason. Stuart tosses and turns in bed half the night before he can go to sleep; he feels troubled, apprehensive, and

vague

uneasy but cannot really say why. He is probably experiencing a _____ fear, a state commonly called *anxiety*.

vague

38. A condition in which a person feels a _____ fear or apprehension

anxiety

and uneasiness for no clearly specified reason is the state of _____ .

39. *Temperament* refers to the *characteristic* level of emotional reactivity of a person. A *mood,* on the other hand, is a more *temporary* state of emotional reactivity. If a person is cheerful most of the time, we say he has a cheerful

temperament

_____ . If a person is usually cheerful but for some reason feels despondent this morning, we say he is in a despondent

mood

_____ .

Temperament

40. _____ refers to the *characteristic* level of emotional

mood

reactivity of a person. A _____ , on the other hand, is a *temporary* state of emotional reactivity.

temporary

41. A mood is a _____ state of emotional reactivity of a per-

characteristic

son, whereas temperament refers to the _____ level of emotional reactivity.

42. In general, emotional experiences enrich our lives, but prolonged or often-repeated emotional tension may be disruptive and may lead to actual illness. *Psychosomatic disorders* constitute a group of illnesses in which the symptoms are those of genuine *organic* ailments, but the *causes* may lie in the patient's *emotional life.* For instance, Mrs. X has an ulcer—an organic ailment, but one that stems from emotional stress due to her inability to cope with feelings of anger and resentment. Therefore Mrs. X is suffering from a

psychosomatic

_____ disorder.

Psychosomatic

43. _____ disorders constitute a group of illnesses in which the symptoms are those of genuine organic ailments, but the causes

emotional

may lie in the patient's _____ life.

44. When an organic ailment is caused by emotional stress, it is called a

psychosomatic disorder

_____ _____ .

psychosomatic

45. Asthma, ulcers, and migraine headaches are _____

disorders

_____ if the causes of these illnesses lie in the patient's emotional life.

self-quiz

Select the alternative that best completes the thought. In some cases several answers are fairly satisfactory; you are to pick the *best* one.

_____ **1.** Anger does not have a particular set of

indicators. Its physiological pattern depends upon

a. whether the emotion occurs in the laboratory or at home
b. what the subject has had to eat

c. the amount of epinephrine secreted

d. how open or inward the expression of anger is

_____ 2. The emotional expression of a ten-year-old child deaf and blind from birth
a. resembled that of an infant
b. resembled the expression and gestures of normal children
c. did not resemble the emotional behavior of normal children
d. revealed that characteristic forms of emotion are essentially learned

_____ 3. The primary occasion for anger is
a. jealousy
b. unjust accusations
c. thwarting of a goal-seeking activity
d. retaliatory action against a person or object

_____ 4. Strangeness as a stimulus to fear in children is
a. the result of conditioning
b. most intense during the first six months of life
c. less potent after the age of ten months
d. probably due to an increased ability to discriminate

_____ 5. Darwin's theory of emotion proposed that
a. our awareness of bodily states involves a feedback from bodily responses
b. emotion is defined by bodily responses that are perceived and labeled
c. the limbic system be recognized as controlling emotion
d. man's behavior is the evolutionary product of a long ancestry

_____ 6. Symptoms of emotion that are controlled by the central nervous system are
a. accelerated heart beat
b. frowning, moaning, and muscular tension
c. "butterflies" in the stomach
d. the flow of tears

_____ 7. Activation theory
a. differentiates one state of emotion from another on a physiological basis

b. conflicts with Darwin's principles

c. proposes that circumstances are unimportant in distinguishing between various emotions

d. maintains that the primary dimension of emotion is arousal

_____ 8. Extreme or pathological fears are known as
a. phobias
b. anxiety states
c. apprehension motives
d. escape anxieties

_____ 9. Studies investigating the differences between fear and anger reveal that the subject who feels fear shows a predominance of
a. epinephrine
b. norepinephrine
c. white corpuscles
d. noradrenalin

_____ 10. "We are afraid because we run." "We are angry because we strike." These seeming paradoxes are important to the

_____ theory of emotion.
a. Darwinian
b. James-Lange
c. activation
d. perceptual-motivational

_____ 11. A song heard during an unhappy experience may always thereafter arouse in the hearer an emotion of unhappiness. This shows that emotions can be
a. conditioned
b. universal
c. innate
d. culturally determined

_____ 12. A person's characteristic level of emotional reactivity is called his
a. temperament
b. mood
c. receptivity
d. complex

_____ 13. Attempts to differentiate emotions on the basis of bodily changes have
a. been largely unsuccessful because the physiological symptoms of different emotions overlap
b. supported the James-Lange theory of emotion
c. shown clear distinctions between the

responses characteristic of rage and
fear
d. shown that the bodily responses to
fear correspond to the action of norepinephrine

_____ 14. Schachter and Singer proposed that an
emotional state depends upon
a. the state of physiological arousal
b. a cognition appropriate to a state of
arousal
c. both of the above
d. neither of the above

_____ 15. The emotional response of the newborn
human is best characterized as
a. general excitement
b. fear
c. cheerfulness
d. a delighted state

_____ 16. Disturbances or damage to bodily organs or tissues that result from emotional stress are called
a. moods
b. temperaments
c. psychosomatic disorders
d. physiological reactions

_____ 17. When we call attention to the pleasantness or unpleasantness of an experience,
we are referring to its
a. emotional state
b. feelings

c. experienced condition
d. affective tone

_____ 18. A moderate increase in tension
a. interferes with learning
b. has no effect on learning
c. aids in learning
d. prevents learning

_____ 19. The person who fears heights and finds
himself on a high place will be restless
until he gets away. In this case the
emotion can be interpreted as a(n)
a. instinct
b. drive
c. conditioned response
d. need

_____ 20. Emotional behavior in the early months
of infancy
a. depends upon the environmental
context
b. depends upon early cognitive cues
c. reflects the infant's internal state of
arousal
d. shows a wide range of emotional re-
sponsiveness

key to self-quiz

20. c	15. a	10. b	5. d
19. b	14. c	9. a	4. d
18. c	13. a	8. a	3. c
17. d	12. a	7. d	2. b
16. c	11. a	6. b	1. d

class exercise

MEASURING EMOTIONAL STATES

introduction

The purpose of this exercise is to determine the
existence of an emotional state in a person. The instructor sets up a situation in which emotion is introduced in one subject but not in another. The class
then measures the subjects' galvanic skin responses
(GSR) and their reaction times.

equipment needed

A GSR apparatus and a stopwatch. If a GSR apparatus is not available, the exercise can be done
using reaction times alone.

procedure

The instructor will select two subjects who will
leave the room while he describes the experiment. One
subject, while absent, will read the description of a
crime that he presumably committed; the other is
simply asked to wait outside the classroom for a few
minutes and told that upon his return he will be given
a brief word-association test. (The "crime" description and the word-association test are given on pages
281–284 of the Appendix. The instructor should make
certain that both of his subjects have not previously
read either of these.)

Mixed randomly among neutral words in the word-
association test are some key words that are related

to the crime. The hypothesis is that the "criminal" will show an emotional reaction to these words, while the subject who knows nothing about the crime will not. Either of two methods can be used to detect an emotional response. The simplest measure is reaction time, which is the time between the presentation of the word and the subject's response. The "guilty" subject should show longer reaction times to the key words than the control subject. A measure requiring more complicated equipment but one that is more sensitive in detecting emotional states is the galvanic skin response (GSR). The GSR is a measure of the changes in electrical resistance of the skin that occur when emotions are aroused. These changes are measured by electrodes attached to the palms of the hands and connected to a recording galvanometer. The GSR is one of the measures used in lie detectors.

treatment of data

One way to analyze the data is to compare the average GSR deflection for the key words with that of the neutral words: the subject with the greatest difference is "guilty." If reaction time is used as a measure of emotional response, the average reaction time to the key words should be compared for the two subjects. The subject with the longest reaction time to these words is the "criminal." It is also possible to look for clues in the responses given by the subjects to the key words.

questions for discussion

1. If both measures were used, which differentiated more clearly between the "guilty" and the "innocent" subjects?

2. Were there any clues in the responses to the key words?

3. What uncontrolled variables might have influenced the results?

4. Do you think that either of these measures would be accurate in identifying a real criminal?

5. Was the GSR measure for neutral words the same for both subjects? If not, what difficulties might be involved in establishing a basal GSR level against which to measure emotional responses?

15 ability testing and intelligence

programed unit

1. All men are alike in many ways; yet each person is *unique*, or *different* from all other human beings, in his physical traits, attitudes, abilities, and other personal characteristics. Were a psychologist interested in studying you as a unique person, he would be interested in those attributes that make you

different   _____ from other people.

unique   **2.** John, like every person, has _____ characteristics that set him apart from other people. The term *individual differences* is used to refer to

differs   the ways in which John _____ from others in his habits, attitudes, physical traits, abilities, and other personal characteristics.

3. One important way in which each of us differs from others is in our abilities.

individual   *Ability testing* is one way of appraising _____ differences in knowledge and skills and in aptitudes and achievements. Were a psychologist interested in how Mary differs from others in her achievements,

ability   aptitudes, skills, and knowledge, he might use _____ testing to determine her general competency in these areas.

4. The study of individual differences in skills and knowledge, achievements

ability   and aptitudes is often carried on by means of _____

testing   _____ .

5. In attempting to appraise one's abilities, psychologists make a distinction between what one can do now and what one might do if he were trained. Ability tests that identify what you can do now, or skills already accomplished, are *achievement tests*. Sally has had two years of typing instruction in high school. Were a psychologist interested in how fast and how accurately

achievement   she can type *now,* he would administer an _____ test.

167

6. When you take your final examination in this course, your instructor will

achievement administer an _____ test to find out how well you have learned the various concepts and generalizations covered in his lectures and the textbook.

7. Ability tests designed to measure *capacity to learn*—that is, to predict what you can accomplish with *training*—are known as *aptitude tests*. Tests de-signed to measure skills already attained, or what a person can do now, are

achievement called _____ tests.

8. Suppose that there are fifty unskilled applicants for a job as machinist and the company intends to train only ten of the fifty applicants to become machinists. An industrial psychologist employed by this company would

aptitude probably administer an _____ test to determine which of the fifty applicants have the greatest capacity to learn to become machinists.

9. Tests designed to measure capacity to learn—that is, to predict what one

aptitude can accomplish with training—are known as _____ tests.

capacity **10.** Aptitude tests are designed to measure _____ to learn, that

training is, to predict what one can accomplish with _____ .

11. Before lawyers are admitted to the bar, they must pass a test of knowledge and understanding of legal precepts. The test they take is an (*achievement/*

achievement *aptitude*) test.

12. If a law school can admit only forty out of several hundred applicants, an

aptitude _____ test might be administered to determine which ap-plicants have the greatest capacity to learn to become skilled lawyers.

achievement **13.** Tests designed to measure skills already attained are called _____ tests. Tests designed to predict what one can accomplish with training or to

aptitude measure capacity to learn are called _____ tests.

ability **14.** Both achievement and aptitude tests are tests of _____ .

15. If test scores are to be used for scientific purposes, they must be *trustworthy.* In scientific terms this means that they must meet two requirements: *reliabil-*

trustworthy *ity* and *validity*. Test scores that are not _____ are not likely to be regarded as useful by scientists.

16. If they are to be regarded as trustworthy, two requirements must be met by all test scores used for scientific purposes. These two requirements are

validity *reliability* and *val*_____ .

17. By *reliability* we mean that the scores are dependable and reproducible, that they measure *consistently* whatever it is they measure. To be regarded

reliability as trustworthy, test scores must have both _____

validity (either order) and _____ .

18. Test scores that measure consistently are said to have the characteristic of

reliability   _____ , since the scores are dependable and reproducible.

19. Few of us would want to use a ruler made of rubber, because the measurements could vary considerably from one measurement to the next and would not give consistent and reproducible results. Such measurements would

reliability   lack _____ .

20. A steel ruler, however, should give us consistent, dependable, and reproducible results from one measurement to the next and would therefore have

reliability   the characteristic of _____ .

21. Psychologist X has developed a new intelligence test, which he has administered to a large group of students. He administered the same test twice to the same group of students and found that the pattern of scores on the second test compared quite closely to the pattern on the first test. Because his test gave consistent results, which are dependable and reproducible, his test

reliability   presumably has _____ .

22. By reliability we mean that the scores are dependable and reproducible, that

consistently   they measure _____ whatever it is they measure.

23. By *validity* we mean that the test scores measure what the tester *intended* to measure. For instance, if your instructor desires to measure what you have learned in this course and his test does measure your actual achievement, his

validity   test has the characteristic of _____ .

24. If your instructor desires to measure knowledge achieved in his course, but his test measures your intelligence rather than your achievement, he is not measuring what he intended to measure and his test therefore would lack

validity   _____ .

25. By validity we mean that the test scores measure what the tester

intended   _____ to measure.

reliability   **26.** By _____ we mean that the scores measure con-

validity   sistently whatever it is they measure; by _____ we mean that the scores measure what the tester intended to measure.

27. A test may be reliable but invalid. That is, a test may measure consistently

intended   yet not measure what the tester _____ to measure.

28. Suppose that a psychologist designed a new test intended to measure intelligence. He administered the same test to the same subjects on two occasions and found that the scores for all subjects on both occasions were quite consistent, but that his test results correlated poorly with those of well-established intelligence tests. His test has reliability but probably lacks

validity   _____ .

29. The psychologist, in attempting to learn how reliable his new test is, administered it twice to the same group of students. To compare the first and second sets of scores, he needs to know the *degree of relationship* between the two sets of scores. This relationship is provided by the *correlation coefficient* (commonly abbreviated as *r*), a term already familiar to you as a measure of the degree of correspondence between two sets of scores. In this case the

coefficient   correlation _____ between the two sets of scores is a *reliability coefficient.*

30. To estimate the degree of relationship between two sets of scores in order to

reliability   find out how reliable a test is, we need a *re*_____ coefficient.

31. Well-constructed psychological tests of ability commonly have reliability coefficients above *r* = .90. The psychologist who designed a new intelligence

90   test should find an *r* of _____ or above for his test if it is to be considered as reliable as other well-constructed ability tests.

32. To measure *validity* we must also have two scores for each person, one being the test score and the other being a score on a *criterion* of some sort. For instance, if we designed a test of ability to sell life insurance and obtained

criterion   scores for a number of persons, we would also need a _____ of some sort, which in this case might be the total value of insurance policies sold by those taking the test.

33. A criterion might be thought of as a standard selected as the goal to be achieved in a task, or as a set of scores or other records against which the success of a predictive test is verified. For instance, if effective life insurance salesmen sell at least $100,000 of insurance in a year, this figure might serve

criterion   as a standard, or _____ .

34. If we want to measure a test's validity, we need not only each person's score

criterion   on the test, but also his scores on a _____ of some sort.

35. To measure validity we need to derive the *degree of relationship* between test scores and a criterion measure. This correlation coefficient is known as a *validity coefficient.* The correlation coefficient that tells us how well the

validity   test measures what it is supposed to measure is a (*validity/reliability*) coefficient.

36. When we derive the degree of relationship between test scores and a criterion

validity   measure, we obtain a _____ coefficient.

37. In using test performance as a basis for selecting candidates, psychologists often use *critical scores.* These are scores selected after experience with tests used for a given purpose; persons scoring below the critical level are rejected

critical   as unlikely to succeed. A _____ score on a scholastic aptitude test for college students is one below which no candidate is accepted for admission.

38. Students applying for admission to college X must have achieved a total scholastic score that places them at or above the fortieth centile. This figure

critical

is a _____ score, since no student obtaining a score that places him below the fortieth centile is permitted to gain admission to this particular college.

39. Alfred Binet invented the intelligence test as we know it and devised a scale of *mental age*. In Binet's system, *average* mental-age (M.A.) scores *correspond* to chronological age (C.A.), that is, to the age determined from the date of birth. Thus, a child of normal intelligence with a chronological age

mental

of ten should have a _____ age of ten.

40. A child with a chronological age of thirteen who has normal intelligence

thirteen

would also have a mental age of _____ .

correspond **41.** If a child has normal intelligence, his mental age will _____ to his chronological age.

Chronological **42.** _____ age refers to the age determined from the date of birth.

43. A bright child's mental age is above his chronological age; one would expect,

below

then, that a dull child's mental age would be _____ his chronological age.

mental **44.** A retarded child has a _____ age below his chronological age.

45. The *intelligence quotient* (I.Q.) is a convenient index of brightness. It expresses intelligence as a ratio of the mental age to chronological age:

$$\text{I.Q.} = 100 \, \frac{\text{Mental age (M.A.)}}{\text{Chronological age (C.A.)}}$$

The 100 is used as a multiplier to remove the decimal point and to make the average I.Q. have a value of 100. If a child with a chronological age of nine

100

has a mental age of nine, his I.Q., or intelligence quotient, is _____ .

46. What is Tom's I.Q. if his mental age is eight and his chronological age is

80

ten? _____

47. If a child has an I.Q. *below 70,* he is considered *mentally subnormal.* If a child has an I.Q. of *140 or above,* he is considered *gifted.* If Jack has a mental age of fourteen and a chronological age of ten, his I.Q. would be

140

_____ .

70 **48.** Persons with I.Q.'s below _____ are considered mentally subnormal;

140 those with I.Q.'s of _____ or above are considered gifted.

49. As the text points out, however, these cut-off points are quite arbitrary. Whether a person with an I.Q. below 70 is considered mentally

subnormal

_____ depends upon his social skills and the complexity of the environment in which he lives. Whether a person with an I.Q. above

gifted
140, supposedly a _____ individual, succeeds in using his ability depends largely upon his social adjustment and motivation.

50. Two of the most widely used intelligence tests are the *Stanford-Binet* and the *Wechsler Intelligence Scale*. The Stanford-_____ is a revision of

Binet

Binet
the earlier test devised by Alfred _____ .

Stanford
51. The _____-Binet Intelligence Test, like the earlier Binet tests,

mental
is a _____-*age scale*. It consists of a number of different items at

age
each *age level*. The number of test items passed at each _____ level determines the child's *mental-age score*.

Intelligence Scale
52. The Wechsler _____ _____ is *not* a mental-age scale. The test items are grouped according to *type* of item rather

level
than age _____ . The child obtains *separate* scores on twelve sub-tests. Six of these subtests are *verbal,* testing such abilities as mathematical

subtests
reasoning, vocabulary, and recall of series of digits; the other six *sub*_____ are nonverbal, or *performance,* tests that involve assembling picture puzzles, manipulating blocks to form specific designs, or recognizing the missing

Wechsler
detail in a picture. The final I.Q. score on the _____

Intelligence
_____ Scale is obtained by averaging all the

subtest
*sub*_____ scores. Separate I.Q. scores can also be obtained for the sum of the verbal tests and for the sum of the performance tests.

53. Since the test provides more information about a child's abilities than just

age, Wechsler
a single mental-_____ score, or I.Q. score, the _____

Intelligence Scale
_____ _____ is frequently used for diag-

verbal
nostic purposes. By analyzing the scores on both the _____ sub-

performance
(either order)
tests and the _____ subtests, it is possible to determine a child's special abilities and weaknesses.

mental-age
54. To recapitulate: the Stanford-Binet is a _____-_____ scale; it

does not
(*does/does not*) group test items according to type so as to permit a diag-nostic analysis of different abilities. A test that does provide separate scores

Wechsler Intelligence
for various subtests is the _____ _____

Scale
_____ .

55. Johnny is having trouble coping with the work in second grade. His teacher suspects that he is quite bright but that difficulty in recognizing visual pat-terns hinders his reading. Of the two intelligence tests we have discussed, the

Wechsler Intelligence
Scale
_____ _____ _____ might

Stanford-Binet
provide more helpful information than the _____-_____ .

56. What are the abilities that underlie intelligence? One method used to identify clusters of abilities that combine to make up the I.Q. scores obtained on tests

Stanford-Binet	such as the _____-_____ and the Wechsler Intelligence Scale is called *factor analysis*.
analysis	**57.** Factor _____ is a statistical procedure used to determine the *common factors* that contribute to a body of data. The same people are given a large number of tests, each individual test composed of similar items. The scores on all the tests are then intercorrelated. If two tests correlate highly with each other, they have a lot in *common* with each other. Tests that show
common	high intercorrelations have much in _____ with each other.
little	**58.** Tests that have low intercorrelations would have (*little/much*) in common with each other.
factor	**59.** This is the basic method of _____ analysis. It is a statistical procedure that provides a systematic way of finding a small number of *common factors* that can account for a large array of intercorrelations.
analysis	**60.** Factor _____ attempts to discover underlying traits or abilities that produce intelligence test results. In one study by Thurstone an analysis of more than sixty different tests yielded seven *primary abilities*.
common	These primary abilities were the _____ factors that emerged from
factor	the application of _____ analysis.
primary	**61.** Thurstone concluded that these _____ abilities were the basic abilities of which intelligence is fashioned.
	62. A later investigator, Guilford, also used factor analysis and found many more abilities underlying intelligence. Guilford found more abilities than did
Thurstone	*Th*_____ because he broadened the concept of intelligence beyond that measured by the usual I.Q. test.
	63. The usual I.Q. test measures *convergent thinking,* that is, thinking that leads to a specific "correct" answer. A test item such as "How many eggs in a
convergent	dozen?" measures *con*_____ thinking, since it requires a specific correct answer.
convergent	**64.** The question "What is the capital of Italy?" measures _____
correct	thinking, since it requires a specific _____ answer.
	65. Guilford proposed that *divergent thinking,* which is concerned with many "possible" answers rather than a specific correct answer, is an important aspect of intelligence. Divergent thinking is more creative than convergent
possible	thinking because it is concerned with many _____ answers.
	66. The question "How many uses can you think of for a paper clip?" asks for
divergent	a number of possible answers and is thus a measure of _____ thinking.
	67. The item "Imagine all of the things that might happen if the force of
divergent	gravity suddenly disappeared" is a measure of _____ thinking.

correct   **68.** Convergent thinking is concerned with a specific _____ answer,

possible   while divergent thinking is concerned with many _____ answers.

convergent   **69.** Intelligence tests consist of questions that require _____

divergent   thinking, while tests of creativity attempt to measure _____ thinking.

self-quiz

Select the alternative that best completes the thought. In some cases several answers are fairly satisfactory; you are to pick the *best* one.

_____ **1.** Binet tested his items by
    a. factor analysis
    b. studying changes in the proportion of children answering an item correctly at different ages
    c. using cross-cultural methods
    d. using only items that required an ability to memorize

_____ **2.** Guilford has broadened the concept of intellect beyond that of the familiar I.Q. tests. One of his chief concepts is
    a. divergent production
    b. convergent production
    c. primary abilities
    d. factor loading

_____ **3.** A test is valid if it
    a. measures what it is supposed to measure
    b. is dependable and measures consistently
    c. is reproducible
    d. is short and subjective

_____ **4.** When mental age equals chronological age, I.Q.
    a. is at a maximum
    b. is at a minimum
    c. equals 100
    d. cannot be calculated

_____ **5.** The Wechsler Adult Intelligence Scale, unlike the Stanford-Binet,
    a. includes a vocabulary section
    b. is an achievement test
    c. does not yield an I.Q. score

    d. is divided into two parts, a verbal scale and a performance scale

_____ **6.** The intelligence test was invented by
    a. Binet
    b. Terman
    c. Wechsler
    d. Stanford

_____ **7.** When a test is administered to students to predict how well they will do in college, it is classified as a(n)
    a. achievement test
    b. intelligence test
    c. aptitude test
    d. test of primary mental abilities

_____ **8.** The formula $100 \times \dfrac{\text{M.A.}}{\text{C.A.}}$ is equal to the
    a. basal mental age
    b. intelligence quotient
    c. brightness value
    d. aptitude score

_____ **9.** A new intelligence test yielded a reliability coefficient of .94 and a validity coefficient of .20. What conclusion can we draw?
    a. an error in computation has been made, since both coefficients are usually the same
    b. the test is not a satisfactory measure of intelligence
    c. the criterion for establishing validity was undoubtedly inappropriate
    d. the test has considerable promise as a cross-cultural intelligence test

_____ **10.** "Fluid" intelligence
    a. depends upon prior habits

b. is not much influenced by prior learning

c. can be best measured by an achievement test

d. is dependent upon cultural circumstances

_____ 11. Compared to their classmates, the intellectually gifted children studied by Terman were
a. poorer physical specimens
b. less successful as adults
c. poorly adapted socially
d. superior in leadership ability

_____ 12. A child classified as mentally retarded
a. is the same as a mentally defective child
b. suffered brain injury at birth
c. often has a history of retardation in the family
d. usually shows a marked physical weakness

_____ 13. The basal mental age of a child is the mental-age level at which he passes
a. 25 percent of the items
b. 50 percent of the items
c. 75 percent of the items
d. 100 percent of the items

_____ 14. Using factor analysis, Thurstone identified
a. the single general factor involved in intelligence
b. seven primary abilities that make up intelligence
c. people most likely to succeed in scientific research
d. a structure-of-intellect model

_____ 15. Tests designed to predict what one can accomplish with training are called
a. achievement tests
b. aptitude tests
c. intelligence tests
d. preference tests

_____ 16. The distribution of I.Q.'s follows a(n)
a. curve of decreasing gains

b. curve of increasing gains
c. bell-shaped curve
d. S-shaped curve

_____ 17. A measure of creative thinking as related to I.Q. reveals that
a. a high I.Q. means the person will most likely have a high score in creative thinking
b. a high creative-thinking score means a low I.Q. score
c. a high I.Q. is no guarantee of a high creative-thinking score
d. a low creative-thinking score means the person probably has an average I.Q.

_____ 18. Examinations given at the end of the term to see how much you have learned are
a. achievement tests
b. aptitude tests
c. intelligence tests
d. accomplishment tests

_____ 19. Using factor analysis, intercorrelations are found that yield a table of correlations known as a
a. factor loading
b. cluster correlation
c. correlation matrix
d. common-elements table

_____ 20. A critical score might be used in
a. selecting applicants for admission to graduate training
b. determining the validity coefficient of a test
c. determining the reliability coefficient of a test
d. all of the above

key to self-quiz

1. b	6. a	11. d	16. c
2. a	7. c	12. c	17. c
3. a	8. b	13. d	18. a
4. c	9. b	14. b	19. c
5. d	10. b	15. b	20. a

class exercise

INDIVIDUAL DIFFERENCES

introduction

Despite the fact that humans resemble one another in some fundamental ways, they also differ from one another in many important characteristics, such as skills, attitudes, intelligence, aptitudes, interests, and personality. In many practical situations, as in the selection of employees, the measurement of these individual differences is important, especially if one wishes to select the best performers and eliminate the poor performers at a given task. This exercise is intended to show that individual differences exist even on relatively simple tasks.

equipment needed

None

procedure

When your instructor gives you instructions to begin, immediately rearrange the following scrambled sentences to make meaningful sentences. Write your meaningful sentence in the space provided below each scrambled sentence. You will be permitted ten minutes for this task. You may not be able to finish in the time allowed, but do the best you can.

1. MEN THEM LIVES GOOD DO AFTER THE THAT

   _____

2. EYES YOU THEIR UNTIL SHOOT OF WHITES DON'T SEE THE

   _____

3. THE HUMAN WORLD IS THING MOST FREE VALUABLE THE MIND THE IN

   _____

4. TELL YOUR DEVIL GO THE TO STYLE YARN YOUR AND LET

   _____

5. IT MOMENTS WE THAT RARE LIVE ONLY IS AT

   _____

6. DO MUCH TOO KNOWING ANSWERS NOT BLAME ME FOR THE ALL NOT

   _____

7. THE FAULTS CONSCIOUS IS OF TO NONE OF GREATEST BE

   _____

8. MISUNDERSTAND BETTER IS UNDERSTAND LOT A THAN TO LITTLE A IT TO

   _____

9. THE BOASTING IT OF THAT MADE OF CAN SUCCESS BE USE WORST IS

   _____

10. BETTER FOOLISH FOOL THAN WIT A WITTY A

_____

11. FIRST CURIOSITY OF LOT ONLY LOVE IS FOOLISHNESS AND A LITTLE A

_____

12. THE LAUGHTER OF ASTONISHING IS POWER

_____

13. MONEY UNHAPPINESS CURE CANNOT

_____

14. FAILURE GROWS WITH REPUTATION YOUR EVERY

_____

15. HOURS FOR MAN HIMSELF AND WILL HE ABOUT A LISTEN TO TALK

_____

16. THE NOBODY BELIEVE WILL ONE IS THE THING TRUTH

_____

17. MY TRUTH THE TO TELL OF JOKING IS WAY

_____

18. LIVING IS MAKES WORTH THAT LIFE PLEASURE NOT IT

_____

19. A INTELLECTUAL BLUESTOCKING WITHOUT SUBJECTS RAY A HAVING INTELLECT OF MANIA HAS WOMAN IS A WHO A FOR

_____

20. VERY MINDS COMPLEX OF IDEAS SIMPLE WITHIN LIE REACH THE ONLY

_____

Total number unscrambled _____

treatment of data

1. The unscrambled sentences are given on page 285 of the Appendix; if your sentence is meaningful it need not have precisely the same word order as that given in the Appendix. Count the number of meaningful sentences you wrote from the scrambled sentences. Enter your score where it reads "Total number unscrambled _____ ."

2. Your instructor will ask you to submit your score on a small slip of paper so that the data for the class as a whole can be plotted on the graph that appears on page 178.

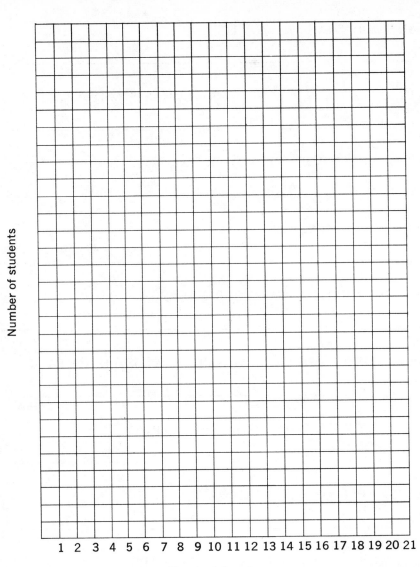

Meaningful sentences

1. Is the curve bell-shaped or skewed?

2. Is there a clustering around the central tendency?

3. Is there more than one mode?

4. Which of the scrambled sentences took the longest time to unscramble? Why?

5. What conclusions regarding individual differences in performing a simple task such as this can you draw?

6. What would you conjecture about the particular abilities of those students who unscrambled the most sentences in the time allotted?

individual exercise

MEASURING INTELLIGENCE

introduction

As yet there is no way of measuring directly the intellectual capacity of an individual. Therefore, psychologists *infer* intellectual capacity from the performance of a person in various test situations. Two widely used individual intelligence tests are the Stanford-Binet and the Wechsler-Bellevue.

The following exercises will give the beginning student some knowledge of the way in which mental age and intelligence quotients are derived, and an awareness of how intelligence quotients may reflect different kinds of intelligence.

equipment needed

None

procedure

Read carefully the instructions given for each set of problems and then attempt to solve them.

I. DETERMINATION OF I.Q. FROM THE STANFORD-BINET

instructions

1. The *mental* age (M.A.) is determined by the number of tests passed. There are six tests at each age level (five to fourteen), so that each test passed counts for two months of mental age. Example: If all the tests through five years are passed, and one of the tests at the six-year level, the mental age is five years, two months.
2. The *chronological* age (C.A.) is the actual age determined from the birth date. It is expressed to the nearest month. Example: A child born on January 1, 1965, has a C.A. of five years, one month, on February 1, 1970.
3. The intelligence quotient (I.Q.) is determined by dividing the mental age (M.A.) by the chronological age (C.A.) and then multiplying by 100. Example: A child of ten years C.A. and twelve years M.A. has an I.Q. of $\frac{12}{10} \times 100$, or 120.

problems

Answers to the following four problems may be found in the Appendix (page 285).

1. David was born on June 15, 1965. On an intelligence test administered June 15, 1970, he passed all of the tests at the four-year level; four tests at the five-year level; two tests at the six-year level; no higher tests were passed. (a) What is David's mental age? (b) What is his I.Q.?
2. John was born on January 1, 1958. He passed the following tests on July 10, 1970: all tests at the nine-year level; five tests at the ten-year level; one test at the eleven-year level; no higher tests were passed. (a) What is his M.A.? (b) his C.A.? (c) his I.Q.?

3. Helen was exactly six years old at the time of testing. She passed all of the five-year tests, five of the six-year tests, three of the seven-year tests, and one of the eight-year tests. (a) What is her M.A.? (b) What is her I.Q.?
4. Peter is eight years old and has an I.Q. of 125. What is his mental age?

II. ADULT INTELLIGENCE

instructions

Below are summaries of the performance of three college students on the Wechsler-Bellevue Intelligence Test.[1] The heading R.S. stands for "raw score," and W.T.S. for "weighted test score." Study the subtest scores as well as the Verbal Scale I.Q., Performance Scale I.Q., and Full Scale I.Q. Then answer the questions that follow.

STUDENT 1

Test	R.S.	W.T.S.
Information	23	16
Comprehension	16	14
Digit span	13	11
Arithmetic	7	9
Similarities	16	13
(Vocabulary)	(30)	(13)
Verbal score*		63
Picture arrangement	6	6
Picture completion	14	14
Block design	38	18
Object assembly	25	16
Digit symbol	61	14
Performance score		68
Total score		131

* Since the verbal scale is based on five tests, and six were given here, we must multiply the total by five-sixths to get the verbal score.

Verbal scale 63	I.Q. 119
Perform. scale 68	I.Q. 124
Full scale 131	I.Q. 124

[1] Courtesy of Dr. Walter T. Plant, San Jose State College, San Jose, California.

STUDENT 2

Test	R.S.	W.T.S.
Information	21	15
Comprehension	16	14
Digit span	13	11
Arithmetic	11	15
Similarities	19	15
(Vocabulary)	(30)	(13)
Verbal score*		69
Picture arrangement	14	12
Picture completion	13	13
Block design	24	11
Object assembly	21	12
Digit symbol	57	14
Performance score		62
Total score		131

* To get the verbal score, we multiply the total by five-sixths.

Verbal scale	69	I.Q.	126
Perform. scale	62	I.Q.	118
Full scale	131	I.Q.	124

STUDENT 3

Test	R.S.	W.T.S.
Information	16	11
Comprehension	13	11
Digit span	12	10
Arithmetic	8	10
Similarities	17	14
(Vocabulary)	(28)	(12)
Verbal score*		57
Picture arrangement	15	13
Picture completion	14	14
Block design	38	17
Object assembly	25	16
Digit symbol	62	15
Performance score		75
Total score		132

* To get the verbal score, we multiply the total by five-sixths.

Verbal scale	57	I.Q.	112
Perform. scale	75	I.Q.	133
Full scale	132	I.Q.	124

questions for discussion

1. Note that the Full Scale I.Q. of all three students is 124. Does this mean that they have the same kind of intelligence?

2. Which two students most resemble each other in intelligence?

3. Why do you suppose Wechsler included both a verbal scale and a performance scale?

4. Which student has the best verbal ability? Would this allow greater chances of success in college? Why or why not?

16 behavior genetics

programed unit

1. Whenever one speaks of *heredity* and *environment,* the question arises as to which is more important to the organism. It is clear that both are of crucial importance. Without reproduction, the organism would not exist; and whenever reproduction takes place, characteristics are transmitted through

   heredity   *h*_____ .

2. It is also clear that the organism cannot live without a(n) _____
   —that is, without food, air, water, and the other conditions necessary for existence.

   environment

3. If we realize that both heredity and environment affect the developing organism, it is only a small step to realize that they must *interact* with each other. For example, there is a *hereditary component* to height, but the height actually attained will depend also upon the variety and adequacy of the

   environment   diet—in other words, upon the _____ .

4. There is also a hereditary component in muscular coordination. However, if the developing organism is given no opportunity to use his muscles—for example, if we raise a child in a box, with no opportunity for movement—his

   will not   coordination (*will/will not*) reach the level of his hereditary possibilities.

5. Even though heredity and environment interact to influence the final development of the organism, we cannot separate out their influences and give the exact proportion of the contribution of each to a given aspect of growth or

   cannot   behavior. If John is 6 feet tall, we (*can/cannot*) make a statement such as, "The fact that John is 6 feet tall is due 60 percent to heredity and 40 percent to environment."

   heredity

6. In most cases the best statement we can make is that _____
   sets upper limits upon our capabilities, and that environmental influences will then determine the extent to which these capabilities will be attained.

7. One of the best ways of investigating the contribution of environment to the attainment of various human capabilities is to use *identical,* or *monozygotic, twins* in research. *Monozygotic* twins develop from the same egg, or ovum, and consequently have *exactly the same heredity.* Thus, monozygotic twins

same   are always of the _____ sex.

8. *Fraternal,* or *dizygotic, twins* develop from two separate ova that have been fertilized by two separate sperm cells. They are *no* more alike genetically than ordinary siblings. We know, then, that they (*do/do not*) have exactly

do not   the same heredity.

monozygotic   9. Identical, or _____ , twins have the very same heredity because they develop from the same ovum that has been fertilized by a single

dizygotic   sperm cell. However, fraternal, or _____ , twins are no more alike genetically than ordinary siblings because they develop from two separate ova that were fertilized by two separate sperm cells.

10. Since monozygotic twins have exactly the same heredity, any differences we

environment   find in them must be due to _____ .

11. If we raise monozygotic twins in different environments and find that one reaches a height of 5 feet 10 inches, while the other reaches a height of only 5 feet 8 inches, we must conclude that this difference could *not* have been

heredity   due to _____ .

monozygotic
(or identical)   12. Because _____ twins have the same, or identical, heredity, they provide useful information in studies investigating the existence of a hereditary component in mental illness. If there is a hereditary component, the incidence of both twins being mentally ill would be much higher

dizygotic (or fraternal)   among monozygotic twins than among _____ twins, who are *not* genetically alike.

13. Research has revealed that if one monozygotic twin is schizophrenic, the other twin is also likely to be schizophrenic. For instance, one study found that in 86.2 percent of the cases, if one monozygotic twin was schizophrenic, the other twin was also schizophrenic. It appears, therefore, that there is a

hereditary   strong _____ component in the susceptibility to at least some forms of mental illness.

14. If heredity is a strong component in the susceptibility to mental illness, you

dizygotic (or fraternal)   would expect a much lower incidence in _____ twins, who are no more alike genetically than ordinary siblings. That is the case; research has shown that in only 14.5 percent of the cases, if one dizygotic twin is schizophrenic, the other dizygotic twin will be schizophrenic.

hereditary   15. It would appear that there is a strong _____ component in the susceptibility to some forms of schizophrenia.

16. *Genetics,* the science of heredity, shows how the *physical* characteristics of offspring derive from the characteristics of parents. For instance, eye color is a physical characteristic that derives from one's parents. Hair color is also a

physical

genetics

_____ characteristic; the study of the inheritance of hair color would thus be part of the study of _____ .

physical, genetics

17. A science that tries to trace the laws governing the inheritance of _____ characteristics is _____ .

18. It is also possible that *behavior* is affected by heredity. The study of the laws governing the inheritance of such psychological characteristics as intelligence, which is studied through behavior, is called *behavior genetics*. For example, psychologists have had some success in breeding strains of rats that seem more intelligent than other rats because they can learn mazes more easily.

behavior

The study of this kind of inheritance is a part of _____ genetics.

Behavior genetics

19. _____ _____ has to do with the study, through behavior, of the genetic transmission of psychological characteristics.

20. The study of the gene distribution throughout groups of individuals that mate with one another and of its consequences for these groups is known as *population genetics*. For instance, by correlating the intelligence of children in a population with that of their parents, it is possible to study the inheritance of intelligence without having to gather family histories over several

population

generations. This is an example of _____ genetics.

21. The basic characteristics of a population of either animals or human beings depend upon the genes existing in those populations. For instance, if we find a strain of rats that has a "wild" temperament and a strain that has a "tame" temperament, we can study their offspring to find out if this trait is trans-

population

mitted genetically. In other words, we are studying _____ genetics.

22. The *hereditary units* that an individual receives from his parents and transmits to his offspring are *carried by* microscopic particles known as *chromosomes,* found within the nucleus of each cell of the body. Each body cell in man has 46 chromosomes. At conception the human being receives 23

chromosomes

chromosomes from the father's sperm and 23 *ch*_____ from the mother's ovum. These 46 chromosomes form 23 *pairs,* which are duplicated in every cell of the body as the individual develops.

chromosomes

23. A fertilized ovum contains 46 _____ , 23 of its own and 23 received from the sperm.

24. The chromosomes are duplicated in every cell of the body as the individual

46

develops. Thus every body cell contains _____ chromosomes arranged

pairs

in 23 _____ .

25. The chromosomes carry the basic units of heredity, which are called *genes*.

genes

Each chromosome carries many of these hereditary units, or _____ .
Like the chromosomes, the genes also occur in pairs; one gene of each pair comes from the sperm chromosome and one gene from the ovum

chromosome

_____ .

26. Chromosomes occur in pairs, and each chromosome contains many pairs of

genes

_____ .

27. In man each chromosome carries more than 1000 genes. Since the fertilized

23

ovum has _____ pairs of chromosomes, the number of genes is high enough to make it extremely unlikely that any two individuals would have the same heredity. The exception would be individuals who develop from the

monozygotic
(or identical)

same ovum, who are called _____ twins.

28. A gene may be either *dominant* or *recessive*. This fact is important in understanding the transmission of heredity. If both members of a gene pair are dominant, the individual will manifest the trait determined by that gene pair.

recessive

If one member of a pair is dominant and the other is *re*_____ , the individual will show the form of the trait characteristic of the dominant gene, but he will also carry the recessive gene, which may show up in his offspring. A recessive form of the trait will be expressed only if both genes are recessive.

will

29. If both members of a gene pair are dominant, the individual (*will/will not*) manifest the trait determined by that gene pair.

30. Brown eyes are dominant and blue are recessive. If a person inherits a gene for brown eyes from his mother and a gene for brown eyes from his father,

brown

the color of his eyes will be _____ . In this case eye color is deter-

dominant

mined by two _____ genes.

31. If one member of a gene pair is dominant and the other is recessive, the

dominant

individual will show the form of the trait expressed by the _____ gene.

32. Mark inherited a gene for brown eyes from his father and a gene for blue

brown

eyes from his mother. His eye color will be _____ .

33. Only if both members of a gene pair are recessive will the individual manifest

recessive

the form of the trait expressed by the _____ gene.

two

34. Margaret has blue eyes. This means that she has _____ (*number*) recessive gene(s) for eye color.

heredity

35. This description of how genes operate in the transmission of *h*_____ is oversimplified (most individual characteristics are determined by more than a single gene pair), but the principle of dominance and recessiveness is basic to genetics and explains why you may possess a feature, characteristic of one of your grandparents, that is not observable in either of your parents.

36. Your parents both have brown eyes but you have blue eyes like your grandmother. Both of your parents must have inherited from their parents a

recessive

_____ gene for blue eyes.

37. The inherited characteristics of a person that can be observed are called

phenotypes. If you have blue eyes, this is an inherited characteristic that can

phenotype

be observed and therefore is a _____ .

phenotype

38. The concept of a _____ refers to the observable inherited characteristics of a person.

39. *Genotypes,* on the other hand, refer to those characteristics that an individual inherits, carries, and *may or may not manifest,* but that he may pass on to his offspring through heredity. If your mother carries a recessive gene for blue eyes (although her eyes are brown), blue-eyedness is a genetic characteristic that she possesses but does not manifest. Blue-eyedness is thus a

genotype

g_____ .

40. When a parent has a characteristic that he does not necessarily manifest but that can be passed on to his offspring through inheritance, we call such a

genotype

characteristic a _____ .

observed

41. A phenotype is a characteristic that can be _____ . A

genotype

_____ cannot always be observed in the individual, because he may not manifest it.

42. If a child inherits a characteristic from his parents, the parent must have had the *genotype* for this characteristic; if the parent did not manifest this trait

phenotype

himself, however, he did *not* have the _____ .

43. The genotype, then, is basic. It may or may not give rise to the

phenotype

*ph*_____ . The phenotype is the surface characteristic; the

genotype

_____ is the basic characteristic without which the phenotype cannot exist.

44. Referring back to our discussion of dominance, a genotype of two dominant genes for a given trait means that the person himself and his offspring will

phenotype

have the dominant trait as a *p*_____ .

45. If a child shows a phenotype of a recessive trait, then each of his parents

recessive

must have had at least one _____ gene for that trait.

46. One special pair of chromosomes determines the offspring's *sex.* Females have two identical sex chromosomes called *X-chromosomes;* males have an *X-* and a *Y-chromosome.* The child inherits one sex chromosome from its

father

mother and one from its _____ .

47. If the child receives an X-chromosome from each parent, it will be a female,

X

since females have two _____-chromosomes.

Y

48. If a child receives an X-chromosome from its mother and a(n) _____-chromosome from its father, it will be a male.

49. Some genes occur on the X-chromosome and not on the Y-chromosome. Such genes are said to be *sex-linked.* Red-green color blindness and hemophilia

sex-linked

(the tendency to bleed excessively) are examples of *sex-_____* traits in man.

two

50. Since females possess _____ (*number*) X-chromosomes, they get a double dose of sex-linked genes, one from each parent. Males only get one

mother

dose of each sex-linked gene, and that dose must come from the *m_____* ,

chromosome

since the father contributes a Y-chromosome instead of an X-_____ .

mother

51. In the male, therefore, all sex-linked characteristics are inherited from the (*mother/father*) .

sex-linked

52. Since the male receives only one dose of each *sex-_____* gene, recessive genes cannot be masked, and the male will manifest any traits

X

carried by the recessive genes of his _____-chromosome. For this reason, sex-linked phenotypes occur much more frequently in males than in females.

53. Red-green color blindness occurs about eight times as often in men as in women. Since this type of color blindness is a recessive trait, a woman who has a dominant gene for normal color vision and a recessive gene for color

will not

blindness (*will/will not*) be colorblind. If she transmits the recessive gene for color blindness to her son, he will be colorblind because he has no dominant gene to mask the trait.

54. Traits that are carried by genes of the X-chromosomes and occur more fre-

sex-linked

quently in men than in women are said to be _____-_____ .

color blindness

Hemophilia and red-green _____ _____ are examples of sex-linked traits.

heredity

55. We have defined a gene as the basic unit of _____ . Recent research in biochemistry gives us a better understanding of the process of hereditary transmission. A gene is actually a *segment* of a complex *protein molecule* called *DNA* (deoxyribonucleic acid), which acts as a unit in transmitting hereditary characteristics.

DNA

56. A gene is a segment of a complex protein molecule called _____ .

57. The DNA molecule is able to divide and replicate itself in every cell in the body as the organism develops, thus providing each cell with its own set of genetic instructions. The biochemical basis of hereditary transmission is pro-

DNA, molecule

vided by the action of _____ , a complex protein _____ .

58. To review: We know that heredity and environment both affect the developing organism. We also know that they interact in the production of the traits

cannot

of the mature organism. However, we (*can/cannot*) make exact statements of the proportion each contributes to the level actually reached for a given trait (for example, height or intelligence). Therefore, if you were to read that a particular person's I.Q. is attributable 80 percent to heredity and 20 percent to environment, you should recognize this as a speculation, since we (*can/*

cannot

cannot) make such precise statements regarding the interaction of heredity and environment.

59. You recall that the study of the genetic transmission of *behavior* is called

behavior

_____ genetics. The study of the gene distribution throughout

population	groups of individuals that mate with one another is known as _____ genetics.
	60. The basic hereditary units that an individual receives from his parents and
genes	transmits to his offspring are the _____ , which are carried by the 23
chromosomes	pairs of _____ within each cell.
recessive	**61.** Since a gene may be either dominant or _____ , a person's underlying inherited characteristics, the genotype, may not always show up
phenotype	in his observable characteristics, or _____ .
	62. The female inherits two X-chromosomes. The male inherits one X- and one
Y	_____-chromosome. Traits transmitted by genes that occur on the
sex-	X-chromosome but not on the Y-chromosome are referred to as _____-
linked	_____ .

self-quiz

Select the alternative that best completes the thought. In some cases several answers are fairly satisfactory; you are to pick the *best* one.

_____ **1.** Behavior genetics is concerned with the
a. inheritance of physical characteristics
b. inheritance of psychological characteristics
c. biochemical nature of heredity
d. all of the above

_____ **2.** The characteristics that an individual manifests are known as the
a. phenotypes
b. genotypes
c. dominant traits
d. recessive traits

_____ **3.** The basic unit of heredity is the
a. gene
b. chromosome
c. RNA
d. DNA

_____ **4.** The chromosomes
a. are found in each blood cell
b. are found within the genes
c. are duplicated in every body cell
d. may be either dominant or recessive

_____ **5.** The individual who possesses one X-

chromosome and one Y-chromosome is
a. colorblind
b. a girl
c. a boy
d. a mongoloid

_____ **6.** The material basis for gene action is a complex substance called
a. DNA
b. amino acids
c. RNA
d. PTC

_____ **7.** The study of gene distribution throughout groups of individuals that mate with one another is known as
a. biochemical genetics
b. population genetics
c. behavior genetics
d. cytogenetics

_____ **8.** Phototaxis in fruit flies refers to the tendency
a. toward intellectual brightness or dullness
b. to be attracted toward a light
c. to go into convulsions when exposed to high-pitched sounds
d. to be either wild or tame

_____ **9.** RNA carries out two different functions:
a. synthesis and coding

b. duplication and coding
c. messenger and duplication
d. messenger and transfer

_____ 10. Studies of foster children indicate that
a. I.Q. tends to drop as a result of emotional readjustment
b. there is no relation between I.Q. and environment
c. I.Q. tends to rise as a result of favorable environment
d. mental age is affected by placement in a good foster home, but I.Q. is not

_____ 11. In humans the evidence is fairly satisfactory that inheritance determines
a. eye and hair color
b. emotionality
c. attitudes
d. personality traits

_____ 12. The underlying hereditary determiners that will be transmitted to the offspring are expressed by the
a. genes
b. chromosomes
c. phenotype
d. genotype

_____ 13. If both parents carry a recessive gene for a particular trait,
a. the trait could show up in some of their offspring
b. the trait will show up only in some of their daughters
c. some of their children are likely to be mentally subnormal
d. some of their children will manifest chromosomal anomalies

_____ 14. Correlations between the I.Q. of a school-age child and that of his parents reveal
a. a negative correlation
b. no correlation
c. a positive correlation
d. an exact correlation of 1.00

_____ 15. Studies correlating the adopted child's I.Q. with that of his foster parents and his biological parents reveal that
a. the correlation is higher with the biological parents

b. the correlation is higher with the foster parents
c. the correlations are the same
d. no significant correlations were found for either comparison

_____ 16. Dizygotic twins
a. are genetically more alike than ordinary siblings
b. develop from the same ovum
c. are always of the same sex
d. need not resemble each other

_____ 17. The studies on the incidence of schizophrenic illness in monozygotic twins suggests that
a. some types of schizophrenia have a strong hereditary component
b. heredity is the determining factor for all types of schizophrenia
c. schizophrenia is definitely psychogenic in origin
d. learning is the crucial factor in the development of the disorder

_____ 18. Monozygotic siblings are the same as
a. fraternal like-sexed twins
b. fraternal twins of the opposite sex
c. ordinary siblings
d. identical twins

_____ 19. Which are the most alike in height and intelligence?
a. dizygotic siblings of the opposite sex
b. monozygotic siblings
c. ordinary siblings
d. dizygotic siblings of the same sex

_____ 20. X-chromosomes
a. carry only dominant genes
b. occur only in females
c. occur only in males
d. carry sex-linked genes

key to self-quiz

20. d	15. a	10. c	5. c
19. b	14. c	9. d	4. c
18. d	13. a	8. b	3. a
17. a	12. d	7. b	2. a
16. d	11. a	6. a	1. b

individual exercise

MENDELIAN THEORY OF INHERITANCE

introduction

The perennial heredity-environment controversy cannot be ignored, since so many erroneous assumptions are made about the contributions of each to the traits and attributes of a person. Some people overstress the importance of hereditary influences. For example, Mr. X incessantly worries that he will be eventually committed to a mental hospital because his grandfather was recently committed and he feels he must have inherited some of his grandfather's genes for psychoses. There appeared an article in the newspaper about a boy who was maltreated and rejected by his natural parents, who felt that he could not be their son because he did not resemble their other four children in appearance or temperament.

Likewise, some people place too much credence in environmental factors. Thus, a student who had difficulty graduating from high school because his I.Q. was in the 80's has a father who insists that if his son is intensively tutored, he can make the grade in a liberal arts course at a nearby college. Or the parents of a mentally defective child wrongly attribute his condition to chicken pox, which he had when he was two years old.

Such confusion can result only in unfortunate consequences for everyone involved. The first task confronting us, then, is to get the facts. If hereditary determinants predominate, as with physical characteristics and certain diseases, there is little that we can do except to acknowledge whatever characteristics we happen to inherit. On the other hand, if environmental influences play a major role, then we can exercise control over characteristics through education, clinical treatment, and the like.

The modern form of the Mendelian theory of inheritance is based upon the conception of *genes* and *chromosomes* transmitted from parents to offspring, each parent giving the child one-half his chromosomes. Since there are *twenty-three* pairs of chromosomes in humans and each chromosome contains a large number of genes, the possible combinations of hereditary factors are great. Thus, even within a given family, it is most unlikely that one child will be exactly like another, except in the case of monozygotic twins.

Even though both members of a pair of genes have the same function, they may exercise the function differently. One member of the pair may be *dominant* and the other *recessive,* or both may be dominant, or both may be recessive. The characteristic controlled by the dominant gene appears in the individual regardless of whether the second member of the pair is recessive. The recessive trait appears in the individual only if both members of the pair of genes are recessive. (This assumes that the trait in question is unitary and controlled by a single gene pair. Few traits are of this kind.)

The following exercises will help to determine whether you understand clearly how heredity works.

equipment needed

None

procedure

1. Below are probability tables for curly (dominant) and straight (recessive) hair. Fill in the tables to show the effect of gene combinations of parents on the traits of their offspring. The gene pairs of the mother and father are listed in the margins of each table. Each square in the table is filled in by drawing from the margins one member of the gene pair from the mother and one from the father, corresponding to the row and column in which the square falls. Now read the four squares in the table as four equal probabilities making up the expected kinds of offspring of parents with this genetic make-up. Write out the description or genetic make-up of the children. The first example has been filled in to show you how this should be done.

   a. Father recessive (aa); mother dominant (AA)

	A	A
a	aA	aA
a	aA	aA

   DESCRIPTION: *All children will have curly hair and be recessive carriers.*

   b. Father dominant (AA); mother recessive (aa)

	a	a
A		
A		

DESCRIPTION: _____

_____

_____

c. Father recessive (aa); mother shows dominant traits but is a recessive carrier (aA)

	a	A
a		
a		

DESCRIPTION: _____

_____

_____

d. Father shows dominant traits but is a recessive carrier (aA); mother shows dominant traits but is a recessive carrier (aA)

	a	A
a		
A		

DESCRIPTION: _____

_____

_____

2. Some traits are sex-linked, that is, determined by genes carried by the X- and Y-chromosomes, the chromosomes that determine sex. The best known of these are hemophilia and red-green color blindness. Such defects exist as recessive genes in the X-chromosomes. Although one of the X-chromosomes may contain the particular recessive gene, it is highly unlikely that both will. Thus, girls, who have two X-chromosomes, generally show no evidence of defect. A boy, however, has only one X-chromosome. The few genes carried by his Y-chromosome will not mask or counteract any defective X-chromosome gene even though the X-chromosome gene may be recessive. Sex-linked characteristics, then, are certain defects that are transmitted in the X-chromosome and appear much more frequently in males than in females.

In the following exercise on the sex-linked

characteristic hemophilia, X represents a dominant gene carried by an X-chromosome, and small x a recessive gene carried by an X-chromosome. Because the genes carried by the Y-chromosome will not mask recessive X-chromosome genes, the Y-chromosome genes act as if they are recessive; consequently a small y will stand for a Y-chromosome gene. The small y is thus also a sign of maleness. Fill in the tables below as you did in the previous exercise.

a. Father normal, no recessive genes for hemophilia (Xy); mother normal but carries a recessive gene for hemophilia (Xx)

	X	x
X		
y		

DESCRIPTION: _____

_____

_____

b. Father hemophiliac (xy); mother normal, with no recessive gene for hemophilia (XX)

	X	X
x		
y		

DESCRIPTION: _____

_____

_____

treatment of data

Answers to the problems may be found in the Appendix on page 285.

questions for discussion

1. Which would prove more efficacious in improving the human race—attempting to improve the heredity or the environment?

2. Colorblind women are much rarer than colorblind men. Why is this true?

3. John's mother says, "John inherited his father's

fussiness about food." Is she correct? Why or why not?

4. Why do monozygotic (identical) twins reared apart resemble one another in intelligence more than dizygotic (fraternal) twins living in the same home?

5. Some of the best data we have on the relative roles of heredity and environment are based upon work with animals rather than with human beings. Why?

6. The genes for many human defects are recessive. Does this fact give any biological authority to the social taboo against marriages between close relatives?

17 theories of personality

programed unit

1. *Personality* is a difficult concept to define, but we will begin by referring to personality as the characteristics and ways of behaving that determine an individual's *unique adjustment* to the environment. According to this definition, every person (*has/does not have*) personality.

has

2. The characteristics and ways of behaving that determine an individual's *unique* adjustment to the environment may be said to make up his

personality

_____ .

3. When we speak of Mark's personality, we are referring to the characteristics and ways of behaving that determine Mark's adjustment to his environment

unique

—an adjustment that, being Mark's alone, is a _____ adjustment.

4. Any characteristics that are important in the individual's unique *personal*

personality

adjustment are included in _____ .

5. Since such factors as appearance, abilities, motives, and emotional reactivity

adjustment

may be important to the individual's personal _____ ,

personality

a description of the individual's _____ must take them into account.

6. Some of the characteristics that influence personality are *inborn,* that is, present at birth. Robert, a large, sturdy baby, lies placidly in his crib and is

inborn

not easily upset. These *in*_____ characteristics, physical size and emotional reactivity, may well influence his personality in later life.

7. John at three weeks of age is a small, frail infant who is fussy and continually

inborn

personality

active. These _____ characteristics may well contribute to his

_____ as an adult.

8. The characteristics that are present at birth constitute the individual's *potential*—a potential that develops through maturation and learning as the person grows up. The experiences that he encounters in growing up shape or modify

potential

the inborn *po*_____ . Some of these experiences are *common experiences,* which most individuals growing up in a certain *culture* share.

9. If a particular culture emphasizes the value of cleanliness and early toilet training, then most individuals growing up in this culture will share

common

_____ experiences in these areas.

10. If a culture expects females to be docile and submissive, then most of the

experiences

girls growing up in this culture will share some common _____ .

inborn (or innate)

These experiences will *modify* the girls' _____ potential. A girl who is active and vigorous as an infant may become more placid as her per-

culture

sonality is shaped or modified by the _____ .

modify

11. Some of the experiences that shape or _____ the person's inborn

culture

potential are common to most individuals in a certain _____ . Other experiences are *unique* or *individual;* they cannot be predicted from knowledge of the culture in which the person was raised.

12. John's father beat him unmercifully when drunk. This would be an example

unique

of an individual or _____ experience for John—one that is not

common

_____ to most boys in his culture.

inborn (or innate)

13. Thus the _____ potential of the individual is shaped or modified

common

by _____ experiences (those shared by most members of the cul-

unique

ture) as well as by _____ or individual experiences to form the

personality

_____ we see in the adult.

14. Many theories attempt to explain and describe personality. One kind of personality theory is *trait theory.* A *trait* is a *persisting characteristic* of personality that can be *measured.* Thus one may think of intelligence as a trait.

trait

Aggressiveness may also be termed a _____ .

15. When we attempt to describe a personality in terms of certain *persisting*

measured

characteristics that can be *m*_____ , we are using a *trait* theory.

persistent

16. A *trait* has two characteristics. It must be *per*_____ and it must be measurable.

17. One measures a trait in an individual by finding his position on a *scale* that is set up to measure that trait. For instance, the trait of intelligence in an individual is measured by comparing him with other people on an I.Q.

scale

_____ .

18. When we measure the traits that make up a personality by finding their positions on a number of scales, we are using _____ theory.

trait

19. Merely listing the specific traits that describe a person, however, does not provide an adequate description of his personality. We need some way of determining how the various traits are organized or related to one another. One method of determining the relationships among traits, used by Cattell, is the technique of *correlation.* You will remember the technique of

correlation

_____ from our discussion in Chapter 1.

20. If several traits cluster together so that an individual who ranks high on one of them tends also to rank high on the others, and an individual who ranks

low

low on one tends to rank _____ on the others, we say that these traits show an *intercorrelation.*

21. When a group of traits cluster together, or show an intercorrelation, they obviously have something in common with one another. This means that one can assign a name to this group and treat it as though it were one trait. Cattell calls what the group has in common a *surface trait.* A *surface trait,*

intercorrelation

then, is determined by the _____ of several traits. The method of analyzing trait intercorrelations and grouping together those traits that intercorrelate is called *cluster analysis.*

22. When a personality test is given to a group of people and it is found that a group of traits from that test correlate highly with one another so that they appear to have something in common, a label may be assigned to what the traits have in common. The intercorrelated traits may be designated as a

surface

single _____ trait.

23. If, for example, people who score high on a personality test scale designed to

high

measure "honesty" also score _____ on scales measuring "loyalty" and

traits, intercorrelated

"fair-mindedness," then these three _____ are *inter* _____ .

fair-mindedness

24. Since the traits of honesty, loyalty, and _____-_____

surface

are intercorrelated, we could group them under a single _____ trait, which might be labeled *integrity.*

25. Cluster analysis is one method of determining what intercorrelating traits have in common. A more refined mathematical technique is *factor analysis.* Cattell calls traits detected by the method of factor analysis *source traits,* to

surface

distinguish them from the _____ traits that are determined by

analysis, Source

cluster _____ . *Sou_____* traits presumably stand for more

surface

basic aspects of the personality than _____ traits.

factor

26. Source traits are detected through the method of _____ analysis. The easier and more superficial method of grouping traits into a smaller number of traits by means of simple correlation is cluster analysis, which

surface, source

yields _____ traits. Factor analysis yields _____ traits;

cluster

_____ analysis yields surface traits.

27. Trait theories attempt to describe a person by measuring on a scale his persisting _____ , or traits. An alternate approach to personality theory attempts to classify people into *types* on the basis of a few *dominant characteristics*. When we say that one person is an introvert while another is an extravert, we are classifying them in terms of their _____ characteristics and are therefore using a *type* theory.

characteristics

dominant

28. A theory that classifies people according to three kinds of body build would be another kind of _____ theory.

type

29. Eysenck has proposed four personality types based on a combination of two dimensions: *stable-unstable* and *introverted-extraverted*. The stable-unstable dimension refers to the degree of *emotional control*. At the stable end of the _____ are those individuals who are generally calm, even-tempered, and not easily aroused. At the unstable end are individuals described as moody, anxious, and restless.

dimension

30. Eysenck's stable-unstable dimension of personality refers to the degree of _____ _____ .

emotional control

31. The introverted-extraverted _____ of personality refers to the extent to which a person's interests are oriented toward the outside world or inward toward himself. The introvert is shy, prefers to work alone, and tends to withdraw into himself in times of stress. The extravert is sociable, prefers to work with others, and tends to lose himself among people in times of stress.

dimension

32. The introverted-extraverted dimension refers to the extent to which a person's interests are oriented toward the _____ world or inward toward _____ .

outside

himself

33. Eysenck's two dimensions of personality are _____-_____ and _____-_____ .

stable-unstable

introverted-extraverted
(either order)

34. By combining these two dimensions Eysenck obtains four personality types: stable-extravert, *stable-in_____* , unstable-extravert, and *un_____-introvert*.

stable-introvert

unstable-introvert

35. Steve is a shy, quiet boy who has few friends. He tends to be moody and irritable. He would probably be classed as a(n) _____-_____ .

unstable-

introvert

36. His sister, Jane, is friendly and outgoing; she enjoys an active social life and is well-liked for her calm and easy-going manner. She would probably be classed as a(n) _____-_____ .

stable-extravert

37. Eysenck's four personality types are _____-_____ , _____-_____ , _____-_____ , and _____-_____ .

stable-extravert
stable-introvert,
unstable-extravert
unstable-introvert
(any order)

38. Eysenck's personality theory classifies people according to a few dominant

type   characteristics. It is thus an example of a _____ theory.

39. One of the dangers of type theories is the assumption that knowing a person's type enables one to make predictions about much of his behavior. A type theory tends to assert too much about an individual and may lead to the use of the *stereotype*. If you assume that a Latin American you have just met is

stereotype   temperamental, this is an example of a _____ .

40. Type theories also tend to neglect *cultural influences* on the individual. If we type a person as a stable-extravert, the tendency is to believe that he will

influences   remain a stable-extravert regardless of cultural _____ .

41. So far we have discussed two kinds of personality theories. Theories that describe a person by measuring his persisting characteristics on a scale are

trait   called _____ theories. Those that classify personality on the basis of a

type   few dominant characteristics are called _____ theories. A third approach to personality is *psychoanalytic theory*. One aspect of psychoanalytic theory is concerned with the development of personality, with how the person got to be the way he is.

psychoanalytic   **42.** The *developmental* aspect of _____ theory emphasizes the influences in early childhood that shape the personality into a relatively enduring structure. As the child progresses toward maturity he encounters different problems at each stage of development. The manner in which he learns to cope with these problems will determine his personality as an adult.

43. In psychoanalytic theory the stages from childhood pleasure to adult sexuality are called the *psychosexual* stages of development. The prefix *psycho-* indicates that the concern is with psychological development; the term *sexual* is used because development is felt to center around bodily pleasure. The

development   stages of psychosexual _____ are the oral, anal, phallic, latent, and genital stages. For a review of the psychosexual stages, see the program for Chapter 3.

44. According to psychoanalytic theory, the individual may fail to cope adequately with the problems associated with a particular stage of

psychosexual   _____ development and may become arrested, or *fixated,* at that stage.

45. For example, a child whose parents are excessively concerned with cleanli-

fixated   ness and insist upon early toilet training may become fi_____ at the anal stage of psychosexual development. A child who is fixated at the

anal   _____ stage will, as an adult, show excessive manifestations of the anal stage in his behavior.

46. Fixations lead to certain forms of *personality structure* associated with the stage at which the person is fixated. Thus a person whose psychosexual

fixated   development was arrested, or _____ , at the anal stage of devel-

personality   opment will display as an adult a certain type of _____ structure.

structure	**47.** The type of personality _____ manifested by a person whose psychosexual development has been _____ at the anal
fixated	
personality	stage is called the *compulsive personality*. The compulsive _____ is characterized by excessive cleanliness, orderliness, obstinacy, and stinginess.

compulsive   **48.** The traits that cluster together to form the _____ personality are excessive cleanliness, orderliness, obstinacy, and stinginess. Psychoanalytic theory proposes that this personality structure arises from ex-

anal   cessive cleanliness training during the _____ stage of psychosexual development.

49. When college men living together in the same residence rated one another on a variety of traits, it was found that there was a positive correlation between the traits of orderliness, obstinacy, and stinginess. In other words, men who

high   were rated high on orderliness tended to be rated _____ on obstinacy and stinginess. These results suggest that these traits do form a pattern that

compulsive personality   resembles the _____ _____ .

50. Many psychologists, however, question whether the origin of the compulsive

anal   personality can be traced solely to harsh toilet training during the _____

psychosexual   stage of _____ development. Parents who are excessive in their demands for cleanliness training may also make excessive demands for conformity, punctuality, neatness, and so on, beyond infancy.

personality   Thus the compulsive _____ structure may develop through continued childhood training in many areas rather than solely from treatment during toilet training. Specific personality structures have been attributed to fixations at other stages of psychosexual development, but the evidence supporting their origin is not strong.

51. In addition to its *developmental* aspect, psychoanalytic theory has a *dynamic* aspect, which focuses on how the different parts of the personality interact

dynamic   *in the present*. When we say that a person is torn between two desires, we are making a statement about the (*dynamic/developmental*) aspects of personality.

52. Freud postulated three parts of the personality, which he maintained were particularly important in understanding personality dynamics. The first of these is the *id,* which is the depository of the innate instinctual drives (sex and aggression). The *id* seeks immediate gratification of primitive impulses without regard to the consequences. If a person acts impulsively, without con-

id   cern for more remote consequences, he is likely to be expressing the _____ portion of his personality.

id   **53.** The irrational, impulsive portion of personality is called the _____ in psychoanalytic theory. It is manifested in early childhood but is never completely outgrown, so that behavior stemming from this part of the personality can be found in the most sober of adults.

54. It is obvious that if the id were given full rein we could never have a civilization. We need a part of the personality that will exert control in such a way as to make our behavior conform to reality, and social constraint. This is called the *ego*. The aspect of personality that takes into account the real

ego

consequences of our search for pleasure is, then, the _____ .

ego

55. The id is the irrational aspect of personality that ignores reality; the _____ is the more rational portion and tries to take reality into account.

id

56. Because it seeks immediate pleasure, the _____ is said to be controlled by the *pleasure principle;* because it conforms to environmental realities, the

ego

_____ is said to be controlled by the *reality principle.*

57. The third part of the personality, according to psychoanalytic theory, is the *superego,* an aspect that develops out of the ego's experiences with social reality and parental prohibitions. Parental commands are made part of the individual, who then feels guilt if he violates this internalized code. The common word for the *superego* is *conscience.* If the ego proposes a course of action that is opportunistic but somewhat in violation of conscience, the

ego, superego

_____ will be opposed by the *s_____* .

58. Let us set up a hypothetical situation involving a young boy, in which his thoughts may be attributed to these three aspects of personality. The boy is angry at one of his classmates and thinks, "I'd sure like to beat him to a

id

pulp!" This statement would be an expression of the _____ . Next the boy thinks, "But he's bigger than I and might beat *me* up." This is the

ego

_____ at work. Finally the boy thinks, "Well, fighting is wrong any-

superego

how." This would be the judgment of the _____ .

59. So far we have discussed several theories of personality. Theories that attempt to describe a personality by the individual's position on a number of

trait

scales or dimensions are called _____ theories. Theories that attempt to classify individuals on the basis of a few dominant characteristics are

type

called _____ theories. A theory that is concerned with both the develop-

psychoanalytic

mental and the dynamic aspects of personality is _____ theory.

60. All these theories assume *consistency* within personality. Some psychologists question whether personality is as consistent as the above-mentioned theories imply. Those who espouse *social behavior theory* maintain that behavior is quite *specific* to the situation or *context* in which it occurs.

behavior, specific

61. Social *be_____* theory proposes that behavior is _____

context

to the situation or _____ in which it occurs.

62. John considers himself to be an "honest" person. He is careful to give the correct change when he works part time as a store clerk, he is scrupulous about filling out his income tax return, and he has never cheated on an examination. However, when he found a wallet full of money on the side-walk, he failed to return it, even though the owner's address was clearly indicated. This example points to the fact that there is no unitary trait that

honesty

we call _____ . Whether a person behaves in an "honest man-

specific

ner" depends upon the _____ situation.

behavior	**63.**	Social *be*_____ theorists maintain that many personality traits are not consistent but depend instead upon the specific _____ in which the behavior occurs.
context (or situation)		

64. An important process in the development of an individual's personality is *identity formation.* As a child grows up he *identifies* with the significant people in his environment—mother, father, teacher, and siblings. When a young boy imitates his father's shaving, he is *identifying* with his father.

identifying

When a little girl dresses up in her mother's clothes, she is _____ with her mother.

65. Boys learn masculine behavior through the process of *identification* with

identification
(or identifying)

their fathers; girls learn feminine behavior through _____ with their mothers.

66. To achieve an identity of his own as an adult, the individual must *integrate* the various separate identifications he has made during his childhood and youth. He cannot be exactly like his father or exactly like his teacher or older brother. He must integrate his earlier identifications to form an

identity

_____ of his own.

integrate **67.** To achieve an identity of his own, a person must _____ his earlier identifications.

68. Adolescents characteristically experiment with various *roles* before they

identity (or personality)

achieve an integrated _____ . In the process of forming their own identity they seek a range of experiences and examine a number of philosophies of life.

69. At one stage a teenager may cut classes and spend his time hanging out with his peers at the local coffee house. At another stage he may turn eagerly toward his studies, spending his free time helping his science teacher develop class demonstrations. This behavior reflects experimentation with various

roles

_____ .

identity **70.** Experimenting with various roles is a necessary step in _____ formation.

71. Not everyone achieves identity formation. Sometimes separate identifications remain unintegrated within the person so that his personality is made of parts that are not self-consistent. Sometimes a person is torn into a variety of inconsistent roles. It is difficult to be at once father's competitive, rough and tough football player and mother's gentle, considerate boy. The experience

role

of incompatible roles such as these is known as _____ *diffusion.*

72. A person torn by many conflicting roles that he is unable to integrate, or

diffusion

unify, within his personality experiences role _____ . He may grow up insecure and unsure of his own identity because the separate identifications have not been assimilated. We say that such a person has not

identity

achieved _____ formation.

self-quiz

Select the alternative that best completes the thought. In some cases several answers are fairly satisfactory; you are to pick the *best* one.

_____ 1. Role diffusion refers to the fact that
  a. each of us has to learn many conflicting roles
  b. separate identifications remain unintegrated
  c. some individuals are bisexual in adult life
  d. certain roles can dominate a person's behavior

_____ 2. According to social behavior theorists, when behavior remains consistent or stable it is because
  a. the physical environment remains stable
  b. the social environment remains stable
  c. intermittent reinforcement fixates behavior so that it remains stable in the face of variable outcomes
  d. all of the above

_____ 3. Unlike the biographer, the scientific student of personality
  a. does not include early childhood in his study
  b. includes the individual's failures as well as his successes
  c. is interested in predicting the behavior of the individual
  d. tries to characterize his subject as an individual

_____ 4. Experimental subjects with a high need for approval tended to
  a. conform under social pressure
  b. inhibit aggressive responses
  c. be cautious in setting goals when there was some risk involved
  d. all of the above

_____ 5. Various roles are assigned to an individual on the basis of his
  a. sex
  b. occupation
  c. culture
  d. all of the above

_____ 6. A personality theory that attempts to describe an individual in terms of a number of measurable characteristics would be a _____ theory.
  a. trait
  b. type
  c. cohesive
  d. temperament

_____ 7. Studies of twins reveal that
  a. monozygotic twins have identical personalities
  b. there is no hereditary factor involved in personality
  c. there may be a tendency to inherit certain personality characteristics
  d. dizygotic twins have identical personalities

_____ 8. Our ordinary social self, realistic and rational, is represented by the
  a. id
  b. ego
  c. superego
  d. conscience

_____ 9. The depository of the innate instinctual drives, motivated by pleasure-seeking impulses, is called the
  a. id
  b. ego
  c. superego
  d. conscience

_____ 10. _____ theories tend to stress continuities in behavior.
  a. Type
  b. Developmental
  c. Trait
  d. all of the above

_____ 11. According to Sheldon, the individual having wide shoulders, narrow hips, and rippling muscles would be classified as a(n)
  a. ectomorph
  b. mesomorph
  c. endomorph
  d. matomorph

_____ 12. Surface traits are found by
  a. studying the clusters of correlations among traits
  b. observing the behavior of a large number of individuals
  c. factor analysis
  d. the use of rating scales

13. One of the limitations of trait theories is that
   a. they do not lend themselves readily to experimentation
   b. so many traits are synonymous in meaning
   c. they fail to describe the organization of traits within the individual
   d. they place too much emphasis on the environmental determinants of behavior

14. Eysenck's two-dimensional theory combines the dimensions
   a. orderly-chaotic and depressed-euphoric
   b. stable-unstable and depressed-euphoric
   c. stable-unstable and introverted-extraverted
   d. introverted-extraverted and orderly-chaotic

15. Cultural pressures impose some personality similarities, but individual personality is not completely predictable from knowledge of the culture because the individual
   a. may have moved often
   b. has some experiences distinctly his own
   c. may speak more than one language
   d. may have close friends from other countries

16. The classic case of Eve White and her multiple personalities shows that
   a. everyone probably has three distinct personalities
   b. personality correlates strongly with body types
   c. the unity of personality is based upon behavioral characteristics
   d. disparity of childhood identification facilitates the achievement of a single identity

17. One danger of type theory is that it
   a. places too much emphasis on cultural influences
   b. tends to assert too much about the individual
   c. does not give enough credit to biological inheritance as a cause of personality characteristics
   d. places too much importance on childhood experiences

18. Social behavior theorists have shifted interest toward the
   a. consistency and generality in personality
   b. coexistence of the developmental and interactive viewpoints
   c. behavior of the individual in a social setting
   d. malleability of behavior and procedures for changing behavior

19. The compulsive personality is characterized by
   a. flexibility and laziness
   b. spontaneity and happiness
   c. curiosity and intelligence
   d. obstinacy and stinginess

20. Type theories of personality attempt to classify people according to
   a. a few dominant characteristics
   b. temperament
   c. a number of measurable traits
   d. an analysis of developmental behavior

key to self-quiz

20. a	15. b	10. d	5. d
19. d	14. c	9. a	4. d
18. d	13. c	8. b	3. c
17. b	12. a	7. c	2. d
16. c	11. b	6. a	1. b

individual exercise

PERSONALITY DESCRIPTION

introduction

The text points out several differences among theories of personality that exist in psychology. The following exercise is designed to give you practical experience with some of these differences.

equipment needed

None

procedure

Write a description of one of your best friends (or someone whom you know very well) from the point of view of

1. a type theory
2. a trait theory
3. psychoanalytic theory

Make the descriptions short but still give as good a description of the person as you can.

questions for discussion

1. Which description was easiest? Why?

2. Which description was longest? Why?

3. Which description do you feel fits the person best? Why?

4. Do you think that some people would be easier to describe in terms of a particular kind of theory (for example, a type theory) than other people would be? Why?

18 personality assessment

programed unit

1. What are some of the characteristics or traits that psychologists can assess in attempting to describe an individual's personality? Two characteristics that are fairly easy to measure are *morphology* (the conformation of the body) and certain aspects of body *physiology*. A person's size, general body build, and attractiveness of appearance are all aspects of _____ .

   morphology

2. Some of the earliest theories of personality were based on type of body build, or _____ . Morphology is a personality characteristic that is fairly (*easy/difficult*) to measure.

   morphology
   easy

3. Measures of body *physiology* include measures of metabolic rate, energy utilization, and reactivity to stressful stimuli. Physiological responses to stress are related to psychological responses to stress. Thus body _____ is a characteristic that influences an individual's personality.

   physiology

4. Psychologists can take measures of _____ and _____ in assessing personality.

   morphology
   physiology
   (either order)

5. Other characteristics that would be considered in assessing an individual's personality are his *intelligence* and special *abilities*. It is customary to distinguish between "intelligence tests" and "personality tests," but this does not deny the fact that _____ is an important aspect of personality. Other abilities, such as musical or artistic _____ , also are relevant to _____ .

   intelligence
   ability (or synonym)
   personality

6. The two groups of personality characteristics subject to assessment that we have discussed so far are (1) _____ and _____ , and (2) _____ and special abilities.

   morphology
   physiology (either order)
   intelligence

7. Another group of characteristics that have been measured in assessing personality are *motivational dispositions* and *needs*. To the extent that

motivational, needs

personality

_____ dispositions and _____ are characteristic of the person over time, they are features of his _____ .

8. Paul has a very strong need for achievement. Since much of his behavior stems from his achievement needs, we (*would/would not*) want to take these needs into account in assessing Paul's personality.

would

9. Besides morphology and _____ , intelligence and other

physiology

abilities

motivational, needs

_____ , psychologists attempt to measure _____ dispositions and _____ in assessing personality. They are also interested in a person's *interests, values,* and *social attitudes.*

10. When a psychologist designs a test to learn what objects or activities you enjoy, he is trying to measure your _____ . When he designs a test to learn what you appreciate the most, what your principles are, he

interests

values

is trying to measure your _____ . When he asks you to respond to a questionnaire seeking your political views, he is trying to measure your

attitudes

social _____ .

11. Four groups of personality characteristics subject to assessment by psychol-

morphology

abilities, dispositions

needs, values

attitudes

ogists are (1) _____ and physiology, (2) intellectual and other _____ , (3) motivational _____ and _____ , and (4) interests, _____ , and social _____ .

12. A fifth category of personality variables includes *expressive,* or *stylistic, traits.* These traits show up in many situations. For instance, some people are talkative wherever they are and regardless of whom they are with. Some people are critical; if this trait is generally characteristic of the personality, it

stylistic

may be considered an expressive, or _____ , trait.

13. An individual may be characteristically sociable in most situations. Sociability

expressive, stylistic
(either order)

would be a(n) _____ , or _____ , trait in his personality make-up.

14. Mark is polite toward everyone and this trait characterizes his personality.

expressive, stylistic
(either order)

It is a(n) _____ , or _____ , trait.

15. We have now described five groups of personality characteristics subject to

morphology
physiology (either order)
intellectual (or
intelligence)
motivational
values, attitudes
expressive, stylistic
(either order)

assessment by psychologists. These are (1) _____ and _____ ; (2) _____ and other abilities; (3) _____ dispositions and needs; (4) interests, _____ , and social _____ ; and (5) _____ , or _____ , traits.

16. In an effort to assess the personality characteristics listed above, psychologists use a variety of techniques. One of the easiest ways to find out something about a person is to *interview* him. An interview may be *unstructured,* in which case the person being interviewed determines largely what is discussed, or it may be *structured* to cover a standard pattern of topics. If you wanted to find out certain specific information about the background of a job applicant, you would probably use a(n) _____ interview.

structured

17. An interview in which the topics discussed are determined largely by the person being interviewed is called a(n) _____ interview. When a standard pattern of topics is covered, the interview is said to be _____ .

unstructured

structured

18. Whether interviewing a person or just carrying on an informal conversation we tend to make judgments about his personality. One technique psychologists use to record judgments of personality characteristics is the *rating scale*. A rating _____ is a device by which a rater can record his judgment of another person according to the traits defined by the scale.

scale

19. The preferred form of rating scale is the *graphic rating scale,* in which each trait is represented by a segmented line; one end of the line indicates one extreme of the trait to be rated, and the other end represents the opposite extreme. The rater places a *check mark* at an appropriate place on the scale to represent the degree to which the subject possesses the trait. With a graphic _____ _____ , judgment is indicated by a check _____ at the appropriate place on the scale.

rating scale

mark

20. Suppose you ask "How well does he control his emotions?" and request an employer to rate his employee by placing a check mark at the appropriate place on a line that runs from "tends to be unresponsive" to "tends to be over-emotional." You are using a _____ _____ scale.

graphic rating

21. The rating scale is one method of assessing personality. Instead of having someone else rate you on various personality _____ , another method of assessment would be to have you rate yourself. A *self-rating* test is called a *personality inventory.*

traits

22. A self-rating test, or personality _____ , usually consists of a number of questions or statements to which the person responds "yes" or "no." Questions such as "Do you daydream a great deal?" or "Do you have frequent headaches?" are the type of items one would find in a personality inventory, or _____-_____ test.

inventory

self-rating

23. A test used in personality assessment in which the person responds to a number of questions about himself is a _____ _____ .

personality

inventory

24. There are hundreds of personality inventories, some of which are designed to appraise a single personality trait and some to measure a multitude of traits to provide an overall estimate of adjustment. We shall discuss three commonly used inventories: (1) the Minnesota Multiphasic Personality Inventory (MMPI), (2) the Edwards Personal Preference Schedule (EPPS); and (3)

Cattell's 16 Personality Factors Questionnaire. One of these three personality inventories, *the Minnesota Multiphasic Personality Inventory* (MMPI), is a

rating

self-_____ personality test designed to detect pathological trends.

MMPI

25. The Minnesota Multiphasic Personality Inventory (abbreviated _____) was designed at the University of Minnesota to measure various phases of personality—thus the word *"multiphasic."* By comparing the individual's test responses with those of patients having known personality disorders, it attempts to detect *pathological* trends in the personality.

Minnesota Multiphasic

pathological

26. The _____ _____ Personality Inventory was designed to measure _____ trends within a personality. Responses on this test are scored according to the correspondence between the answers given by the subject and those given by patients with different kinds of psychological disturbances.

27. The extent to which a person manifests various kinds of psychological disturbances, such as the neuroses and psychoses, are measured by the

Minnesota Multiphasic

_____ _____ Personality Inventory (MMPI).

28. A therapist who wishes to strengthen his diagnosis that a client is severely neurotic or maladjusted enough to be considered psychotic might administer

Minnesota Multiphasic

pathological

the _____ _____ Personality Inventory (MMPI), a test designed to measure _____ trends. However, as the text notes, the MMPI has not been completely successful in distinguishing between neurotic and psychotic individuals.

29. The *Edwards Personal Preference Schedule* is designed to measure *motivational dispositions.* Everyone has motivational dispositions, such as need for dominance, achievement, autonomy, and so on, in various degrees. Therefore,

normal

unlike the MMPI, this test measures characteristics of (*normal/disturbed*) persons.

Edwards Personal

motivational
does not

30. The EPPS, or the _____ _____ Preference Schedule, attempts to measure _____ dispositions. It (*does/does not*) measure pathological trends.

motivational

dispositions, normal

31. Edwards designed his test to measure fifteen basic _____ _____ found in (*normal/disturbed*) people.

32. Whereas the MMPI is a personality inventory designed to measure

pathological

motivational

_____ trends, the EPPS is a personality inventory designed to measure _____ dispositions. Both tests require considerable sophistication to be interpreted properly.

33. The *16 Personality Factors Questionnaire,* which was constructed by Cattell, was established through factor analysis. It is a test designed to give a representative picture of the *whole* personality sphere. It differs in its intent from

pathological

trends

motivational dispositions

both the MMPI, which is designed to measure _____ _____ , and the EPPS, which is designed to measure _____ _____ .

Factors

whole

34. The 16 Personality _____ Questionnaire was designed to measure the _____ sphere of personality. The test was established through factor analysis, a complicated statistical procedure, and yields scores on *sixteen* relatively independent *source traits*—those traits thought to represent the most fundamental and significant characteristics of the total personality.

35. A personality inventory that measures sixteen relatively independent _____ traits is Cattell's _____ _____ _____ Questionnaire, which was designed to measure the _____ personality sphere.

source, 16 Personality

Factors

whole (or synonym)

36. Three commonly used personality inventories are the _____ _____ Personality Inventory, which measures pathological trends; the Edwards Personal _____ _____, which is designed to measure _____ _____ ; and Cattell's 16 _____ _____ Questionnaire, designed to measure sixteen _____ traits representative of the whole personality sphere.

Minnesota

Multiphasic

Preference

Schedule, motivational

dispositions, Personality

Factors, source

37. So far we have discussed three methods of personality assessment. We may find out something about a person through an _____ , which may be structured or unstructured. When we record our judgments of another person by placing a check mark at the appropriate place on a line representing a continuum of a certain trait, we are using a _____ _____ scale. When a person answers questions about himself, he is responding to a self-rating test, or _____ _____ .

interview

graphic

rating

personality

inventory

38. A somewhat different method of personality assessment, in which the individual reveals (projects) himself through his imaginative productions, is a *projective test*. Unlike personality inventories and rating scales, projective tests are *unstructured*, ambiguous, and require the subject to reveal (project) himself by responding imaginatively to ambiguous stimuli. For instance, psychologists often show a subject a series of irregularly shaped inkblots and ask him to tell what the blots suggest to him. Since the inkblots are relatively *unstructured* and *ambiguous* stimuli, an inkblot test is a _____ test.

projective

39. Personality inventories have *fixed alternatives*. That is, the subject is usually required to give a yes-no answer. However, there are no fixed alternatives on projective tests. Projective tests use *un*_____ and ambiguous stimuli to which the subject responds with an *imaginative production.*

unstructured

40. Tests composed of relatively unstructured and ambiguous stimuli that elicit projections of the personality are called _____ tests.

projective

41. Personality inventories have _____ alternatives, whereas projective tests do not.

fixed

42. Projective tests require the subject to reveal himself through his

imaginative

_____ productions.

43. Two commonly used tests are the *Rorschach Inkblot Test* and the *Thematic*

projective

Apperception Test. Since both of these are _____ tests of personality, they utilize stimuli that are relatively unstructured and ambiguous.

Rorschach

44. Two commonly used projective tests are the _____ Inkblot Test and Thematic Apperception Test.

45. The *Rorschach Inkblot Test* consists of a series of cards, each displaying a rather complex inkblot. Subjects taking the Rorschach test, which is a

projective

_____ test of personality, must respond imaginatively by telling what they see on each card. In so doing, they reveal many of their personality characteristics to the examiner, who knows the sort of responses that can be expected to each card.

46. Mr. A is given a series of cards displaying inkblots and is asked to tell the examiner what the cards look like to him, what he sees in the blots, or what the blots remind him of. He is probably being administered the

Rorschach Inkblot

_____ _____ Test of personality, one of several projective tests used by psychologists.

47. The *Thematic Apperception Test,* like the Rorschach test, is also a projective test of personality. It consists of a series of *pictures* about which the subject tells stories. In so doing, he says things about the characters in his stories that

inkblots

really apply to himself. The Rorschach test utilizes _____ as stimuli, whereas the Thematic Apperception Test utilizes a series of pictures.

Thematic

48. The _____ Apperception Test utilizes a series of pictures to which the subject responds with stories. Certain *themes* that recur in the subject's imaginative productions are then analyzed by the psychologist.

49. The *Thematic Apperception Test* is so called because certain "themes" recur in the imaginative productions of a person. "Apperception" means a readiness to perceive in certain ways, based upon prior experience. Hence the subject

picture

interprets an ambiguous stimulus, in this case a _____ , according to his apperceptions and elaborates his stories in terms of preferred themes that reflect personality.

Rorschach Inkblot

50. Both the _____ _____ Test, which utilizes

Thematic Apperception

inkblots, and the _____ _____ Test,

projective

which utilizes pictures, are _____ tests of personality.

51. We have discussed several ways of assessing personality. One method uses

personality inventory

the _____ _____ , which has fixed alternatives, requiring subjects to answer "yes" or "no" to printed questions or statements; another method uses relatively unstructured, ambiguous stim-

projective, Rorschach

uli in *pro*_____ tests of personality such as the _____

Thematic Apperception

Inkblot Test and the _____ _____
Test, in which subjects make up imaginative stories in response to pictures.

rating

scale

interview

personality

inventory, rating

projective

Another instrument of personality assessment is the _____

_____ , by which a rater can record his judgment of another person according to certain defined traits on the scale. Or the rater may simply _____ his subject to find out something about him.

52. Personality assessment may use self-rating devices, as in the _____

_____ , ratings by others, as in _____ scales, or ambiguous stimuli to elicit personality-relevant responses, as in _____ tests.

53. Another means of assessing personality is the direct *observation of behavior* under controlled conditions. Skilled observers record their judgments of individuals as they perform a particular task. For instance, we might assess a

observation

candidate for a particular job by direct _____ of his performance on a task similar to those required in the job.

54. If you needed someone for a job in which leadership was important, you might watch a group of applicants as they attempted to solve a problem that required someone's assuming direction and note which of the applicants took on the role of leader. This would be an example of personality assessment by

observation

means of behavioral _____ .

55. The methods of assessing personality have limitations of various kinds. The text gives a more comprehensive appraisal of these limitations; here we can only point out some of the most common ones. One limitation in the use of

effect

rating scales is the *halo effect*. The halo _____ refers to the tendency to rate someone high on all traits because he makes a good impression on one or two traits, or to rate him low throughout the scale because he

traits

makes a poor impression on one or two _____ .

56. Mr. M has a very friendly and pleasant manner. His employer rates him high on his ability to get along well with others; he also rates Mr. M high on honesty and efficiency although he has little information on which to base his

halo

effect

judgment of the latter two traits. This is an example of how the _____

_____ interferes with objectivity in rating others.

57. The tendency to rate a person high on all traits because he makes a good impression on one or two, or, conversely, to rate a person low throughout the entire rating scale because he makes a poor impression on one or two traits

halo effect

is called the _____ .

rating

scales

58. The halo effect is a possible source of bias in the use of _____

_____ . Personality inventories also have some limitations. One difficulty with personality inventories is that in most cases the "proper" or *"socially desirable"* answer is obvious, so that the person who wants to present himself in a good light can slant his answers accordingly. Many people tend to respond to a personality inventory in a manner that they believe is

desirable

socially _____ .

would not

59. If we suspected that an individual was trying to conceal serious personality disturbance in order to secure a job, we (*would/would not*) test him with a personality inventory.

60. You recall from earlier chapters that tests of all kinds must be reliable and valid. It is difficult to find appropriate *criterion* measures for establishing the

criterion validity of personality tests. Yet, a _____ , or some standard of what constitutes success or failure, is needed.

Rorschach **61.** Projective tests such as the _____ Inkblot Test and the

Apperception Test Thematic _____ _____ are more subtle than personality inventories; that is, it is not as apparent what responses are so-

desirable cially _____ . However, attempts to validate these tests have not been very successful.

62. Projective tests are more subtle than personality inventories, but attempts to

have not validate them (*have/have not*) been successful. Validation requires that an

criterion acceptable standard, or _____ , of measurement be established.

63. The assessment of personality through *behavioral observation* also has its limitations. For instance, it is conceivable that a person may be honest in one situation and quite dishonest in another situation. Before we could put much credence in our observations, we would have to observe a person's

behavior _____ in many different situations to learn how consistently the person we are trying to assess manifests a particular trait.

64. Thus we see that all the current techniques designed to assess personality

halo have their limitations. Rating scales are subject to the _____ effect. Personality inventories are not subtle enough to avoid the tendency to re-

socially desirable spond in a _____ _____ manner. Projec-

Rorschach tive tests such as the _____ Inkblot Test and the

Thematic Apperception _____ _____ Test are more subtle

validity but lack adequate _____ . And behavioral observation may

specific be limited because behavior may be _____ to the situation in which it occurs.

self-quiz

Select the alternative that best completes the thought. In some cases several answers are fairly satisfactory; you are to pick the *best* one.

_____ **1.** The Rorschach test is
a. the best-known standardized paper-and-pencil personality test available
b. easily faked by sophisticated subjects
c. somewhat lacking in subtlety compared to other projective tests
d. lacking in satisfactory validation but still widely used by psychologists

_____ **2.** When a test is designed to measure several aspects of personality at once, it produces
a. a personality inventory
b. a single score
c. dimensions of personality
d. a profile of scores

_____ **3.** David met a beautiful girl at a dance last night. He danced with her only once, and they talked very little, but he describes her today as an unusually in-

telligent person. His reaction illustrates
a. compensation
b. personal disposition
c. the halo effect
d. source traits

____ 4. A measure of personality seeks to find behavior
a. at its best
b. at its worst
c. during emergency situations
d. characteristic of the individual

____ 5. The present personality can be understood according to its developmental history. It is assessed according to
a. present behavior in various environmental contexts
b. behavior patterns in the recent past
c. the changes in personality during childhood
d. the personality of an individual's parents and siblings

____ 6. Some tests are based on the responses of reference groups of individuals who show the characteristics that are being assessed. This method is called
a. empirical construction
b. factor analysis
c. design according to theory
d. correction for stylistic response

____ 7. Unconscious aspects of the personality are more likely to be revealed by
a. projective tests
b. personality inventories
c. forced-choice tests
d. rating scales

____ 8. The Minnesota Multiphasic Personality Inventory
a. gives a single score of introversion-extraversion
b. is most useful in obtaining a measure of ascendancy-submission
c. is designed to detect pathological trends within the personality
d. reveals little difference between responses from delinquents and non-delinquents

____ 9. One disadvantage of Cattell's 16 Personality Factors Questionnaire is that
a. it is less arbitrarily related to pathology
b. it yields scores on 16 relatively independent personality characteristics

c. the individual scales as subtests are too short to be reliable
d. the results do not characterize the fundamental surface traits

____ 10. A person being interviewed is most markedly affected by the
a. setting of the interview
b. time of day of the interview
c. events that occur just before the interview takes place
d. behavior of the interviewer

____ 11. An item that reads "I like to read detective stories" would most likely be found in a
a. projective test
b. forced-choice test
c. personality inventory
d. rating scale

____ 12. The Eysenck Personality Inventory is constructed on the basis of
a. a theory of personality
b. factor analysis
c. individual source traits
d. pathological reference groups

____ 13. One disadvantage of the Edwards Personal Preference Schedule is that it
a. does not allow for stylistic variables
b. is ambiguous because of the "social desirability" scale
c. gives only relative preferences for one pattern of motive over another
d. emphasizes psychopathology

____ 14. If an employer wished to rate an employee according to certain traits revealed on the job, he would probably use a
a. projective test
b. graphic rating scale
c. standardized questionnaire
d. personality inventory

____ 15. Morphology refers to
a. metabolic rate
b. the conformation of the body
c. energy utilization by the body
d. reactivity to stressful stimuli

____ 16. A measure of interest that has been used in occupational guidance is the
a. Strong Vocational Interest Blank
b. Scale of Values
c. Stanford-Binet Intelligence Test
d. Personal Preference Selection

17. When an interview follows a standard pattern, assuring that all relevant topics are covered, it is described as
a. informative
b. diagnostic
c. prognostic
d. structured

18. An example of a projective test is the
a. Rorschach Inkblot Test
b. Minnesota Multiphasic Personality Inventory
c. Strong Vocational Preference Blank
d. 16 Personality Factors Questionnaire

19. The difference between personality inventories and ability tests is that the former
a. are more susceptible to dishonest answers
b. must be validated against a criterion

c. deal with the subject's best performance
d. are not scored objectively

20. The psychologist uses the Thematic Apperception Test to analyze
a. whether the subject sees human movement in the stimuli
b. form and shading responses
c. themes that occur in a person's imaginative productions
d. the trait profile

key to self-quiz

20. c	15. b	10. d	5. a
19. a	14. b	9. c	4. d
18. a	13. c	8. c	3. c
17. d	12. a	7. a	2. d
16. a	11. c	6. a	1. d

class exercise

A PROJECTIVE TEST

introduction

The Rorschach test, introduced by Dr. Hermann Rorschach in 1921, consists of a series of complex inkblots. A subject is asked to tell what he sees in each inkblot and his responses are then scored and interpreted by experienced testers.

In this demonstration we will use the inkblot provided below, which is similar to one of the Rorschach inkblots; it was constructed by spilling some ink on a piece of paper and creasing it in the middle. The exercise is designed to demonstrate that people looking at the same blot will see different things. No attempt at interpretation will be made by your instructor.

equipment needed

The inkblot presented here.

procedure

Your instructor will ask six volunteers, preferably three men and three women, to leave the room. While they are out of the room, write below what the blot looks like to you. They will be called in one at a time and will be asked to relate what the blot looks like to them or what it makes them think of. You are to write each student's response in the space provided below.

Your own impression:

Student 1:

Student 2:

Student 3:

Student 4:

Student 5:

Student 6:

questions for discussion

1. Were there differences in the responses of the six subjects? If so, why?

2. Although the sample used was small, did there seem to be sex differences in perception?

3. Do you think people "project" aspects of their personality in responding to such a blot?

4. What would be the advantages of using stimuli as unstructured as this? The disadvantages?

5. How does this test differ from the Thematic Apperception Test?

6. Would it be easy to derive objective scoring methods for a test of this type?

19 conflict and adjustment

programed unit

1. No matter how resourceful one may be in coping with problems, *conflict* is inevitable. Each of us has a number of motives that are active at the same time, and the goals to which they lead may be *mutually exclusive.* When a person is torn between two motives or goals, we say he is experiencing

conflict _____ .

motives   **2.** A person experiences conflict when he is torn between two _____

exclusive   or goals that are mutually _____ .

3. A conflict is the simultaneous presence of mutually exclusive motives or

goals _____ . When we say that you cannot have your cake and eat it

conflict   too, we are acknowledging the fact of _____ .

4. Conflicts involve a choice between alternatives. If we consider only two alternatives, we can describe conflicts as being of three types: *approach-approach, avoidance-avoidance,* and *approach-avoidance.* We say that a person is in a conflict situation when he has mutually exclusive motives or

goals _____ .

5. When a person has two *desirable* but mutually exclusive goals, he is temporarily torn between them. Because both goals are attractive to him, he experiences an *approach-approach conflict.* For instance, Sarah is a member of the college chorus and is looking forward to their Christmas concert. A boy she likes very much asks her to go skiing the same weekend. Because

approach-   these incentives are both attractive, she has an _____-

approach   _____ conflict.

6. Mary has two boy friends, both of whom propose marriage to her. Because she has to make a choice between two attractive incentives, she has an

approach-approach

_____-_____ conflict.

7. Sometimes we are given a choice between two *unattractive* alternatives, that is, both incentives are negative. This is an *avoidance-avoidance* conflict. Steve dislikes college and feels unable to keep up with his classmates. However, if he drops out of school he will encounter his parents' wrath and lose their financial support—a prospect he also dislikes. Since these alternatives

avoidance-avoidance

are both unattractive, he has an _____-_____ conflict.

8. Phil has a choice between suffering from a toothache or going to the dentist

avoidance-
avoidance

to have his tooth drilled. He also has an _____-_____ conflict.

9. Sometimes an incentive or goal is at once *desirable* and *undesirable,* both *positive* and *negative.* Such a state produces an *approach-avoidance* conflict. For instance, Mary is overweight and realizes she should diet, but she is very fond of ice cream. She is torn between the desire to eat ice cream and

approach-avoidance

the desire to lose weight. She has an _____-_____ conflict.

positive
negative

positive
negative (either order)

10. In an approach-approach conflict, both incentives are (*positive/negative*). In an avoidance-avoidance conflict, both incentives are (*positive/negative*). In an approach-avoidance conflict, an incentive may be both _____ and _____ .

11. One's attitude toward the incentive in an approach-avoidance conflict is *ambivalent.* To be ambivalent is both to like and dislike something at the same time. Bobby finds his baby sister appealing but dislikes the amount of

ambivalent

attention she receives; his attitude toward his sister is _____ .

12. Martha wants to ride a horse but is afraid of being thrown. Her attitude to-

ambivalent

ward the horse is _____ .

approach-approach
approach-avoidance
avoidance-
avoidance (any order)
approach-avoidance

13. The three main types of conflict are _____-_____ , _____-_____ , and _____-_____ . Ambivalent attitudes are characteristic of _____-_____ conflicts.

14. A continuing or unresolved conflict is a source of *frustration.* When a person's progress toward a desired goal is blocked, we say that he encounters

frustration

fr_____ . A frustrating situation is one in which progress toward a goal is blocked, delayed, or otherwise interfered with.

15. David wants to play on the college tennis team, but the amount of time required for practice may interfere with his studies and cause him to lose his

approach-avoidance

scholarship. He has an _____-_____ conflict that is a source of

frustration

flict that is a source of _____ .

frustration	**16.** Conflicts are not the only source of _____ . Anything
goal	that hinders progress toward a _____ may constitute a frustrating situation. *Obstacles* and *deficiencies* are thus sources of frustration.
	17. Ann wants to fly home to be with her family for the holidays, but her plane is grounded because of snow. In this case the weather is an obstacle to the
frustration	attainment of her goal and is thus a source of _____ .
deficiencies	**18.** Obstacles and _____ can both be sources of
deficiencies	frustration. Blind, deaf, and other handicapped people have _____ that keep them from attaining certain goals and are consequently sources of frustration.
conflicts	**19.** Since obstacles, deficiencies, and _____ can all block progress
goal	toward a _____ , they are sources of frustration.
	20. Frustration—whether it is the result of conflicts, deficiencies, or obstacles—may have a number of immediate consequences. One common consequence is a state of *restlessness* and *tension*. Bill has neglected his studies throughout the semester and is now staying up late to cram for the final exam. If he chain smokes and frequently paces around his room, he is displaying restless-
tension	ness and _____ as an immediate consequence of his frustration.
	21. Restlessness and tension are common immediate consequences of
frustration	_____ . Another immediate consequence may be destructiveness, or *aggression*. If Tommy kicks his older sister in the shins
aggression	when she takes his ball away from him, he is displaying _____ toward his sister as a consequence of frustration.
	22. When a frustrated person directly attacks the frustrating object or person, we say he is displaying *direct* aggression. If, after Tommy's sister takes the
direct	ball away from him, he kicks her, he is displaying _____ aggres-
is not	sion. If he kicks the door instead, he (*is/is not*) displaying direct aggression.
	23. If we cannot satisfactorily express our aggression against the source of frustration, we may shift, or *displace,* the aggression toward an innocent person or object. Sandra, who is angry with her father, pulls the cat's tail. She is
displaced	probably exhibiting _____ aggression.
	24. The football player who has caught and then dropped a pass stamps the
displaced	ground. This is an example of _____ aggression.
	25. Sometimes when frustrated we may simply act indifferent or attempt to withdraw from the situation—that is, we may react with *apathy*. Ann, who has been told that she cannot attend a movie with her friends, does not display active aggression but goes to her room and sulks. Her behavior could be
apathy	described as _____ , which is diametrically opposed to aggression.
	26. The immediate consequences of frustration we have discussed so far include
tension, displaced	restlessness and _____ , direct or *dis*_____ aggression, and
apathy	_____ .

27. When problems become too much for us, we sometimes seek the "solution" of escape into a dream world, a solution through *fantasy* rather than through realistic means. Fantasy is (*more/less*) difficult to observe directly than aggression.

more

28. Mr. L has just learned that another employee has been promoted to the job he was hoping to get. If Mr. L constructs a daydream in which he pictures his rival as being a complete failure in the new assignment, he is engaging

fantasy

in _____ as a consequence of frustration.

29. Bill, who postponed his studying until the night before the final exam, has learned that he has failed the exam and may have to leave school. He returns to his room, shuts the door, and sits quietly staring out the window. Based on his *observed* behavior, we can say that, of the four immediate consequences of frustration we have studied so far, Bill is *not* displaying

restlessness (or tension)
aggression (either order)
apathy, fantasy

_____ or _____ . However,

he *might* be demonstrating _____ or engaging in _____ .

30. Another possible consequence of frustration is *stereotypy* in behavior, that is, a tendency to *blind, repetitive, fixated* behavior. The same faulty behavior that produced the frustration is repeated again and again; the organism has lost its flexibility in problem-solving. *Stereotypy* is more easily identified in laboratory animals than in human beings; in contrast, direct or displaced

aggression

_____ can easily be observed in humans.

stereotypy

31. The tendency to blind, repetitive, fixated behavior, called _____ , is another consequence of frustration.

32. Behavior in response to frustration sometimes shows a childish quality. Such behavior, in which the individual returns to behavior patterns characteristic of an earlier stage of development, is called *regression*. A return to thumb-sucking or a lapse in toilet training in a young child may be an example of

regression

_____ as a consequence of frustration.

33. We have examined six behavior patterns that may occur as immediate conse-

restlessness

quences of frustration. These are _____ and

tension, direct, displaced,
apathy, fantasy,
stereotypy,
regression (any order)

_____ , aggression (either _____ or _____),

_____ , _____ , _____ , and

_____ .

34. Continuing frustration that is resolved may have more enduring conse-quences. The term *defense mechanisms* is used to identify certain habitual modes of adjustment that *protect* the individual's *self-esteem* and *defend* him *against anxiety* when he is faced with continuing frustration. The

defense

_____ mechanisms arise in response to continuing frustration.

35. Defense mechanisms are modes of adjustment that protect self-esteem and

anxiety

defend against _____ when we are faced with continuing frustration.

36. Defense mechanisms serve two useful functions: they protect _____-_____ and defend against _____ .

self-esteem, anxiety

37. All defense mechanisms have in common the quality of *self-deception,* which takes two chief forms, *denial* and *disguise.* We utilize defense mechanisms to protect self-esteem and to defend against _____ .

anxiety

38. Self-deception is characteristic of all defense mechanisms. This self-deception takes two chief forms: _____ and disguise.

denial

39. The defense mechanisms involve deceiving ourselves about the nature of impulses, memories, or actions that might otherwise cause us anxiety or lower our self-esteem. We deceive ourselves by _____*ing* the existence of these impulses, memories, or actions or by _____*ing* their expression.

denying
disguising

40. We can identify at least six main kinds of _____ mechanisms: (1) *rationalization,* (2) *projection,* (3) *reaction-formation,* (4) *dissociation,* (5) *repression,* and (6) *substitution.*

defense

41. Assigning logical reasons or plausible excuses for what we do impulsively is known as *rationalization.* The statement, "I'd have been here on time but my alarm clock didn't go off," might very well be a _____ .

rationalization

42. A young boy refused to share his candy with his younger sister and gave as the reason, "If I give her some candy, it will only make her teeth decay." If the boy is giving a "good" reason but not the "true" reason for not sharing, he is using the defense mechanism of _____ .

rationalization

43. In _____ we give "good" reasons but not "true" reasons for our behavior.

rationalization

44. In *projection* we protect ourselves from recognizing our own *undesirable* qualities by assigning them in an exaggerated amount to other people, thereby justifying our own tendencies. If a man says, "You can't trust people any farther than you can throw them," it is possible that he himself has been untrustworthy in the past and is attempting to protect himself from acknowledging his own failings by using the mechanism of _____ .

projection

45. Attributing to others traits we find undesirable in ourselves describes the defense mechanism known as _____ .

projection

46. Jeff is overly critical but does not readily acknowledge this as one of his traits. He is overheard saying that his roommate is a very critical person. Jeff is attributing to another individual an undesirable trait that he himself possesses. This illustrates the mechanism of _____ .

projection

47. In projection we protect ourselves from recognizing our own _____ qualities by assigning them in an exaggerated amount to other people.

undesirable

48. "Most people cheat on examinations," says Mark. In order to justify his own

projection

unacknowledged tendencies, he is assuring himself that everyone else cheats on examinations. This example also illustrates _____ .

49. In *reaction-formation* we *conceal a motive* from ourselves by giving strong expression to its *opposite*. The mother who unconsciously resents the demands and restrictions upon her time that result from having a child may be excessively fussy and particular in her care of the child, devoting more time than is necessary. She conceals her real motives through the mechanism of

reaction-formation

reaction-_____ .

50. Concealing a motive by giving strong expression to its opposite describes the

reaction-formation

defense mechanism known as _____-_____ .

opposite

51. When we conceal a motive by giving strong expression to its _____ , we are using the defense mechanism known as reaction-formation.

52. Mrs. Z, once an alcoholic but now a teetotaler, is an ardent prohibitionist and engages in a personal crusade to convert everyone from drinking any kind of alcoholic beverage. She may be displaying the defense mechanism

reaction-formation

called _____-_____ .

53. In *dissociation* there is a *splitting* of aspects of behavior or experiences that normally occur together. For instance, when someone has hurt us, we usually

dissociation

feel angry and strike back, but in _____ we may deny to ourselves our own angry feelings.

54. Two manifestations of dissociation are *compulsive movements,* actions that the person feels compelled to repeat over and over again and that are split off from the feelings appropriate to them, and *excessive theorizing,* in which talking or thinking about something becomes a substitute for action. Both manifestations illustrate a key characteristic of dissociation: the

splitting

_____ of aspects of behavior that normally go together.

compulsive

55. Two manifestations of dissociation are _____ movements

theorizing

and excessive _____ . The text discusses possible explanations of both.

56. The defense mechanism whereby we assign logical reasons or plausible ex-

rationalization

cuses for what we do impulsively is known as _____ .

self-deception

Like all defense mechanisms, it contains an element of *self-_____* .

57. An individual who attributes to others qualities that he finds undesirable in

projection

himself is engaging in _____ .

58. The mechanism that shows a splitting of aspects of behavior that normally

dissociation

occur together is known as _____ .

59. In *repression* an impulse or memory that might provoke feelings of guilt is completely denied, that is, it *disappears from awareness*. Mr. X was very drunk last night and did several things that would be extremely damaging

repression

to his self-esteem. Now he does not remember anything he did or said. This total forgetting may be an example of _____ .

60. A ten-year-old boy has strong feelings of hostility and resentment toward his father. Yet he has been brought up to love his parents. To protect himself from guilt, he has succeeded in burying these feelings of hostility and is not even aware that they exist. The defense mechanism known as

repression

_____ is operating in this case.

guilt

61. In repression an impulse or memory that might provoke feelings of g_____

awareness

is denied entirely, so that it disappears from _____ .

62. The defense mechanism by which we conceal a motive by giving strong

reaction-formation

expression to its opposite is known as _____-_____ ; the mechanism by which we deny an unacceptable impulse, causing it to

repression

disappear from awareness, is known as _____ .

63. Finally, let us consider the defense mechanism of *substitution,* whereby *approved* goals are substituted for *disapproved* ones, and activities that have possibilities of *success* are entered upon instead of activities that are doomed to *failure.* Substitution is sometimes divided into two forms: *sublimation* and *compensation.* The student who is poor in academic subjects may work even

compensate

harder at athletics in order to *com*_____ for his academic deficiencies.

64. In *sublimation* socially unacceptable motives find expression in socially acceptable form. Thus the desire for sexual gratification, if frustrated, may be sublimated in the writing of love poetry. Sublimation is one form of

substitution

_____ .

65. Writing, painting, and other artistic activities are often explained as the

sublimation

_____ of sexual motives. But they might also be explained as compensation, that is, the strenuous effort to make up for failure or weakness in one activity by excelling in another.

substitution

66. Both sublimation and compensation are forms of _____ ,

approved, disapproved

whereby _____ goals are substituted for _____

success

ones, and activities that have possibilities of _____ are entered

failure

upon instead of activities that are doomed to _____ .

67. We have talked about defense mechanisms as a means of protecting the in-

self-esteem, anxiety

dividual's _____-_____ and defending him against _____ . Although defense mechanisms are not the best way of coping with conflicts, they may contribute toward satisfactory adjustment by helping the individual endure frustrating situations until he can learn more *mature* and *realistic* ways of solving problems.

68. To the extent that defense mechanisms help the person through difficult

realistic

times until he can learn more mature and _____ ways of coping with his problems, they contribute toward satisfactory adjustment.

69.

mature

If, however, the individual continues to rely upon defense mechanisms so that he is never forced to learn more _____ and realistic ways of behaving, then such mechanisms would constitute a barrier to satisfactory

adjustment

_____ .

self-quiz

Select the alternative that best completes the thought. In some cases several answers are fairly satisfactory; you are to pick the *best* one.

_____ 1. Compulsive movements illustrate a form of
   a. regression
   b. projection
   c. dissociation
   d. sublimation

_____ 2. When two interesting classes are scheduled for the same period, this presents a(n)
   a. approach-approach conflict
   b. double approach-avoidance conflict
   c. avoidance-avoidance conflict
   d. approach-avoidance conflict

_____ 3. The attitude toward a goal at once wanted and not wanted produces a(n)
   a. approach-approach conflict
   b. double approach-avoidance conflict
   c. avoidance-avoidance conflict
   d. approach-avoidance conflict

_____ 4. Increased drive
   a. affects only approach gradients
   b. affects only avoidance gradients
   c. lowers all gradients
   d. raises all gradients

_____ 5. Frustration as defined in this book refers to
   a. an unpleasant emotional state
   b. thwarting circumstances
   c. the consequences of blocked goal-seeking
   d. the various types of conflict

_____ 6. An aggressive action against an innocent person or object rather than against the actual cause of the frustration is described as
   a. redirected
   b. channeled

   c. displaced
   d. indirect

_____ 7. Studies of the reactions of concentration-camp prisoners who were subjected to extremely frustrating experiences of long duration revealed that many of them became
   a. apathetic
   b. prone to projection
   c. excessive rationalizers
   d. victims of reaction-formation

_____ 8. When we have two attractive goals, starting toward one of them
   a. results in an approach-avoidance conflict
   b. increases the tendency to go toward the other goal
   c. causes us to become vacillating and indecisive
   d. increases the tendency to go toward it

_____ 9. The child who lay on the floor reciting nursery rhymes in the frustration experiment dealt with his problem through
   a. aggression
   b. indifference
   c. fantasy
   d. withdrawal

_____ 10. Defense mechanisms
   a. can serve a useful purpose
   b. are genuinely satisfying
   c. prevent rational problem-solving from ever occurring
   d. are always damaging

_____ 11. The tendency to exhibit repetitive or fixated behavior in the face of frustration is called
   a. fantasy
   b. apathy
   c. stereotypy
   d. aggression

12. Which of the following types of conflict is most likely to lead to a tendency to escape making a choice?
    a. conflict between two positive goals
    b. conflict within the person
    c. conflict between a positive and a negative goal
    d. conflict between two negative incentives

13. Primitivation is a
    a. state of severe deprivation
    b. type of regression
    c. state of withdrawal and indifference
    d. kind of fantasy experience

14. Reaction-formation means that
    a. one substitutes an approved goal for a disapproved goal
    b. a person conceals a motive from himself by giving strong expression to its opposite
    c. an individual gives good reasons, but not the real reasons, for his behavior
    d. one incorporates the values and behavior of someone he admires

15. Devices that protect the individual's self-esteem and defend him against excessive anxiety are called
    a. defense mechanisms
    b. anxiety escape
    c. esteem maintenance
    d. adjustment responses

16. All defense mechanisms have in common the quality of
    a. repression
    b. regression
    c. amnesia
    d. self-deception

17. Substitution takes two forms:
    a. sublimation and compensation
    b. displacement and condensation
    c. suppression and dissociation
    d. repression and regression

18. Projection is
    a. assigning logical reasons for what we do impulsively
    b. assigning our own undesirable qualities to other people
    c. expressing the opposite of the motive we wish to conceal
    d. a kind of reaction-formation

19. When subjects respond to a post-hypnotic suggestion, they sometimes feel so embarrassed that they _____ the behavior.
    a. repress
    b. rationalize
    c. project
    d. sublimate

20. The process whereby socially unacceptable motives find expression in socially acceptable forms is called
    a. compensation
    b. sublimation
    c. repression
    d. rationalization

key to self-quiz

20. b	15. a	10. a	5. b
19. b	14. b	9. c	4. d
18. b	13. b	8. d	3. d
17. a	12. d	7. a	2. a
16. d	11. c	6. c	1. c

individual exercise

ANALYSIS OF CONFLICTS

introduction

Everyone has problems at some time or another. Problems result quite naturally from the frustration of needs or from conflict between needs. Who of us has not felt the discomfort of having two opposing desires, impulses, needs, drives, tendencies?

Several aspects of conflict are usually considered by the psychologist. He is interested in whether the conflict is superficial or deep, mild or intense, infrequent or frequent. When conflicts are deep-seated and intense, they sometimes usurp too much of a person's energy and time because they are related to fundamental aspects of the personality and cannot be resolved as readily as most mild and superficial conflicts. Human happiness depends to some extent upon how well we resolve our conflicts, and often our adjustment hinges more on being emotionally healthy than it does on having material conveniences or ideal social arrangements.

We can name but a few of the vast variety of conflicts that people experience in our culture. There are conflicts between the desire to achieve and the fear of failure, between being dominant and being submissive, between being independent and being dependent, between gratifying sexual impulses and maintaining moral standards. There is a host of other conflicts involving incompatible wishes, beliefs, values, duties, ambitions, and ideals.

equipment needed

None

procedure

The following material, recorded from various phases of counseling interviews with students, depicts conflicts of various kinds. Seldom in counseling are the conflicts of the simple, precise types found in textbooks. Nevertheless, it is sometimes possible to classify them by the types given in the text: *approach-approach, approach-avoidance,* and *avoidance-avoidance conflicts.* Sometimes a student expresses in a few statements all three types of conflict or several conflicts of the same type.

After each excerpt from the student interviews, you are to summarize in the space provided the conflict(s) expressed. Then opposite each statement of a conflict, write whether it is an approach-approach, approach-avoidance, or avoidance-avoidance type of conflict.

As you read the cases you will see that some of the conflicts can be easily and unambiguously identified; others have multiple determiners and, depending upon your interpretation, can be identified in one of several ways. Because some of the cases can be interpreted in different ways, depending upon the judgment of the reader, no answers are provided in the Appendix.

Male, Age Nineteen

"I'd sort of like to major in sociology because I find it so interesting, but my parents, especially my father, think that it's impractical from a financial point of view. He thinks I should major in business administration, dentistry, or something like that, where the money is. I wonder whether I should continue with my business courses, which I find rather dull, because being a success is important to me, or should I major

in something like sociology even though there is an element of financial insecurity that goes along with it? I really don't know what would be best."

Statement of conflict   **Type of conflict**

Female, Age Eighteen

"I'd like to quit my sorority, but I don't think I could take the feelings of ostracism I'd have to endure every time I'd run into one of my so-called sisters. Besides, my parents would probably be very upset about it. If you knew my mother and how status-conscious she is, you'd understand my predicament better."

Statement of conflict   **Type of conflict**

Male, Age Eighteen

"I don't want to come here crying on anyone's shoulder about my problems because I think I should be old enough to make my own decisions, but the pressure has been building up to a point where something has to be done. To put the whole thing in a nutshell, here's my problem—I'd like to quit school because I don't think I'm college material or have what it takes to be successful. But if I did quit, it would hurt my parents too much because they've sacrificed all these years to save money to send me to college."

Statement of conflict   **Type of conflict**

Female, Age Twenty-one

"I'm the sort of person who likes to eat his cake and have it too. I mean I have to make a decision about whom I'm going to go steady with. John has a lot in his favor but so has Phil. John is the tactful sort. He's got lots of ambition and wants to make something of himself, and I do think he'll make an excellent engineer because he's so good at math. As far as his appearance is concerned, I'd say he's average. But I sometimes wonder if our interests aren't miles apart, and there are other things about him that make me wonder if we'd really make a success of marriage if it ever came to that. Phil is more the passive type, and I wish he were a little more aggressive. But he's intelligent and gifted in so many things. Phil likes to travel a lot and so do I. I forgot to tell you that John isn't the gadabout type—he's more the homebody sort of person and he doesn't like camping and that sort of thing. Phil thinks he'd like State Department work. I suppose if I married him, it would mean a chance to travel—something I've always wanted. But Phil isn't the warm, affectionate type of person, and that's really what bothers me about him. It seems to me that I'd be more like a welcome appendage as far as he's concerned, and I'm afraid his other interests would always come first."

Statement of conflict   **Type of conflict**

Male, Age Twenty-one

"I come from a mixed-up family. Maybe that's why I'm such a mixed-up character. My mother's more or less Puritanical in her outlook on life: 'Be honest, get to the top, be of good character, keep your nose to the grindstone, blah, blah, blah.'—I could go on and on with her tune. And in a way I respect her and her judgment. She's worked hard and you might say she's made a success of her life in some ways. Now my father is quite different. It's no wonder their marriage was a flop. He ran around with other women even when he was married; and while I've always been fond of him, I didn't like that about him. And his philosophy of life is so different from Mom's: 'Live today—tomorrow who knows? Don't be a sucker if you get the chance to make an easy buck, slap people on the back if it'll help you get ahead, etc., etc.' In a way, they're both immature and corny in their outlook on life, but just the same I've grown up with these two different orientations, you might call them, and it's not easy knowing what to think is right any more."

Statement of conflict   **Type of conflict**

Female, Age Nineteen

"I don't know whether to quit school now or take a chance on finishing the semester. My midsemester grades were really sad. I don't know if it's because my study habits are poor or if it's because I'm just too dumb for college work. To be truthful, I didn't want to go to college in the first place. I'm going just to please my mother. Sounds silly, doesn't it? I wanted to take up beauty operating when I left high school, but my mother is so persistent about getting a college education. She'd like me to be a nurse, I guess. If I don't quit, I'll be miserable. If I do quit, mother will be miserable. So it looks as though somebody has to be miserable, and the question is, who should it be?"

Statement of conflict   **Type of conflict**

Female, Age Eighteen

"I've been going with Bill the past few months, and I'd like to break off the affair, but I don't know how to without hurting his feelings. He's very considerate and all, but I've met somebody else now who is much more appealing to me. But I just can't stand to hurt Bill's feelings."

Statement of conflict   **Type of conflict**

Male, Age Nineteen

"All my life I've grown up with the idea that women were a bunch of angels—untouchables, sacred, or something like that. I know most guys would laugh if they heard me talk like this, but it's true. I've heard various guys talk about girls they know who evidently don't have morals or scruples. What I'm trying to find out is does it pay to be noble around women? I've been out on dates, and I sometimes wonder if I'm not so good around them that they think I'm sort of odd or weird because I don't fool around. Maybe they think I'm a drip. Yet I always thought women would respect you if you didn't get fresh with them. A couple of times I felt like trying something, but I was afraid of what they might think of me."

questions for discussion

1. Which type of conflict was easiest to identify?

2. Which type of conflict was most difficult to identify?

3. Which type of conflict would be easiest to resolve?

4. Which type of conflict would be the most difficult to resolve?

5. Are these conflicts quite prevalent among college students?

6. What other types of conflicts do college students experience?

conflict and adjustment   **225**

behavior disorders

programed unit

1. Some people are able to handle stress and conflict better than others, but there is no such thing as an ideally adjusted person. We can, however, conceive of a *continuum of adjustment,* with highly adaptive behavior at one end and complete helplessness and self-defeating behavior at the other. Since most people are neither highly adaptive nor completely helpless in their behavior,

    continuum
    they would fall somewhere near the middle of the adjustment *con_____* .

2. Before we go on to consider maladjusted or disordered behavior, we should get some idea of what we mean by "good adjustment." First, the well-adjusted person experiences *conflicts,* but he is not unduly distressed by them. He is able to handle his conflicts in a *realistic* manner. To be well adjusted,

    conflicts
    then, does not mean to be without _____ .

3. The maladjusted person often tries to solve his conflicts and problems by denying them; the well-adjusted person faces his problems and deals with

    realistic
    them in a *re_____* manner.

4. To be well adjusted does not necessarily mean that one must conform to the values of his society. The well-adjusted person may be a conformist or a nonconformist, just as a maladjusted person may be a conformist or a non-

    well-adjusted
    conformist. The difference is that the _____-_____
    person has a realistic view of whatever conflicts his position entails.

5. The adjusted person, then, accepts his own and others' shortcomings and

    realistic
    faces his problems in a _____ manner.

6. The well-adjusted person is also *productive.* He has a spontaneity in work and in social relations that we think of as creative, as using his potentialities to the full. He may not be brilliant or especially talented, but whatever his endowments, he is able to use them in productive activity. Thus one can be

productive

equally _____ as a homemaker, a teacher, or as a creative artist.

well adjusted

7. The key to this concept is that the person who is _____ _____ will use his endowments, whether meager or ample, in productive activity.

8. The well-adjusted person has a *zest for living*. He does not have to drive himself to do what he should do, but enters into activities with enthusiasm. Chronic fatigue and lack of energy are frequently symptoms of unresolved

conflicts

emotional *con*_____ .

zest

9. Enthusiasm and _____ for living are thus qualities that describe the well-adjusted person.

10. A well-adjusted person has the capacity to form satisfying affectionate relationships with other people. From earlier chapters, you recall that the capacity to trust others and to form affectionate relationships with them is learned

early

(*early*/*late*) in life.

11. Another characteristic of the well-adjusted person is his capacity to form

affectionate

satisfying, _____ relationships with others.

12. A well-adjusted person also has some *awareness* of his own *motives* and

feelings

feelings; he does not try to hide important motives and _____ from himself.

13. A well-adjusted person, then, may be distinguished from a poorly adjusted person on the basis of five characteristics: (1) he does not deny his conflicts

realistic, productive

but faces them in a *re*_____ manner; (2) he is _____ , that is, he can use his potentialities and powers; (3) he has enthusiasm and

zest

_____ for living; (4) he has the capacity to form satisfying,

affectionate

_____ relationships with other people; and (5) he

awareness

has some _____ of his own motives and feelings.

14. We run into a thorny problem when we try to give a precise definition of *abnormality*. One definition is based upon *statistical frequency:* what is normal falls within the middle range and what is statistically infrequent or

abnormal

deviant from the norm might be considered _____ .

statistical

15. It becomes immediately apparent that the _____ frequency definition of abnormality has serious limitations because people who are highly gifted intellectually deviate from the norm, yet we do not consider them abnormal.

16. A second method of classifying behavior as normal or abnormal is by determining whether the behavior is in accord with *society's standards*. Anthropological studies have revealed, however, that what is considered normal in one society may be considered abnormal in another. Therefore, this definition of abnormality, which really constitutes a *social* definition, also has its limitations. For example, homosexuality has been, and still is, considered normal

abnormal

behavior in some cultures, but in our culture it is considered _____ .

17. A definition of abnormality in terms of _____ frequency is not satisfactory because some very desirable traits may fall outside the normal range. Likewise, we cannot be content with a _____ definition of abnormality, since the standards of normality and abnormality vary from one culture to the next.

statistical

social

18. Probably the most important means of defining maladjusted or abnormal behavior is according to the *degree of impairment* in functioning. If a person is so immobilized by conflict and anxiety or by brain disturbance that he cannot cope with everyday responsibilities, or if his behavior threatens harm to himself or someone else, he would be considered (*normal/abnormal*).

abnormal

19. Similarly, a person who is severely impaired in his social relations to the extent that he lives constantly in a dream world would also be considered (*normal/abnormal*).

abnormal

20. Three types of definition of abnormality are (1) *statistical frequency,* (2) *social,* and (3) *impairment.* Of these three, probably _____ is the best definition, since it depicts a person who is so crippled by conflict and anxiety or brain disturbance that he cannot fend for himself in meeting the problems of everyday living.

impairment

21. Behavior disorders are usually thought of as falling into two classes according to their degree of severity. These are the *neuroses* (singular, *neurosis*) and the *psychoses* (singular, *psychosis*). The *neurotic* disorders, the less severe types of behavior disorder, may be viewed as exaggerated forms of the normal *defense mechanisms* used in an attempt to resolve a persistent conflict. When a person cannot achieve a realistic solution to a persistent conflict but instead habitually resorts to exaggerated forms of defense mechanisms, he may be considered _____*tic.*

neurotic

22. The neuroses are characterized by the habitual use of exaggerated forms of the normal _____ mechanisms in response to a persistent conflict.

defense

23. Unresolved conflicts create *anxiety.* Consequently, it is not surprising that the chief symptom of neurosis is *an_____* .

anxiety

24. We noted in the preceding chapter that defense mechanisms serve to protect our self-esteem and to defend against _____ . If a person cannot resolve a persistent conflict, he either remains in a state of anxiety or he resorts to habitual use of one of the _____ _____ , often in exaggerated form, to defend against anxiety.

anxiety

defense mechanisms

25. All people resort to defense mechanisms at one time or another. It is only when these defenses become the dominant method of problem-solving that the person is called _____ .

neurotic

26. Anxiety is the chief symptom of the _____ . Sometimes the anxiety is very obvious—the individual appears tense, restless, and may be unable to eat or sleep. *Anxiety reactions* are a type of neurosis in which the chief symptom, _____ , is obvious.

neuroses

anxiety

anxiety   **27.**   In the type of neurosis called _____ reactions the person habitually appears tense and restless, and he reacts to even the slightest difficulty with strong feelings of anxiety.

28.   Since the unresolved conflicts that underlie a neurosis are frequently *unconscious,* the person suffering from an anxiety reaction usually has no clear idea of why he feels so tense and apprehensive. The reasons behind his anxiety

unconscious   are usually *un*_____ .

29.   When a person feels tense and anxious much of the time without being able

anxiety   to specify exactly what he is afraid of, he is suffering from an _____

reaction   _____ .

30.   In anxiety reactions the person's anxiety is quite apparent. In another type of neurosis, called *conversion reaction,* the anxiety is *converted* into *physical*

symptoms   *symptoms.* These physical _____ have no organic cause; they serve unconscious purposes of the patient.

31.   A pilot becomes afraid to fly following an emergency landing in which he nearly lost his life. He develops a paralysis of the right arm for which the

conversion   doctors can find no organic basis. This is an example of a _____ reaction.

32.   A woman is afraid that her husband may leave her. She suddenly loses her sight so that she is totally dependent upon his care. Since no physical cause can be found for her blindness, this appears to be another case of a

conversion reaction   _____ _____ .

physical   **33.**   In conversion reactions anxiety is converted into _____ symptoms that serve unconscious purposes for the individual. It should be emphasized, however, that the person is not faking. In conversion

reactions   _____ the physical disability seems quite real to him, and

unconscious   the purposes served are *un*_____ .

34.   In anxiety reactions the anxiety is quite obvious. In conversion reactions, however, the person usually seems calm and relaxed. His anxiety is

converted   _____ into physical symptoms. He may be somewhat concerned about his physical condition, but he is not overwhelmed by anxiety.

35.   The chief symptom in all types of neurosis is anxiety. The anxiety may be

anxiety reaction   readily apparent, as in a(n) _____ _____ , or it

conversion   may be converted into physical symptoms, as in a(n) _____

reaction   _____ .

reactions   **36.**   A third type of neurosis is the *phobic* reaction. Phobic _____ are *excessive fears* of certain situations in the *absence of real danger.* Jane is so fearful of closed places that she will never take the elevator to her ninth-floor office but insists upon climbing the stairs instead. She has a

phobic reaction   _____ _____ .

37. Tom is so fearful of fire that he cannot stay in a room in which there is a fire burning in the fireplace. Since Tom's fear is excessive in a situation in which

phobic
there is no real danger, it is another example of a _____

reaction
_____ .

absence
38. Phobic reactions are excessive fears in the _____ of real danger. The assumption is that the anxiety that stems from some other conflict in the individual's life is channeled into a highly specific fear.

anxiety
39. So far we have discussed three kinds of neurotic disorders: (1) _____ reactions, in which feelings of tension and anxiety are predominant; (2)

conversion
_____ reactions, in which the anxiety is converted into

phobic
a physical symptom; and (3) _____ reactions, in which the person experiences excessive, irrational fear in the absence of real danger. The fourth major type of neurosis is the *obsessive-compulsive* reaction.

40. *Obsessive-compulsive* reactions take three forms: (1) *obsessive thoughts,* (2) *compulsive acts,* and (3) a *combination* of obsessive thoughts and com-

obsessive
pulsive acts. You might guess that a person with _____ thoughts has persistently unwelcome, disturbing thoughts and that a person with a compulsion has an irresistible urge to repeat a certain stereotyped or

act
ritualistic _____ .

41. *Obsessive thoughts* frequently involve unacceptable aggressive or sexual impulses that are quite foreign to the conscious feelings of the person who has them. Because these unacceptable impulses would cause great anxiety if the person acknowledged them as his real feelings, they are repressed and appear

obsessive
as _____ thoughts that the individual experiences as not being really his own.

impulses
42. Obsessive thoughts thus involve unacceptable _____ that the person cannot acknowledge as his own.

43. A young mother had frequent thoughts of murdering her two small children. She professed nothing but love for them and maintained that "these awful thoughts that pop into my head" had nothing to do with her real feelings.

obsessive
In this case _____ thoughts protected the mother from the anxiety she would feel were she to acknowledge these impulses as her own.

44. *Compulsive acts* are stereotyped or ritualistic acts that are designed to protect the individual from feelings of anxiety or guilt. A young boy who suffered guilt feelings whenever he masturbated felt compelled to scrub his hands

compulsive
many times a day. In this case the _____ act served to relieve his feelings of guilt.

45. Obsessive thoughts and compulsive acts thus serve to protect the individual

anxiety
against _____ or guilt. They are characteristic of an

obsessive-compulsive
_____-_____ reaction.

46. We have discussed four major types of neuroses, all of which are character-

anxiety, conversion
ized by anxiety: (1) _____ reactions; (2) _____

reactions, in which anxiety is converted into physical symptoms; (3)

phobic   _____ reactions, in which there is excessive fear in the absence of

obsessive-compulsive   real danger; and (4) _____-_____ reactions, in which a person has persistent, unpleasant thoughts or feels the need to perform a ritualistic act of some sort to ward off aggressive or sexual impulses he does not wish to acknowledge to himself.

47. *Psychotic* disorders are much more serious than neuroses. The personality is disorganized and normal social functioning is greatly impaired. The psychotic individual often requires hospitalization. While the neurotic tries to cope with

psychotic   his anxiety in order to continue functioning, the p_____ is no longer able to function adequately and to some extent has lost contact with reality.

48. Some psychoses are due to *physical* damage or malfunctioning. These are called the *organic* psychoses. Others are called *functional* psychoses because

physical   no *ph*_____ basis for them can be demonstrated.

49. *Manic-depressive* reactions are a form of functional psychosis characterized by recurrent and exaggerated mood swings from the normal to either the depressive phase (deep depression) or the manic phase (wild excitement). If a person feels complete worthlessness and despondency, we might suspect

manic-depressive   that he is in the depressive phase of a _____-_____ reaction.

50. Most people suffering from manic-depressive reactions do not exhibit both phases of the mood cycle. They tend to swing from normal to one of the extreme phases. Thus, if a person at times felt normal and at other times

manic   felt deep depression, never showing the *m*_____ phase of the disorder, he could still be classified as manic-depressive.

51. Schizophrenic reactions are the most common of the functional psychoses and are characterized by a split between the thought processes and the emotions. For example, a schizophrenic may smile as he describes a sad event, showing an emotion that is inappropriate to the thought being expressed. *Withdrawal from reality* is also a common characteristic of a

schizophrenic   *sch*_____ reaction.

schizophrenic   52. In a *sch*_____ reaction a person may have *hallucinations*. That is, he may hear voices or see visions that are not there. A person suffer-

reality   ing from this disorder often seems to withdraw from *r*_____ity in order to build a more satisfying fantasy world of his own.

53. Likewise, a schizophrenic may have *delusions,* which are simply *false beliefs* that are clung to in spite of contrary evidence and common sense. Do not

hallucinations   confuse delusions with _____ , such as "hearing voices," which refer to false *sensory perceptions* without an appropriate external stimulus.

54. Patient X thinks he is God and has come back to earth to save us. He is

delusion   evidently experiencing a _____ , since he is clinging to a false

belief. Patient Y hears voices talking to him and threatening him that no one
else hears. He is probably experiencing a _____ .

hallucination

beliefs

perceptions

55. Delusions are false _____ , whereas hallucinations are false
sensory _____ .

56. We have mentioned several *symptoms* of schizophrenia. The schizophrenic
may experience *disturbances of affect,* which means that his affect, or emotion, may be inappropriate to the thoughts he is expressing or the situation
in which he finds himself. He may experience *delusions* and *hallucinations.*
He may exhibit *autism,* which means that he is absorbed in an inner fantasy
life that he finds more satisfying than the real world. He often manifests
"bizarre" behavior, such as peculiar gestures, movements, and repetitive acts.
His speech and writing are often incoherent and disconnected, indicating
disturbances of thought. These are all symptoms of the psychosis we call

schizophrenia

symptoms

_____ , although any one schizophrenic will
usually not exhibit all of these _____ .

57. A person who becomes so absorbed in his inner fantasy life that he loses
contact with the world of reality is showing the symptom of schizophrenia

autism

that we call _____ .

58. One of the symptoms of schizophrenia, in which withdrawal from reality is
accompanied by almost complete absorption in an inner fantasy life, is called

autism

hallucinations

delusions

bizarre

affect

_____ . Some of the other symptoms include withdrawal, or a loss
of interest in the realistic environment; _____ ,
which are false sensory perceptions, and _____ , which are
false beliefs; " _____ " behavior, such as peculiar gestures and
movements; disturbances of _____ as well as disturbances of
thought.

59. A two-category scheme for classifying schizophrenia has been proposed. The
scheme is not based upon a patient's current symptoms, but rather upon his
pre-illness adjustment and the prognosis for recovery. *Process schizophrenia*
is one category; it involves a history of *long-term, progressive deterioration* in
adjustment. Because the illness has been long-term, you might guess that the

poor

prognosis for recovery is relatively (*good/poor*).

60. The second category is *reactive schizophrenia,* in which the person has had a
fairly adequate adjustment in his past history but the illness has been
precipitated by some sudden severe *stress,* such as death of a loved one or
loss of a job. You might surmise that for reactive schizophrenia the prognosis

good

for recovery is relatively (*good/poor*).

Process

poor

Reactive

stress

good

61. _____ schizophrenia involves a history of long-term, progressive deterioration in adjustment, and the prognosis is relatively _____ .
_____ schizophrenia, however, involves a history of fairly
adequate adjustment but is precipitated by sudden _____ , and the
prognosis is relatively _____ .

62. We have discussed two major types of psychosis, the most common type being _____ , which is characterized by disturbances of affect and by withdrawal from reality. The _____-_____ psychosis involves violent mood swings.

schizophrenia

manic-

depressive

63. The *antisocial* or *psychopathic* reaction differs from both the neuroses and psychoses in that it is manifested by a life-long history of socially deviant behavior and the individual experiences little, if any, anxiety. Because the *psychopath* is antisocial and is frequently in conflict with the law, he is more likely to be found in a (*hospital/prison*).

prison

64. The chief characteristic of the *psychopath* is that he lacks moral development, or *conscience*. He is highly impulsive, manipulative, seeks immediate gratification of his needs, and cannot tolerate frustration. "I want what I want when I want it" sums up the behavior of the _____ .

psychopath

65. The _____ 's chief characteristic is his lack of _____ . He acts impulsively, like a young child, has little tolerance of _____ , and seeks immediate _____ of his needs.

psychopath's

conscience

frustration

gratification

66. We mentioned that psychoses due to physical damage or malfunctioning of the brain and nervous system are called organic psychoses, while psychoses for which no physical basis can be found are called *fu*_____ psychoses. Since as yet no one has found any physical basis for the neuroses, they are classed as _____ disorders.

functional

functional

67. In some disorders emotional or psychological factors can bring about changes in parts of the body other than the nervous system; these are called *psychosomatic* disorders. Duodenal ulcers brought about by emotional stress would be an example of a _____ disorder.

psychosomatic

68. Although asthma is related to certain allergies, asthmatic attacks are frequently triggered by emotional factors. Thus we can say that asthma may be in some cases a _____ disorder.

psychosomatic

69. Psychosomatic disorders come about through the effect of psychological or _____ factors on the body.

emotional

70. Let's review. The chief symptom of the neuroses is _____ . The four major types of neuroses include _____ reactions, in which anxiety is predominant; _____ reactions, in which the anxiety is converted into a physical symptom of some sort, such as paralysis, blindness, or deafness; _____ reactions, in which the patient suffers excessive fear in the absence of real danger; and, finally, _____-_____ reactions, in which persistently disturbing thoughts keep recurring or the person feels an irresistible urge to carry out some ritualistic act as a means of warding off dangerous impulses.

anxiety

anxiety

conversion

phobic

obsessive-

compulsive

schizophrenia

Manic-

depressive

Psychopathic

71. The psychotic reactions are more severe disorders, of which the most common is _____ , which is often characterized by withdrawal from reality into one's own private world. _____ reactions, which are characterized by violent mood swings, are another type of psychosis. _____ reactions are characterized by socially deviant behavior; persons with this disorder usually are impulsive, lacking in conscience, cannot tolerate frustration, and seek immediate gratification of their needs.

psychosomatic

72. Finally, we have the _____ disorders, in which organic symptoms, such as duodenal ulcers, originate in psychological factors.

self-quiz

Select the alternative that best completes the thought. In some cases several answers are fairly satisfactory; you are to pick the *best* one.

_____ 1. A psychogenic or functional illness is one that
   a. is associated with severe organic changes in the brain
   b. shows no identifiable organic change in the brain or nervous system
   c. occurs at birth
   d. is associated with alcoholism, tumors, and epilepsy

_____ 2. The manic phase of the manic-depressive reaction is characterized by
   a. extreme fatigue
   b. despondency
   c. sadness
   d. excitement

_____ 3. The chief symptom of neurosis is
   a. insomnia
   b. loss of appetite
   c. anxiety
   d. hallucinations

_____ 4. In conversion reactions
   a. physical symptoms appear without an underlying organic cause
   b. the individual has strong feelings of inadequacy yet maintains unrealistically high standards
   c. there are irresistible urges to repeat a certain stereotyped act
   d. there is an excessive fear in the absence of real danger

_____ 5. The individual who has given up the struggle of trying to function in the world and lost contact with reality is called a(n)
   a. psychotic
   b. neurotic
   c. phobic
   d. obsessive-compulsive

_____ 6. Manic-depressive reactions occur more frequently among
   a. the upper class
   b. adolescents
   c. people who have high-pressure jobs
   d. the offspring of manic-depressives

_____ 7. The man who fears that his friends and relatives are poisoning him and complains that he is being followed and talked about when there is no real basis for these suspicions is called
   a. autistic
   b. neurotic
   c. paranoid
   d. hypermanic

_____ 8. A person with an intense fear of closed places suffers from a(n)
   a. obsessive-compulsive reaction
   b. phobic reaction
   c. anxiety reaction
   d. conversion reaction

_____ 9. Withdrawal from reality is usually accompanied by absorption in an inner fantasy life. This state of self-absorption is known as

a. a catatonic stupor
b. autism
c. a delusion
d. a hallucination

_____ **10.** Disturbances of affect and thought processes, withdrawal, delusions, hallucinations, and autism characterize
a. paranoia
b. schizophrenia
c. manic-depression
d. conversion reactions

_____ **11.** The individual who suffers from an antisocial or psychopathic reaction is characterized by
a. signs of anxiety and guilt
b. despondency and sadness
c. extreme fatigue
d. lack of moral development

_____ **12.** Neurotic reactions
a. are exaggerated forms of normal defense mechanisms
b. are very adaptive, particularly under stress
c. are easily distinguishable from one another
d. all manifest the same degree of anxiety

_____ **13.** A process schizophrenic
a. has an adequate premorbid social development, with the illness being precipitated by a sudden stress
b. has a good prognosis for recovery
c. has a history of long-term deterioration in adjustment
d. shows persistent hallucinations

_____ **14.** The neurotic reaction with the least amount of observable anxiety is the
a. anxiety reaction
b. phobic reaction
c. obsessive-compulsive reaction
d. conversion reaction

_____ **15.** The well-adjusted person has all but *one* of these characteristics:
a. he is productive
b. he attacks his problems in a realistic manner
c. he is a social conformist
d. he has the capacity to form intimate relationships

_____ **16.** An estimated one-half of all neuropsychiatric hospital beds are occupied by patients diagnosed as
a. schizophrenic
b. manic-depressive
c. obsessive-compulsive
d. neurotic

_____ **17.** What are the three types of definitions used in diagnosing abnormality?
a. statistical, social, and degree of impairment
b. psychological, social, and degree of impairment
c. physiological, statistical, and social
d. physiological, psychological, and social

_____ **18.** Anxiety that is not associated with a particular stimulus event or object but occurs in a wide variety of situations is termed
a. free-floating
b. bound
c. diffuse
d. vague

_____ **19.** When an individual has an overwhelming feeling that something dreadful is about to happen—a feeling accompanied by heart palpitations, rapid breathing and faintness—it is called a(n)
a. obsessive-compulsive reaction
b. phobic reaction
c. acute anxiety attack
d. conversion reaction

_____ **20.** One form of obsessive-compulsive reaction is
a. free-floating anxiety
b. bound anxiety
c. obsessive thoughts
d. compulsive thoughts

key to self-quiz

20. c	15. c	10. b	5. a
19. c	14. d	9. b	4. a
18. a	13. c	8. b	3. c
17. a	12. a	7. c	2. d
16. a	11. d	6. d	1. b

individual exercise

CLASSIFICATION OF BEHAVIOR DISORDERS

equipment needed

None

procedure

Descriptions of people with various kinds of disorders follow. In each instance, attempt to classify the kind of disorder exhibited by the patient. The *neurotic reactions* include anxiety reactions, conversion reactions, phobic reactions, and obsessive-compulsive reactions. The *psychotic reactions* include two functional psychoses, manic-depressive reactions and schizophrenic reactions, as well as psychoses owing to organic conditions. *Psychopathic reaction* is a separate category not included under the neuroses or psychoses.

The correct diagnoses are given on page 285 of the Appendix.

Case 1

John, a patient at the state mental hospital, appears to be happy and elated. He frequently makes humorous remarks, laughs at them himself, and is successful in making others laugh too. In expressing his thoughts he jumps from one topic to another without following any particular course. If, while he is talking about his family, the psychiatrist suddenly interjects a comment about the weather, John immediately switches his conversation to the weather or any other topic the psychiatrist introduces. Furthermore, he is hyperactive. He is either drumming with his fingers, playing with a pencil, or engaging others with his rapid talk. There is no deterioration of intellectual and emotional faculties, however. His present illness will probably be followed by several years of "normal" behavior.

Case 2

Jack, a patient in a mental hospital, has been hearing for several months the same voice, which makes derogatory accusations about his being a sexually immoral pervert. This same voice often commands him to do such things as throw furniture out of the window. His speech is monotonous except when he is talking about his troubles, at which time it becomes quite animated and vehement. His sentence structure is often shattered and his statements are usually incoherent, since they consist of a sequence of apparently unconnected words. An example of his "word-salad" is "The pipe tail on the bed, the TV said, a brown came out of the lawn, the flowers are board walk." He also coins new words such as "lapicator," which he said was an important chemical that will be used to purify the world.

Case 3

Jim, a soldier, is in an Army medical hospital. He complains of a loss of sensation in his fingers. He also complains that he cannot see, although a competent oculist examined his eyes and found nothing wrong. It seems strange that Jim is calm about his disorder even to the point of feeling indifferent about it. Except for this, his personality seems intact.

Case 4

Jane has been referred to a psychiatrist by her local physician, who can find nothing physically wrong with her. She complains, however, of feeling that something terrible is going to happen to her or to her family. She realizes that her fear is irrational, but she can't seem to help it. She has also become fearful of doing things she formerly did without any apprehension whatsoever, such as going to dances and driving her car. One might describe her as being in a state of apprehension about practically everything. Jane herself is not certain what she fears, and she seems to lack insight into the etiology of her present condition.

Case 5

Margaret, an eighteen-year-old girl, is afraid to be alone at home or to go alone more than one block away from home. She is particularly afraid of being in a room by herself. She becomes panicky when alone and reports she has the feeling that the walls are closing in on her.

Case 6

Bill is an extremely orderly, clean, stubborn, and stingy person. He expects everything in the house to be spotless at all times. He insists that every chair, napkin, ashtray, and book be in its proper place. His wife loves him but finds it very difficult to keep the house in the rigid order he demands. He tends to have some time-consuming rituals connected with dressing and personal care, such as arranging his toilet articles in a particular order, rinsing his face exactly five times after shaving, laying out all of his clothes in a fixed sequence and making sure that he puts them on in that order.

Case 7

Ralph is a highly impulsive person who has difficulty making plans or sticking to a job for any length of time. He has been fired from several jobs because he was caught stealing or because of frequent absences due to periodic drinking and gambling sprees. He always blames his employer for his dismissal and will not admit that his own behavior is responsible for his poor job history. Women tend to find him charming and personable, but they soon tire of his irresponsible behavior, frequent financial sponging, and general lack of consideration. His quick temper and disregard for social regulations have brought him into frequent brushes with the law, but he usually manages to charm his way out and has never been convicted of a crime.

He appears to feel little guilt or anxiety regarding his behavior.

questions for discussion

1. Which of the symptoms shown by neurotic patients are most common (in less extreme form) among mentally healthy people?

2. Is the classification normal-neurotic-psychotic one of degree or one of kind?

3. In what way does the psychopathic personality differ from individuals classed as psychotic or neurotic?

21

psychotherapy and related techniques

programed unit

1. When a person is seriously disturbed emotionally, what can be done? *Psychotherapy* is one method of treatment. If you know that "therapy" means treatment, you can guess that *psychotherapy* is treatment by

psychological   _____ means. *Somatotherapy,* on the other hand, is a method of treatment that is not psychological, but biological, in that it treats the body (*soma*) with drugs, surgery, electroshock, or other physiological means.

Somatotherapy

psychotherapy

2. *Som_____* is carried out by persons with medical training and is

of less intrinsic interest to a psychologist than *ps_____* , which involves treatment by psychological means.

3. The individuals active in the treatment of behavior disorders are the *psychiatrist,* who is a physician, the *clinical psychologist,* the *psychiatric social worker,* and, in mental hospitals, the *psychiatric nurse.* Since the only person who can assume *medical* responsibility for the patient is a physician, this is

psychiatrist   the function of the _____ .

4. Some psychiatrists are psychoanalysts and follow the therapeutic methods formulated by Freud, but most psychiatrists are not trained in psychoanalysis

somatotherapy   and use other methods of treatment, including *somato_____* . A psychoanalyst today is almost always a psychiatrist, but a psychiatrist

is not   (*is/is not*) always a psychoanalyst.

5. The *clinical psychologist* usually has a Ph.D. degree in psychology and has special training in the fields of diagnostic testing, psychotherapy, and research. He is not trained in medicine, however, and cannot assume

medical   *m_____* responsibility for his patients.

6. The *psychiatric social worker* usually has a Master's degree in social work and has special training in interviewing, writing case histories, and carrying treatment procedures into the home and community. Neither the psychiatric social worker nor the clinical psychologist is trained in medicine, however, and therefore they (*can/cannot*) assume medical responsibility for patients.

cannot

7. A staff member who administers diagnostic tests, such as the Rorschach and the Minnesota Multiphasic Personality Inventory, to a group of mental patients as part of a research study is probably a (*psychiatrist/psychiatric social worker/clinical psychologist*).

clinical psychologist

8. The (*clinical psychologist/psychiatric social worker*) usually develops case histories on mental patients and carries treatment procedures into the home and the community.

psychiatric social worker

9. In mental hospitals, the *psychiatric nurse* is also an important team member because she (or he) has had special training in nursing as well as in the handling of mental patients and is of immense help to the _____ , who is responsible for whatever medical treatment is prescribed.

psychiatrist

10. You will remember that psychoanalysis was discussed as a theory of personality. We will now consider psychoanalysis as a method of psychotherapy. One of the foundations of this method is called *free association*. In this approach the patient is told to say, without selection or editing, everything that enters his mind. In order to get the patient to put repressed thoughts into words, the psychoanalyst will ask him to talk, to ramble, not to think too much about what he is saying, and not to suppress anything. This is the technique of _____ _____ .

free association

11. When one says a word, it will be associated, through past experience, with other words. For instance, if one says "grass," the word "green" may come to mind. If the patient allows this type of association to continue freely, without censorship, he may bring out repressed thoughts and feelings by following the technique of _____ _____ .

free association

12. The technique of _____ _____ assumes that as the patient continues to talk without editing his words, he will utter words and feelings that are associated with his problem and that these will give the analyst and eventually the patient the information they need to work toward a cure.

free association

13. If a person has repressed certain thoughts, feelings, and impulses, they are (*conscious/unconscious*). The psychoanalyst, by using the method of free association, helps the client bring to *conscious* awareness that which has been repressed.

unconscious

14. A person in treatment often represses certain thoughts and feelings because they make him feel too uncomfortable. He therefore *resists* their recall during his analytic treatment. You might guess that one of the tasks of the analyst is to help the patient overcome his _____*ance* so that they, together, can deal with these unpleasant unconscious thoughts and feelings.

resistance

15. Patient C is late for his appointment and, when he does show up, he states that he cannot recall something he wished to share with the analyst. This is

resistance

resistance

an example of _____ . That is, consciously the patient wishes to recall, but unconscious blocks hinder recall. And the fact that he

was late for his appointment might also be interpreted as _____ .

16. In order to help the client to overcome *resistance* and to better understand himself, the psychoanalyst will make *interpretations* of his behavior. He may, for instance, call the patient's attention to his resistance to treatment by pointing out to him that he was late for his appointment and that he cannot recall what he wished to share with the therapist. Psychoanalysts use

interpretation

_____ to help the client overcome his resistances to treatment and to help him understand himself better.

17. The psychoanalyst helps the client understand some of the deeper meanings of his free associations as well as his dreams. He helps the client make *interpretations* of his behavior. A client recalls the manifest content of a nightmare he had last night, for instance, but he cannot understand the dream's latent content, or what the dream means or implies. With the help

interpretation

of the analyst, however, he may be able to make an _____ of what the dream really means.

resistance

18. It is not unusual for a client to have some _____ to treatment, since his symptoms are often less painful and stressful to him than the *reality* of some of his conflicts and feelings. To help him deal with what

free

has been repressed, the analyst may use _____ association and make

interpretations

_____ of the deeper meanings of the client's associations and dreams.

19. On a conscious level, the patient wishes to get well and to feel good. But on

resistance

an unconscious level, he may show _____ to treatment by coming late for appointments and by frequent blocking of what he wished to relate to the therapist.

20. During therapy the patient will often *transfer* to the analyst emotional reactions that he has had to others who were important to him. This tendency is

transference

called *tr_____ence.* By analyzing these reactions, which often are not appropriate to the actual relationship of the analyst and the patient, the analyst gets clues to the patient's difficulties.

21. If a patient acts toward an analyst in the way he used to act toward his father or mother or some other significant person in his life, we would call

transference

this a manifestation of _____ .

22. Sometimes a patient acts in a hostile manner toward the analyst when the latter

transference

has given him no reason to do so. This is interpreted as _____ , since the patient is responding emotionally toward the analyst as though he were someone else.

23. In the permissive atmosphere of the therapist's office it is sometimes possible for a patient to relive a past situation that had strong emotional aspects and to express this emotion *freely,* as he had been unable to do in the original situation. This process, called *abreaction,* often brings the patient some relief from tension. If a patient relives a situation in which his father treated him

unfairly and freely expresses the anger that he could not express then, he is

abreaction experiencing _____ .

24. A free expression of _____ that was felt but not expressed in
emotion
abreaction an earlier situation is known as _____ .

25. At the time of his father's funeral Peter suppressed his feelings of anguish
because they might be regarded as unmanly. Now that Peter is in therapy
and relating the experience to an uncritical listener, the former suppressed
feelings are expressed and he cries and sobs freely. We would say Peter is
abreaction now experiencing what psychoanalysts call _____ .

freely 26. Abreaction is like catharsis in that pent-up feelings are _____ly expressed in a permissive setting.

abreaction 27. A form of emotional cleansing, called _____ by psychoanalysts, sometimes takes place in therapy; by itself, it does not eliminate
the causes of conflict, though the patient may feel some relief from tension.

28. When a patient understands the roots of his conflict, he has achieved *insight*.
For instance, Sue now understands the relationship between some of her
symptoms and some early life experiences. In other words, she has achieved
insight some measure of _____ into her difficulties.

29. Stan now understands that he forms an immediate dislike of anyone in a
supervisory capacity over him because the first authority figure in his life, his
father, both bossed and belittled him unmercifully. We would say that Stan
insight now has some _____ into his hatred for authority figures.

30. As a patient is on the road to recovery, he goes through a process known as
working through. In this process, he examines the same conflicts over and
over again as they have appeared in a variety of situations throughout his
Working life, and learns to face them in a more mature way. _____
through is part of the process of becoming adjusted, which is a matter of
learning to face reality.

31. Since the patient will often face his conflicts over and over again outside
working through the therapist's office, it follows that the _____ _____
process will continue in many situations in everyday life.

psychotherapy 32. Psychoanalysis is a method of _____*therapy* that accents the unconscious determinants of personality.

33. A form of psychotherapy that differs from psychoanalysis is *client-centered*
therapy. This form of therapy assumes that the client can work out his own
problems if the therapist provides the right psychological atmosphere. The
therapist does not instruct the client to free associate, nor does he interpret
psychoanalyst the client's statements and behavior as would a _____ .
Instead he attempts to *reflect* and to *clarify* the feelings of the client and to
see things from the client's point of view, his *frame of reference*, as it is
sometimes referred to.

34. The client-centered therapist tries to see things from the client's frame of

reference   _____ . He *accepts* the client and his statements and feel-

accept   ings so that the client may begin to *acc*_____ himself.

client-centered   **35.**   In _____-_____ therapy the therapist mainly accepts, reflects, and clarifies the views of the client so that the client can
understand himself better.

       36.   Since the therapist accepts the client and shows the client that he does, the

more   client should give evidence that he accepts himself (*more/less*) at the end of
the therapy than he did at the beginning.

client-centered   **37.**   An assumption made in _____-_____ therapy is
that the client has the capacity to deal with his psychological situation and
with himself.

       38.   One of the main tenets of client-centered therapy is that the therapist must

reference   try to adopt the frame of _____ of the client. That is, he

client   must try to see things as the _____ sees them.

       39.   Thus far we have discussed two different kinds of psychotherapy.

Psychoanalysis   _____ is a form of treatment by psychological means in which the therapist uses free association and interpretation

client-centered   as techniques of treatment. In _____-_____ therapy,
the therapist tries to adopt the frame of reference of the client and to reflect
and clarify his feelings. The assumption in this form of treatment is that the
client has resources to solve his own problems in an accepting relationship
with another.

frame   **40.**   A client-centered therapist tries to adopt the _____ of reference, or

reflect, clarify   viewpoint, of his client and also tries to _____ and _____
(either order)   the feelings of his client.

       41.   Still a third form of psychotherapy is *behavior therapy,* which differs from
both psychoanalysis and client-centered therapy in that it is based upon the
principles of learning theory. The assumption in this kind of therapy is that if

unlearned   maladaptive behavior is *learned,* it can also be *unl*_____ by having
the person learn new or more appropriate responses in place of the maladaptive responses.

       42.   Because we are trying to change the *behavior* of a maladjusted organism by

learning   means of certain principles of _____ , we call this method

behavior   _____ therapy.

       43.   If a severe shock is administered to a cat every time it approaches a feeding
cage, it will, of course, become *anxious* and *fearful.* The cat wishes to eat
because it is hungry, but it dreads the pain from the electric shock. The cat
may even manifest neurotic behavior because it has been placed in an

avoidance   approach-_____ conflict that cannot be resolved. The

anxiety   maladaptive response learned by the cat in this situation is *a*_____ .

       44.   The *maladaptive* anxiety reaction one has learned in one situation or under certain conditions may *generalize* to other situations. Thus, our anxious cat may refuse to eat not only in the feeding cage but also in other places in the experimental room, even though the other places are perfectly safe. Its

maladaptive

behavior is certainly *mal*_____ , because it is hungry but re-

generalized

fuses to eat even in safe places. Its anxiety reaction has _____ to other situations.

45. We wish now to use _____ therapy on this cat so that it will

behavior

learn that it is safe to eat. We shall have to eliminate, or extinguish, the

maladaptive

*mal*_____ behavior. How do we go about doing this, using what we know about the principles of learning?

46. Because the cat's maladaptive behavior has been learned through condition-

extinguish

ing, perhaps we can use *counter-conditioning* to weaken or *ex*_____ the maladaptive responses by strengthening incompatible or antagonistic responses.

47. Psychologists use _____-conditioning to help extinguish a

counter

maladaptive response. That is, the organism learns some new response through weakening or extinguishing the maladaptive response.

48. The prime task is to destroy or _____ the anxiety

extinguish

response, or maladaptive response, by making it possible for the normal response of eating to occur.

49. Since the cat is anxious and refuses to eat anywhere in the experimental

generalized

room because its anxiety has *g*_____ from the feeding place to other places in the experimental room, perhaps we can get it to eat

far removed from

if we place the food (*near/far removed from*) the original feeding place.

50. Once the cat learns it can eat in one place without experiencing any pain, it

anxiety

can overcome its *a*_____ reactions.

51. Once the cat learns it can eat, we can place the feeding cup in *gradual* steps closer to the original feeding place. If, after one successful feeding at a place far from the original feeding place, we set the feeding cup very near the

anxious

original place, the cat would surely become _____ again and

maladaptive, gradual

manifest *m*_____ behavior. Thus the steps must be _____ .

52. Once the cat is able to eat in the cage where it had originally been shocked and shows no sign of being anxious, we have probably cured it of its anxiety

conditioning

by means of counter-_____ . In other words, we have extinguished the anxious, maladaptive behavior it had learned by strengthening incompatible or antagonistic responses.

53. We can treat human subjects who exhibit anxiety in a similar manner by asking them to list the sorts of situations that are anxiety-producing for them. We can then ascertain and rank in a sort of *hierarchy* the situations that are most and least anxiety-provoking. Such a list is called an *anxiety hierarchy* because we have ranked these situations from the least to the

most

_____ anxiety-provoking.

54. When a therapist ranks from low to high those situations that a particular

anxiety

client finds most anxiety-provoking, he is establishing an _____ hierarchy.

55. From what we have learned about behavior therapy from the illustration of the maladapted cat in the feeding situation, we may surmise that, as we study

least

the anxiety hierarchy, we would start with situations that are (*most/least*) anxiety-provoking for our subject.

56. We can ask our subject to *relax* and instruct him to visualize the least

anxiety

_____-provoking situation. If he remains relaxed and appears not to be anxious, we can then *gradually* proceed to the next anxiety-provoking situation on the list.

57. We continue in this manner until the situation that originally provoked the most anxiety now elicits only relaxation. Thus, we have conditioned our

relaxation

subject to respond with _____ to situations that initially produced an anxiety response.

conditioning

58. Both examples above illustrate counter-_____,

maladaptive

whereby a _____ response is extinguished and replaced

behavior

by an adaptive one. This is one technique used in _____ therapy. The text discusses other methods used by behavior therapists.

59. Since most emotional problems stem from difficulties in relating to other people, it makes sense sometimes to practice in *groups*. Such therapy is called,

group

appropriately enough, *gr_____ therapy.*

60. When therapy is carried out with a therapist and more than one client, we

group

call it _____ therapy. Group therapy saves time, gives the individual the feeling that his problems are not unique—that others are "in the same boat"—and provides opportunities to learn better ways of interacting with other people. All the methods of psychotherapy that we have discussed have been used, often in modified form, in group therapy.

61. *Encounter groups* are a popular offshoot of group therapy. The main differ-

encounter

ence is that *en_____* groups are aimed at teaching people how to relate more openly to one another rather than at solving emotional problems or treating behavior disorders.

groups

62. Encounter _____, also known as *T-groups* or *sensitivity groups,* emphasize learning how to express one's feelings more openly. They may help a person achieve a better understanding of how he interacts with others, but they are not designed to treat emotional problems or behavior

disorders

_____ .

encounter

63. T-group and sensitivity group are other names for a(n) _____

group

_____ .

64. We have discussed three major approaches to psychotherapy. The method that uses free association to bring repressed impulses and thoughts to con-

psychoanalysis

scious awareness is called _____ . When a

therapist makes no attempt to interpret what the patient says but simply
reflects and clarifies the patient's feelings, he is using _____-
_____ therapy. The method of psychotherapy that is based
upon learning-theory principles is called _____ _____ .

client-
centered

behavior therapy

65. Psychotherapy is the treatment of behavior disorders by psychological means.
Treatment by physiological means is called *so*_____ .
Some forms of somatotherapy used in the past, such as electroshock and
brain surgery, have had little success. The most promising type of somatotherapy in use today is *chemotherapy.*

somatotherapy

66. Chemotherapy, which uses drugs to modify behavior, is the most promising
type of _____ used today. *Tranquilizers,* such
as reserpine and chlorpromazine, have been very effective in calming disturbed and anxious patients and making them more amenable to treatment
by psychological means, or _____ .

somatotherapy

psychotherapy

67. The therapeutic use of drugs to modify behavior is called _____ .
Some of the most effective drugs for calming disturbed patients are the
_____ .

chemotherapy

tranquilizers

self-quiz

Select the alternative that best completes the thought.
In some cases several answers are fairly satisfactory;
you are to pick the *best* one.

_____ **1.** Client-centered therapists
  a. reflect and clarify feelings
  b. make insightful interpretations
  c. probe skillfully into the client's prob-
    lems
  d. maximize transference as a technique
    of treatment

_____ **2.** Psychoanalytic cure usually results from
  a. sudden insight into relationships be-
    tween present symptoms and early
    experiences
  b. the sudden recall of some traumatic
    experience that the patient has re-
    pressed
  c. a long, gradual increase in self-
    knowledge
  d. learning more acceptable behavior

_____ **3.** When counter-conditioning is used as a
  therapeutic technique
  a. maladaptive responses are weakened

or eliminated by strengthening an-
    tagonistic responses
  b. anxiety is increased to effect an al-
    teration in behavior
  c. the patient is placed in a restricted
    environment with no anxiety-provok-
    ing stimuli present
  d. modification of behavior depends
    upon the patient's understanding of
    his unconscious motives

_____ **4.** In client-centered therapy the therapist
  a. structures the sessions so that the
    client arrives at his own insights
    and makes his own decisions
  b. carefully directs the patient's atten-
    tion to specific topics
  c. tries to relate the patient's present
    problems to his early history
  d. gathers a case history to facilitate
    understanding of the client

_____ **5.** The tendency of the patient to make
  the therapist the object of emotional response is known as
  a. abreaction

b. resistance
c. working through
d. transference

6. The greatest advances among the somatotherapies have been made in the area of
   a. insulin-shock therapy
   b. chemotherapy
   c. electroshock therapy
   d. psychosurgery

7. Somatotherapy attempts to
   a. correct physical problems through psychological methods
   b. bring about behavior change through communication between patient and therapist
   c. change behavior by working with patients in groups
   d. change behavior through physiological methods

8. Studies show that children identified as having emotional problems in elementary school grades
   a. do not outgrow such problems as a matter of development
   b. usually overcome these problems as they grow older
   c. adjust rapidly when they are held back a grade
   d. should be placed in special classes

9. The incidence of psychosis is highest among
   a. the lower class
   b. the middle class
   c. the upper class
   d. immigrants

10. When the patient is asked to say everything that enters his mind, without selection, this is called
    a. free imagery
    b. free association
    c. thought purging
    d. feeling awareness

11. The patient who represses the recall of certain thoughts and feelings must overcome his
    a. resistance
    b. blockage
    c. preoccupation
    d. mind-barrier

12. The use of tranquilizers for the treatment of behavior disorders is called
    a. psychopharmacology
    b. psychochemistry
    c. chemotherapy
    d. medicotherapy

13. Traditional therapists and psychoanalysts criticize behavior therapy because they feel
    a. it is not client-centered
    b. it deals with the symptoms and leaves the conflict unresolved
    c. that only a superficial relationship is developed between the patient and therapist
    d. that the therapist maintains too objective an approach to the client's problem

14. Reinforcing socially appropriate behavior in hospital wards with chronic patients has been highly successful. This kind of system is called a
    a. right-response reward system
    b. token economy
    c. reinforcement progress program
    d. behavior inducement system

15. The subjects who made the greatest number of snake-approach responses after receiving behavior therapy treatment were in the
    a. live modeling with participation group
    b. desensitization group
    c. symbolic modeling group
    d. control group

16. The psychotherapeutic approach that attempts to apply the principles of learning to the treatment of neurotic disorders is called
    a. conditioned therapy
    b. psychoanalysis
    c. nondirective therapy
    d. behavior therapy

17. A large number of psychotherapists use an eclectic approach, which means they use
    a. group therapy
    b. encounter groups
    c. family therapy
    d. a variety of methods

18. Alcoholics Anonymous and Synanon

try to help their clients work out their problems through

a. psychoanalysis
b. client-centered therapy
c. group therapy
d. behavior therapy

_____ 19. In behavior therapy the therapist discovers the situations that produce anxiety. The patient is then conditioned to respond to these situations with

a. indifference
b. relaxation
c. withdrawal
d. fatigue

_____ 20. The administration and interpretation of psychological tests is usually done by a

a. psychiatrist
b. psychoanalyst
c. clinical psychologist
d. psychiatric social worker

key to self-quiz

20. c	15. a	10. b	5. d
19. b	14. b	9. a	4. a
18. c	13. b	8. a	3. a
17. d	12. c	7. d	2. c
16. d	11. a	6. b	1. a

individual exercise

FREE ASSOCIATION

introduction

This is a very simple exercise, but it will give you a better feeling for what goes on in therapy and a better understanding of why certain kinds of therapy take so long.

The main technique in psychoanalytic therapy is free association. The therapist instructs the client to say whatever comes into his mind. There should be no attempt to censor any material that comes to consciousness—it should all be verbalized, no matter how irrelevant, unimportant, or embarrassing it may seem.

equipment needed

None required, but if a tape recorder is available it would be useful.

procedure

This technique appears to be a simple thing to carry out. In order to get some idea of what it is like, follow these instructions: Go to a room in which you know you will not be disturbed—go to any lengths you feel necessary in order to do this. Some students have waited until they were at home and the rest of their family was away. When you are *sure* that you are alone and no one else can hear you, try to follow the rules for free association. Say everything *aloud* in a clear tone.

If possible it would be instructive to tape record your free associations so that you can analyze them later.

questions for discussion

1. Was it easy to do? If not, why do you think it was not?

2. Can you imagine what it would be like to do this in the presence of another person?

3. How long do you think it would take you to be able to do this in the presence of another person?

4. Can you trace some of the cues that made one thought lead to another?

social psychology

programed unit

1. Man's behavior is influenced by the *social context* in which it occurs. *Social psychology* is concerned with how a person *behaves* in the presence of others and how his behavior is influenced by them. When we study behavior in a

social   social context, we are studying _____ psychology.

behaves   **2.** Social psychology is concerned with how a person _____ in the presence of others—how he perceives other people and is influenced by them.

3. The *impressions* we form of another person are influenced by more than that person's observable characteristics. Two people might observe the same per-

impressions   son and form quite different *imp*_____ of him.

impression   **4.** One factor that influences our _____ of another person is our *emotional state* at the time. Studies have shown that people in a state of fear tend to judge others as appearing fearful. If John is happy and Bill is worried, their impression of their newly arrived roommate is likely to be

different   (*the same/different*).

5. A person's *self-perception* will also affect his impression of others. People who view themselves as having certain desirable traits tend to assign these

traits   _____ to individuals they like more than to those they dislike. John views himself as quite masculine. He is likely to judge his friend Mark as

more   (*more/less*) masculine than Fred, whom he dislikes.

6. Thus we see that our impression or perception of another person may be in-

emotional   fluenced by our _____ state as well as by our

self-perception   *self-*_____ . The text discusses other factors that in-fluence our perception of another person and the bases for liking or disliking him.

7. Social behavior in man is influenced by the *rules* and *expectations* of the society in which he lives. The complex interrelationship of these rules and

expectations

structure

_____ form the *social structure* of the society. Social _____ is especially concerned with behavior that is affected by rank, or position, or role.

8. When we refer to the rules and expectations of a society, especially with regard to behavior that is affected by rank or position within the society, we

social structure

speak of _____ _____ .

structure

9. The social _____ of most societies arranges relationships in some sort of hierarchy. If this hierarchy is rigid, if the positions in it are fixed by birth and cannot be changed without extreme difficulty, it is called a *caste* system.

10. A social structure in which rank and position are fixed by birth and in which

caste

change is difficult, if not impossible, is called a _____ system.

birth

11. Since rank and position were fixed by _____ in the old system in India, it could be called a caste system.

12. A *class* system, on the other hand, is much less rigid. It is composed of groups of people with certain common characteristics, but the boundaries

classes

between the _____ are much less firm than the boundaries between the groups in a caste system.

class

13. The United States has, in general, a _____ system. The boundaries are not rigid and it is possible for a person to move between classes. This movement between classes is called *social mobility*.

14. However, the black person in American society has been subject to a system

caste

that approaches a _____ system. This is true because he was born into a certain position and it has been very difficult for him to move out of it. This situation is changing, but for a long time the black person has had

social

little _____ mobility.

mobility

15. In a caste system there is little social _____ . This means that

class

there is practically no movement between castes. In a _____ system, however, social mobility is much greater.

16. The ease with which one can change his position in the hierarchy of a social

social mobility

structure is known as _____ _____ .

17. Both caste and class refer to groups within a society that have some common characteristics. You will be rejected by the groups above you and you will reject persons from the groups below you if you belong to a group in a

caste, class

_____ system. This is also true in a _____ system, but the rejection will not be so severe or so final. In the class system it is possible for the person in the lower class to achieve membership in a higher group.

18. Any group to which a person belongs and with which he identifies himself is

in-group	known as an *in-group*. If a person belongs to a fraternity, his fraternity brothers probably constitute his _____-_____ .
in-group	**19.** Any group to which a person belongs and with which he identifies himself is known as a(n) _____-_____ .
out	**20.** For an in-group to exist and be identified, there must be people *outside* its boundaries. You might expect that the people who are *not* members of a particular social grouping—a country club, perhaps, or even a football squad —would constitute, for that in-group, an _____-*group*.
out- groups	**21.** Groups with which an individual does *not* identify are, for him, _____-_____ .
in-group out-group	**22.** The gang to which a delinquent boy belongs is his _____-_____ . For a boy who conforms to the standards, customs, and norms of his society, a delinquent gang of boys would be an _____-_____ .
stereotype	**23.** The existence of in-groups and out-groups leads to perceptual distortions. One such form of distortion is a *stereotype*. You can probably fill in the sentence "All (so-and-sos) are (such-and-such)" from examples you have heard or perhaps even used yourself. Such a statement expresses a _____ .
group	**24.** Stereotyping exists when people attribute to an individual characteristics that they believe to be typical of the _____ to which they assign him.
stereotype	**25.** A stereotype is a generalization, usually about a social or national group, according to which individuals are assigned traits they may not possess. To believe that all Latin Americans are hot-tempered is to _____ this group.
scapegoats	**26.** The existence of in-groups and out-groups also leads to intergroup conflict. One such type of conflict is *scapegoating*. Scapegoating is a form of *displaced aggression* in which an innocent victim is blamed or punished as the source of the scapegoater's frustration. Hitler, for instance, found it convenient to blame the Jews for Germany's plight. For Hitler, the Jews were convenient _____ .
displaced	**27.** Scapegoating is a form of _____ aggression in which an innocent victim is blamed or punished as the source of the scapegoater's frustration.
scapegoating	**28.** In _____ , displaced aggression is directed toward an innocent victim.
destructive	**29.** Usually we control our *aggressive* or *destructive* impulses. But there are occasions, as in riots or mob violence, when normally restrained people engage in aggressive or _____ behavior as part of a large group.
group	**30.** When a person is part of a large _____ or mob, he tends to lose his

feeling of individuality. The term *deindividuation* has been coined to describe the process by which a person may lose his feeling of individuality in a group and may as a consequence act more irresponsibly than he would otherwise.

31. When people are responding not as individuals but as part of a group, then

deindividuation

there is a certain amount of _____ . Since they tend to respond not as identified individuals but as part of an anonymous

group

_____ , they feel less responsible for their actions.

32. When people do not have an individual identity but are part of a faceless

more

mob, they are (*more/less*) apt to behave irresponsibly.

33. The process by which individuals lose their identity and respond as part of a

deindividuation

group rather than as individuals is called _____ .

34. In one fraternity initiation the members wear masks, while in another fraternity they do not. We would expect the members of the first fraternity to be

more

(*more/less*) aggressive in their treatment of the pledges than the second group.

35. Anything that reduces a person's sense of identity, such as wearing a

mask, mob (or group)

_____ or being part of a faceless _____ , may lead to

deindividuation

_____ . Both of these factors contribute to the type of senseless violence perpetrated by groups such as the Ku Klux Klan.

36. A *social norm* of conduct is a type of social behavior that is expected in a given situation. Obviously, one can understand this behavior only in refer-

social

ence to the group that expects it. In other words, a _____ norm makes sense to the group in which it originated. It may or may not make sense to anyone outside that group.

37. We have certain expected eating behavior in our society. We train children to eat with a fork rather than with their fingers. We *expect* them to eat in

social norm

this way. Thus we have set a _____ _____ for eating.

38. The society in general sets social norms for such things as hair length. Certain subgroups in the society may set different social norms. Thus, when we see an adolescent male with exceedingly long hair, it is not legitimate to deduce

social norm

that he is rebelling against a _____ _____ . He may be a nonconformist in regard to the society in general but a slavish conformist to his own particular subgroup.

39. Studies show that the more strongly a member is attracted to a group, the more his perceptions and actions tend to *conform* to the *group norms*. If John is strongly attracted to the other members of his gang, one would expect

conform

him to _____ to their norms.

group

40. One tends to conform to _____ norms if one is strongly attracted to a particular group.

41. The *attitudes* and *opinions* that people have are important influences on their social behavior. An attitude represents both an *orientation* toward or away from some object, concept, or situation, and a *readiness to respond* in a predetermined way to these or related objects, concepts, or situations. If you are oriented to feel a sense of irritation when you hear the terms "hippie" or "radical," you may have an unfavorable _____ toward these groups.

attitude

42. Similarly, if you react approvingly when you hear someone labeled a "conservative," you may be oriented toward conservative groups (however you define "conservative") and may be ready to _____ in a predetermined way to such groups.

respond

43. An _____ represents both an orientation toward or away from an object, concept, or situation, and a _____ to respond in a predetermined way to these or related objects, concepts, or situations.

attitude
readiness

44. Attitudes grade into *opinions* and there is no sharp difference between them. One possible distinction is that an opinion involves some kind of *expectation* or *prediction* (not merely a preference) and can always be *put into words*. For instance, if someone says, "I don't think we will have another Depression," he is making a prediction in words and is therefore voicing an _____ .

opinion

45. An _____ involves some kind of expectation or prediction and can always be put into words.

opinion

46. Attitudes may be partly unconscious. But an opinion can always be verbalized, that is, put into _____ .

words

47. An opinion usually involves some sort of expectation or _____ .

prediction

48. If you say, "I think that federal aid to education is desirable," you are expressing an (*attitude*/*opinion*). If you say, "I think the Democrats will win the next election," you are expressing an (*attitude*/*opinion*).

attitude
opinion

49. When investigators ask a group of people how they expect to vote in the next election, they are conducting a *public* _____ *survey*.

opinion

50. You would expect psychologists to be interested in *measuring* attitudes and _____ . The text describes the problems involved in constructing questionnaires to _____ attitudes and opinions.

opinions
measure

51. One method of _____ attitudes and opinions uses *free-answer* or *open* questions, that is, questions to which the respondents must reply in their own words. If you were asked "How do you feel about legalized abortion?", this would be an example of a free-_____ or open question. One of the shortcomings of questionnaires using the _____-answer or _____ question is that they are often difficult to interpret and analyze statistically.

measuring

answer
free-
open

measuring 52. Another method of _____ attitudes and opinions uses questions that can be answered by a number of *fixed alternatives*. Suppose you were asked "What is your opinion regarding legalized abortion?" and were requested to check one of the following alternatives.

(a) All abortions should be prohibited by law.
(b) Abortions should be permitted only when the life of the mother is at stake.
(c) Abortions should be permitted whenever there is evidence that the physical or mental well-being of the mother or fetus is in jeopardy.
(d) There should be no legal restriction on abortion.

fixed This question illustrates the method of _____ alternatives.

alternatives 53. The method of fixed _____ is easier to analyze

open statistically than a questionnaire using free-answer or _____ questions. Its disadvantage is that by not allowing the person to answer as he wishes we are not always sure how he interprets the question or what he intends by his answer.

fixed-alternative 54. Opinion questionnaires can utilize _____-_____

open questions or free-answer or _____ questions. In some cases it proves useful to employ both methods in constructing an effective questionnaire.

55. In addition to his interest in what people's attitudes are, the social psychologist is also concerned with how attitudes change. A general theory, called *consistency theory*, holds that a person wants his *attitudes* to be consistent with each other and with his *behavior*. If he finds them inconsistent, he tries in some way to reduce this discrepancy. He may alter his attitudes, or his

behavior _____ , or both.

attitudes 56. Consistency theory maintains that a person wants his _____ to be consistent with each other and with his behavior. If he finds that they

both are inconsistent, he tends to alter his attitudes, his behavior, or _____ . Three closely related variants of consistency theory are covered in the text. Here we will be concerned only with the general theory.

57. If we like a person and he makes a statement with which we agree, then there is no inconsistency between our attitude toward him and our attitude concerning what he says. If, on the other hand, a person we dislike agrees with our opinion or likes something we like, then we are faced with an

inconsistency _____ .

58. If a senator whom we admire votes against legislation designed to lower the voting age—legislation that we strongly support—then we are faced with an

inconsistency _____ between our attitude toward the senator and our favorable attitude toward the legislation he has vetoed.

59. To reduce this inconsistency we can do one of two things. We can form a

less (*more/less*) favorable attitude toward the senator, or we can change our views concerning the legislation. Which move we make depends upon how extreme our view is concerning either the person or the proposition.

theory 60. According to consistency _____ , a person likes his set of beliefs

consistent to be _____ . If he finds them inconsistent, he tries to

discrepancy (or synonym)	reduce the _____ by making some changes in his set of beliefs.

61. Much (though not all) of the influence people exert to change the attitudes of others is carried on through *communication*. While some communication is carried on face-to-face, we are also subject to influences from *mass media* —that is, organs of communication, such as television or the newspapers, that reach very large, or mass, audiences. A speaker addressing a group of fifty persons in a lecture hall (*is/is not*) using one of the mass means of communication.

is not

62. Radio and motion pictures reach large masses of people; they are examples of what are called the _____ media of communication.

mass

63. Social psychologists are naturally interested in studying the effect of newspapers and magazines, radio, television, and motion pictures—that is, the mass _____ of communication—upon the opinions and attitudes of their audiences.

media

64. Many factors can influence the *effectiveness* of a communication. One factor is the *credibility of the source*, that is, how much confidence the listener has in the source of the communication. Your confidence in a speaker will help to determine the _____ of his communication.

effectiveness

65. Suppose you hear a lecture given by a well-known doctor in favor of legalizing the use of marijuana. You are more likely to develop a favorable attitude toward the drug than you would if you heard the same lecture given by a man who had just served a jail term for selling marijuana. This is an example of how the _____ of the source can influence the effectiveness of a communication.

credibility

66. One factor that can influence the effectiveness of a communication is the credibility of the _____ . Another factor is the extent to which the communication arouses fear. The degree of *fear arousal* helps to determine the _____ of the communication.

source

effectiveness

67. The experimental results are not clear-cut, but they indicate that the effects of fear _____ depend upon how anxious the person is about the topic to begin with. At low levels of initial anxiety, fear arousal is effective in producing attitude change; when initial anxiety is high, further fear arousal may mobilize defenses and produce a *resistance to change*.

arousal

68. A heavy smoker who is worried about the possibility of lung cancer sees a TV commercial emphasizing the dangers of smoking; a teen-age boy who has experimented with only a few cigarettes sees the same commercial. If the assumption about the relationship between initial anxiety level and the effects of fear arousal is true, we would expect the most attitude change on the part of the (*heavy smoker/teen-age boy*).

teen-age boy

low

69. Fear arousal appears to be most effective when initial anxiety is _____ . When initial anxiety is high, fear arousal may mobilize defenses and produce a resistance to _____ .

change

70. We have mentioned two of a number of factors that can influence the effectiveness of a communication. They are the credibility of the _____

source

fear arousal

and the degree of _____ _____ .

self-quiz

Select the alternative that best completes the thought. In some cases several answers are fairly satisfactory; you are to pick the *best* one.

_____ 1. More suicides are found among
a. the very poor
b. the well-to-do
c. black people
d. people who have many restraints on their actions

_____ 2. A social group having boundaries that cannot be crossed without severe social punishment defines a
a. culture
b. civilization
c. caste
d. class

_____ 3. In a study in which an observer assigned responsibility for another's actions, the responsibility was determined
a. by the importance of the people involved in the act
b. by the outcome of the act
c. in an impartial manner
d. by the amount of education of the observer

_____ 4. People who view themselves as having certain desirable traits tend to assign these characteristics to others
a. who are important and influential
b. whom they like
c. whom they dislike
d. toward whom they feel neutral

_____ 5. One distinction that has been made between attitudes and opinions is that an opinion
a. may be partly unconscious
b. involves an expectation or prediction
c. cannot necessarily be verbalized
d. involves a preference

_____ 6. One of the social processes that leads

to a lowered threshold for destructive behavior is called
a. perspective distortion
b. regressive behavior
c. anonymity
d. deindividuation

_____ 7. The objects of scapegoating are characterized by
a. never having been a scapegoat before
b. posing a real threat that will be eliminated through scapegoating
c. being easily identifiable and accessible
d. being intellectual, selfish, and mercenary

_____ 8. An example of a social norm is
a. eating when hungry
b. sleeping when tired
c. stopping a car at a red light
d. putting on a coat when cold

_____ 9. A person is more apt to sign a petition if
a. there are three people circulating it
b. the petitioners first approach the person by phone
c. the petitioners first bring a pamphlet on the topic
d. there are a number of signatures already on the petition

_____ 10. The term "risky-shift" refers to the
a. change to greater willingness to take a risk
b. point at which the individual yields to the majority opinion
c. point at which the individual no longer conforms to the majority opinion
d. degree to which the individual is compelled to engage in scapegoating

_____ 11. Two important concepts involved in the definition of an attitude are

a. scapegoating and group pressure
b. conformity and emotion
c. motivation and risky-shift
d. orientation and readiness to respond

_____ 12. A likes B, and A also likes C. He finds out B and C like each other. This is an example of
a. a balanced state
b. a simple condition
c. an unbalanced state
d. perception equilibrium

_____ 13. The theory that focuses attention on the aftereffects of decision-making is known as the
a. congruity theory
b. balance model
c. theory of cognitive dissonance
d. equilibrium theory

_____ 14. In studies of TV viewing by children it was found that
a. the higher the child's intelligence, the less time he spent before the TV screen
b. viewing violence on TV made children more aggressive
c. the higher the child's intelligence, the more time he spent before the TV screen
d. children spend twice as much time in free play as in watching TV

_____ 15. Conformity is usually best obtained by using
a. strong fear appeal
b. moderate fear appeal
c. minimal fear appeal
d. a low-credibility source

_____ 16. In the study of upward and downward social mobility in six different countries, the country with the highest upward social mobility was _____ and the

country with the highest downward social mobility was _____ .
a. United States/Japan
b. Switzerland/Germany
c. Sweden/France
d. Germany/Sweden

_____ 17. Congruity, balance, and cognitive dissonance theories are all concerned with
a. opinion sampling
b. compliance
c. conformity to social influences
d. attitude change

_____ 18. One disadvantage of the free-answer question is that
a. it is difficult to analyze statistically
b. it is not certain how the respondent interprets the question
c. the meaning of the answer is not always clear
d. all of the above

_____ 19. The congruity theory was formulated by
a. Osgood and Tannenbaum
b. Festinger and Carlsmith
c. Heider
d. Allport

_____ 20. The heavy smoker who denies the evidence that smoking is harmful is engaging in
a. stereotyped behavior
b. wishful thinking
c. habit formation
d. dissonance reduction

key to self-quiz

20. d	15. b	10. a	5. b
19. a	14. a	9. d	4. b
18. a	13. c	8. c	3. b
17. d	12. a	7. c	2. c
16. b	11. d	6. d	1. b

individual or class exercise

CONFORMITY TO RULES

introduction

In order to function effectively and to provide for the safety and welfare of its people any society must establish certain rules and regulations governing behavior. Social psychologists are interested in the factors that produce conformity to society's rules. The purpose of this exercise is to investigate some of the variables that influence an individual motorist's conformity to the rule requiring him to stop at a stop sign.

equipment needed

Clipboard and pencil.

procedure

Select a four-way stop intersection (marked by stop signs, not a traffic light) with a moderate flow of traffic. It should be an intersection where you can watch the traffic from all four directions without being too conspicuous.

For a 45-minute period observe each car that approaches the intersection and record the information specified on the data sheet given on page 258. You will need to decide first whether the car (1) comes to a full stop at the intersection, (2) slows down but does not make a complete stop, or (3) makes little or no attempt to slow down. You should spend a few minutes observing the cars before starting your recording period in order to get an idea of how to classify the various degrees of "stopping." Exclude from your records those cars that are forced to stop because they were either behind another car or blocked by cross traffic.

After deciding upon the appropriate conformity category, note the sex of the driver, approximate age (under or over 25), and whether or not the driver is traveling alone. Place a tally mark in the appropriate box on the data sheet. For example, if the driver was a female, over 25, traveling with two children, and she made no attempt to slow down, you would place a tally mark in the bottom row in the box to the far right. If the driver was a male, under 25, traveling alone, and he came to a full stop, your tally mark would go in the top box of the extreme left-hand column. Obviously, if the car does not stop you will have to make some quick judgments as to age, sex, and companion.

treatment of data

Either you may analyze only your own data or the instructor may collect the data sheets from the entire class and provide you with the class totals in each category for your analysis.

1. Compute the overall percentage of individuals who made a full stop (that is, those who were rated as falling in Conformity Category 1).

_____%

2. Compute the percentage of males who made a full stop, and do the same for females.

males _____%

females _____%

3. Compute the percentage of individuals under 25 who made a full stop, and do the same for those over 25.

under 25 _____%

over 25 _____%

4. Compute the percentage of times a full stop was made when the driver was alone, and the percentage when he was accompanied by one or more riders.

alone _____%

accompanied _____%

questions for discussion

1. Do most people comply with the regulation requiring a full stop at stop signs?

2. Does the degree of compliance or conformity depend upon the age and sex of the drivers? Is compliance influenced by whether or not the driver is alone?

3. In calculating our percentages, only Conformity Category 1 was considered. Do we gain any additional information by examining the percentage of drivers that fell in categories 2 and 3?

4. What other variables besides those recorded in this study seemed to predict conformity behavior? For example, did you get the impression that factors such as type or condition of the car, or the apparent socioeconomic status of the driver, were related to conformity?

5. How accurate do you think your judgments were concerning stopping behavior and the other variables? Would it have been worthwhile to have had several judges rather than a single observer making ratings?

6. If you were to make a large-scale study of this type of conformity behavior, what changes would you make in the research procedure?

DATA SHEET

| | | | Conformity Categories | | |
			1. Full stop	2. Considerable slowing but not full stop	3. Little or no slowing
Alone	Under 25	Male			
		Female			
	Over 25	Male			
		Female			
With others	Under 25	Male			
		Female			
	Over 25	Male			
		Female			

psychology and society

programed unit

1.   Psychology shares with other sciences a responsibility to help solve the enormous problems confronting mankind today. Problems of overpopulation, exhaustion of natural resources, environmental pollution, and the control of nuclear weapons must be solved if mankind is to survive. Behavioral scientists must join forces with workers in the other sciences if a solution is to be found. To understand how science contributes to man's welfare let us look at some distinctions that are made among *basic research, applied research,* and *development.* Although, as we shall see, the areas overlap, scientific research

applied

development

  can be divided into the three categories of basic research, _____

research, and _____ .

2.   Basic research seeks to understand the *relationships between events.* The

research

basic

relationships

findings of basic _____ may well have practical applications,

but the goal of the worker in _____ research is to discover the

_____ between events.

3.   A scientist working in the area of basic research is motivated by a desire to

events

practical

discover the relationships between _____ . His discoveries may or

may not have immediate _____ applications.

4.   A psychologist who runs rats in a T-maze in an attempt to discover the relationship between speed of running and amount of reinforcement is engaged

basic research, are not

in _____ _____ . His findings (*are/are not*) directly relevant to problems of learning in the classroom.

5.   Another psychologist studies how newborn infants respond with eye movements to objects presented at different distances. His research would prob-

basic research

ably be classified as _____ _____ .

6. A third psychologist is working on the problem of how mathematical concepts should be presented to the student for the most efficient learning— that is, how best to *apply* basic research on concept learning to classroom instruction. He does his experiments with second graders in a school class-

applied

research

room. His research would probably be classified as _____

_____ .

7. As we have said, there is no clear-cut distinction between basic and

applied

_____ research. Basic research may have immediate practical applications. A laboratory study on the effectiveness of mental imagery on the long-term retention of paired-associates may have practical

applications

_____ for learning a foreign language in the class-room.

8. Applied research frequently must be implemented by technological *development*. For example, research on computer-assisted instruction, which would

applied research

be classified as _____ _____ , necessitates the development of equipment such as color display screens, special electric type-writers, and audio systems to present the programed material in the most effective manner.

development

9. Technological _____ , requiring the assistance of specialists other than research scientists, may be needed to implement

applied

_____ research.

10. Thus we see that research, whether it be in psychology, engineering, biology,

basic

or any other scientific field, can be roughly classified as _____ or

applied

_____ , although frequently the two categories overlap. Applied

development

research may need to be implemented by technological _____ before it can serve the needs of mankind.

11. To put research findings into practice also may require the training of *professionals*. For example, research may yield data bearing upon the treatment

professionals

of schizophrenia, but _____ such as psychia-trists, clinical psychologists, and psychiatric social workers must be trained to apply the results in actual work with schizophrenic patients.

12. The text discusses how these types of research interrelate and how they bear upon policy-making in regard to the larger problems of society. One way of providing *guidelines* for policy decisions concerning social problems would

indicators

be to construct *social indicators*. Social _____ would show, on the basis of available data, how well we are progressing in such areas as health, education, public safety, crime, poverty, social mobility, protection of the physical environment, and so on.

13. The number of first admissions to neuropsychiatric hospitals each year would

social indicator

be a _____ _____ telling us something about the status of the nation's mental health.

14. The proportion of crimes committed each year by juveniles would be a social indicator _____ _____ telling us how well we are coping with the problems of our youth.

15. Social indicators can be developed in many areas to show the current status
guidelines and to provide g_____ for *future policy*. Because of the psychologist's experience in survey research, test construction, and studies of attitude change, he can play a major role in the development and interpreta-
indicators tion of social _____ .

policy **16.** In recommending future _____ it is helpful to be able to make some forecasts about the future, to make predictions about the course of
future large-scale social processes. One method of forecasting the _____ is *trend analysis*.

17. If we know the number of mental patients cared for in various private, state, and government hospitals each year for the past ten years, and we know also the rate of population growth over these years, we can predict, or
forecast _____ , with fair accuracy the number of hospital beds that will be required to care for mental patients ten years from now. We are
trend, trend analyzing the tr_____ in population growth and the tr_____ in incidence of mental illness.

analysis **18.** One difficulty with trend _____ is that it does not take into account new events that have not affected the trend in the past but may influence the future. For example, the trend in population growth may well be affected by widespread use of more effective methods of birth control. If this were the case, prediction of the size of the population ten years hence,
overestimate based upon past growth, may well (*overestimate/underestimate*) the actual population size in ten years.

19. Similarly, if a new and startlingly effective treatment for schizophrenia were
prediction discovered within the next few years, the *pre*_____ concerning the treatment facilities required in ten years would probably be an (*over-*
overestimation *estimation/underestimation*).

analysis **20.** To improve prediction based upon trend _____ the method
judgment of *expert judgment* is used. The method of expert _____
experts utilizes the knowledge of *ex*_____ in various fields to assess those
trends factors that may well modify future *tr*_____ .

21. When the predictions of experts in a number of fields are synthesized to take into account the interdependencies of their predictions, the method is known
impact matrix as the *cross-impact matrix method*. The cross-_____ _____
experts method synthesizes the predictions of a number of _____ to
forecast arrive at a more accurate *fore*_____ of future events.

22. For psychologists, economists, engineers, biologists, and other scientists to work individually on social problems is not the most efficient way of reaching a solution. More effective would be the establishment of multidisciplinary *institutes* where scientists from various fields, or disciplines, would pool their knowledge and abilities in a concerted attack upon social problems. Because

multidisciplinary

the problems that confront society span many scientific areas, a *multi-* _____ approach would be the most effective.

23. A multidisciplinary institute would provide an arrangement whereby scientists

disciplines

from many fields, or _____ , could share their skills and knowledge.

24. A science concerned with solving human problems soon encounters *issues of*

value

value. One issue of _____ is *respect for privacy.* To answer questions about social problems we need to know a great deal about people. But protection of privacy has always been one of the principal values of our society.

25. One issue that psychologists must be concerned with, then, is the respect for

privacy

_____ . Although accurate information about the welfare of the nation's citizens is necessary to guide public policy, it is essential that information-gathering not violate the individual's right to privacy.

value   26. Another issue of _____ is respect for *freedom of choice.* For example, as techniques for modifying behavior become more powerful, therapists must be aware of their potential for control over the patient's behavior and must be alert to the danger of imposing their own values upon the patient.

27. Techniques for modifying behavior can, if uncontrolled, pose a threat to

choice

freedom of _____ .

28. Among the issues of value that may soon pose problems for psychologists

privacy

freedom

we have mentioned only two, respect for _____ and respect for _____ of choice. In working toward the construction of social policies that will lead to the amelioration of social ills and the creation of a better society, psychologists must be aware of these and many other issues.

Note: The last part of Chapter 23 is a section entitled "Psychology and the problems of society," which explores some of the considerations that must apply in making psychology and the social sciences pertinent to the large-scale social problems. This section should be particularly interesting to those who are considering further study of psychology.

self-quiz

Select the alternative that best completes the thought. In some cases several answers are fairly satisfactory; you are to pick the *best* one.

_____ 1. The preservation of confidentiality in research should be the responsibility of the
a. government
b. interviewee
c. investigator
d. National Academy of Sciences

_____ 2. A science concerned with solving human problems must face the issue of
a. human values
b. the protection of privacy
c. political pressures
d. all of the above

_____ 3. One suggestion for making research in the behavioral sciences relate more directly to social problems is to establish

a. a commission for organizing research efforts
b. a library complex to make research available to all
c. multidisciplinary institutes
d. a magazine to include articles from specialists of different fields

_____ 4. It is possible to predict the number of persons who will be killed over a holiday weekend or the number of doctoral degrees to be given in a future year by means of
a. social indicators
b. expert judgment
c. trend analysis
d. interpolation equations

_____ 5. Which of the following would most likely be classed as technological research and development?
a. computer-assisted instruction
b. role of RNA in memory
c. eyelid conditioning
d. study of eye movements in reading

_____ 6. The distinction between "little science" and "big science" is based upon the
a. relevance of the research to society
b. degree to which it attacks crucial problems
c. number of important scientists working in the science
d. amounts of money required to sustain the science

_____ 7. The step that is often closely associated with applied research is
a. development
b. testing
c. sampling
d. reviewing

_____ 8. The Delphi method refers to
a. predictions made by palmists and spiritualists
b. the prediction of the future by means of trend analysis
c. predictions made from past experience
d. the use of expert judgment in forecasting

_____ 9. Which of the following has expressed the fear that techniques of behavior control may be a threat to individual freedom?

a. Skinner
b. Rogers
c. Kelman
d. Maslow

_____ 10. If social indicators are to be useful they should be
a. derived from a broad base of firm data
b. based primarily on the judgments of experts
c. based on the cross-impact matrix method
d. derived by the Delphi method

_____ 11. In the future, psychology will probably shift its emphasis to research on the
a. problems of individuals
b. physiological correlates of behavior
c. problems of groups and societies
d. problems of mental health

_____ 12. Studies have shown that children of the same age may differ widely in ability. Yet many schools still maintain a "lock-step" program in which all pupils in the same grade receive the same instruction. This discrepancy points up the fact that
a. educational psychologists have not been active in research
b. most teachers are resistant to change
c. student response to curriculum is largely ignored
d. innovations in education require well-informed school boards, parents, and teachers

_____ 13. Which of the following is a disadvantage of trend analysis as a method of forecasting the future?
a. by using expert judgments it sometimes lacks objectivity
b. its predictions are accurate for only a few years in the future
c. it fails to take into account new events that have not affected past trends
d. all of the above

_____ 14. Social mobility refers to
a. the use of social indicators to improve prediction
b. the transition from rural to urban living
c. societies with a class rather than caste system

d. the opportunity to improve one's social status

____ 15. In order for man to relate successfully to the technological changes in his environment, science must place a greater emphasis upon
a. analysis and explanation
b. applied technology
c. synthesis and design
d. research and development

____ 16. A method that synthesizes the predictions of experts in a number of fields to forecast the future is called
a. factor analysis
b. trend analysis
c. expert judgment
d. the cross-impact matrix method

____ 17. The evaluation of large-scale remedial programs, such as Head Start or the Job Corps, is difficult because
a. the programs may be carried out in an uneven way so that they are effective in some places and not in others
b. the programs may not be of sufficient scale to show up in social indicators
c. most changes are the result of multiple causal factors
d. all of the above

____ 18. Social indicators should be used to

a. provide guidelines for policy decisions regarding social problems
b. help people conform to social standards
c. indicate future social problems
d. supplement the use of trend analysis

____ 19. A psychologist studying the effect of different schedules of reinforcement on bar-pressing in the rat is engaged in _____ research.
a. applied
b. developmental
c. basic
d. cognitive

____ 20. Which of the following statements concerning the relationship between basic and applied research is most accurate?
a. basic research precedes applied research
b. they require quite different research techniques
c. applied research is the utilization of basic research
d. there is continual feedback between the two types of research

key to self-quiz

20. d	15. c	10. a	5. a
19. c	14. d	9. b	4. c
18. a	13. c	8. d	3. c
17. d	12. d	7. a	2. d
16. d	11. c	6. d	1. c

APPENDIX

statistical methods and measurement

programed unit

1.   If we administer a test to 1000 students and enter their scores in a notebook, we will be recording information about the test results in the form of *raw*

raw   *scores*. The scores are called _____ because these are the data as they were collected; they have not been changed in any way.

2.   The number a person receives on any measure (height, weight, a test, and

raw   so on) is called a _____ score because it has not been manipulated in any way—it remains just as it was collected.

3.   Raw data become comprehensible if they are presented in the form of a *frequency distribution*. If we follow a common procedure, we may list each possible score and record next to it the number of people who made that score. In this way the raw data is rearranged as a frequency

distribution   _____ .

4.   Whenever we take raw data and arrange it so that we can tell how many

frequency   people made each possible score, we have a _____

distribution   _____ .

5.   Since we cannot keep 1000 raw scores in mind at any one time, it would be very convenient if we could *describe* these scores more simply. There are a number of ways to describe (or summarize) frequency distributions; all of them, so long as they merely *describe* the distribution, are classified as *descriptive statistics*. Whenever we use a number (for example, an average)

descriptive   to describe a distribution, we are using a _____ statistic.

6.   Professor X, who has given a test to a large class, wishes to compute the

average score in order to describe how well his students as a whole have

descriptive
statistic

performed. The professor is using a _____

_____ .

7. Anyone who describes a distribution of scores by the use of summarizing or

descriptive statistics

simplifying scores is using _____ _____ .

8. One descriptive statistic, used very often, is called the *mean;* it is nothing more than the familiar arithmetic average. In order to determine the *mean* of a distribution of scores, one merely sums (that is, adds up) all the scores and *divides* by the *number* of scores. If you sum the raw scores and divide

mean

by the number of scores, you have computed the _____ .

9. John has taken eight tests during a semester, each of which counts equally toward his final grade. To get an idea of how well he has done, he sums the numerical grades received on the tests and divides the sum by eight. He has

mean

computed a _____ grade.

10. In order to compute a mean, one sums all the raw scores and divides by the

number

_____ of scores.

11. Another descriptive statistic is called the *median*. The *median* is defined as the middle score of the distribution. This statistic is obtained by arranging all the scores from low to high and counting in to the middle from either

median

end. The middle score is the _____ score. If the number of cases is even, one simply averages the cases on either side of the middle. For

median

instance, with 10 cases, the _____ is the average of the fifth and sixth scores when they are arranged from low to high.

12. Put another way, if we find the score that divides the distribution in half, we

median

have found the _____ .

13. The *mode* is the score that appears most *frequently* in the distribution. We find the mode by merely examining the distribution; it requires no computation. Whenever we are talking about the score that occurs most frequently,

mode

we are talking about the _____ .

frequently (or synonym)

14. The mode, then, is the score that appears most _____ in the distribution.

descriptive

15. The mean, the median, and the mode are all _____ statistics. They simply describe the distribution of scores.

16. Let us illustrate the way these three statistics may differ by using an example. Let us consider the salaries of five men. Assume that Jim earns $5000 a year, Tom earns $10,000, Harry also earns $10,000, Bob earns $20,000, and Mack earns $155,000. First let us compute the *mean* salary. To make

divide

this computation, sum all the salaries and _____ by the number of salaries. (*Use a separate sheet for this computation and keep it in view.*)

5
$40,000

17. When we sum the salaries of the five men, and divide by _____ , we arrive at a mean salary of $_____ .

$10,000

18. Next find the *median* salary. The median is the salary in the middle of the distribution. Arranging the five salaries in order from high to low and counting in to the middle yields a median of $_____ .

$10,000

19. Finally we examine the distribution to find the *modal* salary. It is obvious that the *mode* of the distribution is $_____ , since this is the salary that appears most often in the distribution.

same, larger

20. It now becomes clear that these three statistics may be very different from one another. In this particular example, the mode and median both take on the _____ value, but the mean is much _____ . If you were given the mode of a distribution and thought that you were getting the mean, you would be receiving a distorted picture of the true state of affairs.

range

21. Once we have a mean, it is often helpful to know whether the scores are all very close to the mean or whether they are spread from very low to very high. In other words, we would like to have a *measure of variation* to describe whether the scores vary a lot or just a little. One measure of variation is the *range,* which is the spread from the lowest to the highest score. If the instructor says that the scores on a test went from a low of 32 to a high of 93, he is giving the _____ of scores.

variation

22. The range is one measure of _____ .

range

23. John got a 63 on a test. His roommate asked him how well the others in the class did, and he replied that the scores ran from 40 to 74. John was describing the variation of scores in terms of their _____ .

mean

variation

24. Most scores are not the same as the mean; that is, they deviate from the mean. The *standard deviation* is a frequently used measure of the amount by which scores deviate or depart from their _____ . The standard deviation is thus another measure of _____ .

deviation

25. The lower-case Greek letter σ is frequently used as an abbreviation for the standard _____ . The formula for computing the standard deviation is as follows:

$$\sigma = \sqrt{\frac{\text{Sum of } d^2}{N}}$$

The deviation, *d,* for each score is first computed by subtracting the score from the mean. Next, the *d* for each score is squared, and then the squared deviations for all the scores are summed.

deviations

scores

26. Statisticians use *N* as a shorthand for the number of scores. When we divide the sum of the squared _____ by *N,* we are dividing by the number of _____ .

27. In computing the *standard deviation,* then, the first step is to determine the

square

deviation of each raw score from the mean. The second step is to _____ each of these deviations.

28. In the third step, sum these squared deviations and then divide by *N*. To

deviation

square

N

review: The first step is to determine the _____ of each raw score from the mean. The second step is to _____ each of these deviations. Third, sum the squared deviations and divide by _____ .

29. When we then take the *square root* of the result of step three, we arrive at

standard deviation

the _____ _____ .

30. To recapitulate: First, determine the deviations of the raw scores from the

mean, deviations

sum

root, standard

deviation

_____ ; second, square each of these _____ ; third, _____ these squared deviations and divide by *N*. Finally, take the square _____ of the result to obtain the _____ _____ .

31. Let us consider the following example to show how a standard deviation is calculated. For the sake of simplicity, we will use only a few scores. Suppose a test is given to five people and the scores are as follows: 11, 13, 14, 15, 17.

14

In this case the mean would be _____ . (*Use a separate sheet of paper.*)

32. For the score of 11, the deviation from the mean (obtained by subtracting the score from the mean) is 3. Squaring this we would arrive at the number

9

_____ .

1

1

33. The deviation of the score of 13 would be _____ . Squaring this we would arrive at the number _____ .

0

0

34. The deviation of the score of 14 would be _____ . Squaring this yields _____ .

35. The deviation of the score of 15 would be −1 (14 − 15 = −1). Squaring

1

−1 yields _____ .

−3

9

36. The deviation of the score of 17 would be _____ . Squaring this yields _____ .

37. We now have the squared deviation of each of the scores. In other words, we have completed steps one and two in the sequence mentioned above and are ready to move on to step three in the computation of the standard devia-

sum

5

tion. In step three we _____ the squared deviations and divide by *N*. In this case *N* equals _____ .

4

38. When the operations in step three are carried out, we arrive at _____ (*number*) as a result.

39. We now perform the final operation; we take the square root of the result
of step three. The square root of 4 is _____ .

2

2   **40.** Therefore the standard deviation of this distribution of scores is _____ .

standard   **41.** We have examined two *measures of variation:* the range and the _____
deviation.

variation   **42.** The range and the standard deviation are both measures of _____ .
Since these two statistics merely *describe* the distribution, they are classified

descriptive   as _____ statistics.

43. We often wish to say something about large groups of people, for example,
the population of China, or the population of the United States, or all college
students, or all students at a particular college. The group we wish to talk
about is called the *population,* whether it contains 50,000,000 or 100
people. In research, the total group we wish to make our statements about

population   is called the _____ .

44. Professor Jones wishes to find out whether English males are taller than
German males. Since he wants to say something about both English males

populations   and German males, these are his _____*s.*

45. It is obvious that Professor Jones will not have enough time or money to
test all English and German males. Therefore he will have to be satisfied to
test fewer than all of them. In a way he has the same problem that a customs inspector has. The customs inspector wants to make sure that no one
brings in contraband, but he hasn't time to inspect everyone's luggage.
Therefore he selects some of the people and inspects their baggage thoroughly.

sample   He has drawn a *sample* of the total population. A _____ , then, is

population   a smaller number of cases that is drawn from the _____ .

46. Whenever one selects and tests a smaller number of cases from the total

sample   population he is interested in, he has drawn a _____ from the
population.

47. A sample should be selected in such a way that it is *representative* of the
total population. Otherwise, we cannot make reasonable *inferences* about

population   the total _____ based solely on information obtained
from the sample.

48. A sample that is not representative of the population will not allow us to

inferences   make reasonable _____ about the population.

49. One way of obtaining a representative sample is to select it at *random.* To do
this, we can put the names of the members of the population in a hat and
draw out the number we need, or use any other means of selection that will
guarantee that *every person in the population has an equal chance of being
chosen.* When we draw a sample in such a way that each individual in the

random

population has an equal chance of being chosen, we have drawn a r_____ sample.

50. A key feature of a random sample is that each individual in the population

equal chance

has an _____ _____ of being chosen.

51. If we collect data on a sample of 100 people in a town of 1000 people and then make statements about the *entire* population of the town on the basis of this data, we cannot be *sure* our statements are correct. Only if we collect

population

data on the entire _____ of the town can we be sure that any statements based upon the data will be correct for the whole population.

52. When we make statements about a population on the basis of a sample, we *infer* that what is true about the sample will also be approximately true for the entire population. A statement about a population based upon a sample

inference

of that population is called a(n) _____*ence*. We can never be com-

sure (or synonym)

pletely _____ that such an inference is correct.

53. Another way of putting this is to say that when we make an inference about a population from a sample, we have only a certain probability that our statement is correct for the population as a whole. The probability of our statement being true would be 100 percent only if we had data on the

entire (or synonym)

_____ population.

54. The smaller the size of the sample, the smaller the probability of making a correct inference about the population. Since we are making inferences

population

about the _____ , based on *statistics* that are computed

sample

from only a _____ of the population, we call this process *statistical inference.*

55. When the Gallup poll interviews a small number of people and makes a prediction about who will be elected President of the United States, a

statistical inference

_____ _____ _____ is being made.

56. Suppose a researcher is interested in the population of a particular college with 10,000 students. He goes to the college directory and takes each hun-

random

dredth name, thus drawing a _____ sample of the population of students at that college.

57. He tests this sample of students and, on the basis of their scores alone, he

population

makes statements about the entire _____ of the col-

statistical

lege. When he does this, he is making a _____

inference

_____ .

58. Suppose we gave an intelligence test to all the people in the United States and then plotted on a graph the scores and the number of people who got each score. We plot the number of people on the vertical axis and their horizontal

scores on the *hor*_____ axis, In schematic form the graph would look like the illustration below.

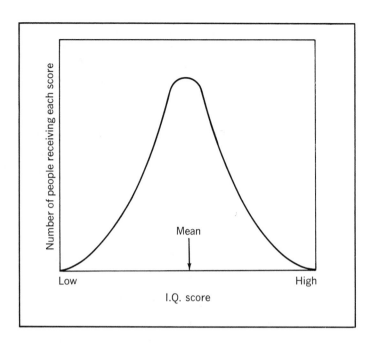

59. This graph represents a *frequency distribution* of scores. Looking at the graph, we find that there are relatively few people who got very low scores and that the number of people who got any particular score (*increases/decreases*) as we move upward toward the mean. As we move past the mean to the right, there are fewer and fewer people getting the higher scores and very few getting the highest scores.

increases

60. Note that the curve of the frequency distribution is *symmetric* in form; that is, the part of the curve below the mean is a mirror image of the part

above

_____ the mean. Symmetry implies that for every score a fixed distance above the mean there is a corresponding score the same distance

below

_____ the mean, so that the number of people receiving each score will be the same.

frequency

61. The curve of the _____ distribution shown above is not only symmetric in form but also is shaped very much like a bell. A frequency-

bell

distribution curve that is symmetric and also _____-*shaped* is called a *normal curve*.

distribution

62. When we plot a frequency _____ and get a curve

normal

that is bell-shaped, we call this curve a _____ curve.

63. For a normal curve the mean, median, and mode all have the same value. There are the same number of cases below and above the middle of the distribution; for every score below the mean there is another score the same distance above the mean; and the number of cases receiving a score a given distance below the mean is matched by an equal number of cases receiving a score the same distance above the mean. In other words, the two halves of

symmetric

the curve are _____ .

fifty   **64.** If fifty people have a score of 80 and the mean is 100, then _____ (*number*) people can be expected to have a score of 120 if the curve is a normal curve.

65. If we actually administered the Stanford-Binet intelligence test to all the people in the United States, we would find that the frequency distribution of scores would take the form of a normal curve. The *mean* of the scores would be 100 and the *standard deviation* would be 16. The standard devia-

variation   tion, as you will remember, is a measure of *var*_____ .

66. Statisticians often talk about a score as being one or more standard deviations away from the mean. If the mean of the scores on an intelligence test is 100 and the standard deviation is 16, a score of 84 would be said to be one

below   standard deviation _____ the mean.

67. One of the properties of the normal curve is that *68 percent* of all the cases in the distribution will have scores that lie between one standard deviation below and one above the mean. The normal curve is so defined that this will *always* be true. If a distribution of intelligence test scores fits a normal curve,

68   _____ percent of the cases will have scores between one standard devia-

above   tion below the mean and one standard deviation _____ the mean. This characteristic of the normal curve is shown in the illustration below, in which new labels have been added to the normal curve with which you are already familiar.

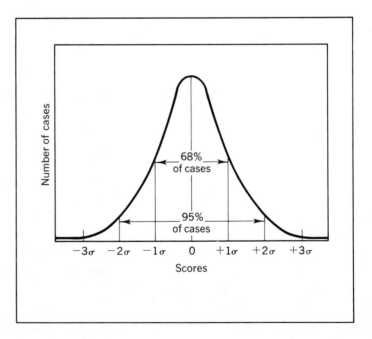

68. As you already know, the Greek letter σ is the abbreviation for standard

below   deviation. Thus -1σ means one standard deviation _____ the mean.

69. Referring again to the intelligence test with a mean of 100 and a standard deviation of 16, the score that is one standard deviation below the mean is

84   _____ (*number*).

116   **70.** The score that is one standard deviation above the mean would be _____ .

71. Therefore, if we group all the people with scores between 84 and 116 on the

68   intelligence test, we will have _____ percent of the population.

72. If we look again at the new illustration of the normal curve, we see that 95 percent of the population have scores that lie between *two* standard deviations below the mean and two standard deviations above the mean. To go back to the intelligence test with a mean of 100 and a standard deviation of

132   16, 95 percent of the population will have scores between 68 and _____ .

73. If 68 percent of the population have scores that lie between one standard deviation below the mean and one standard deviation above the mean on

34   the normal curve, then it follows that _____ percent of the population have scores between one standard deviation below the mean and the mean itself.

74. In other words, in our example, 34 percent of the population have scores

100   between 84 and _____ .

75. If 95 percent of the population have scores between two standard deviations below the mean and two standard deviations above the mean, then 47.5 percent of the population have scores between two standard deviations above the mean and the mean itself. In our example, then, 47.5 percent of the

132   population have scores between 100 and _____ .

76. Again looking at our illustration of the normal curve, we can see that almost all of the people (over 99 percent) have scores that lie between three

above   standard deviations below the mean and three standard deviations _____ the mean. Thus for practical purposes virtually all of the scores fall between

three   minus and plus _____ standard deviations from the mean.

77. To use our example once more, we would expect that practically all the people who took the intelligence test (mean = 100, standard deviation = 16)

52, 148   would have scores between _____ and _____ .

78. As a quick example of how one can use the concept of the standard deviation on the normal curve, let us suppose that John had a score of 148 on the intelligence test. Knowing the mean and the standard deviation of that test, John can be sure that he has earned one of the very highest scores, since

three   his score is _____ standard deviations above the mean. In other words, he knows how his score compares with those from the population at large.

Note: The Appendix in the text can be only an introduction to the subject of statistics. In turn, this programed unit can be only an introduction to that material. You have learned about some of the basic terms and techniques of statistical analysis, but several concepts that are treated in the text have not even been mentioned in this program. You should, however, find it easier to master the text treatment if you have understood the concepts presented here.

self-quiz

Select the alternative that best completes the thought. In some cases several answers are fairly satisfactory; you are to pick the *best* one.

_____ 1. The mode of a distribution is the
a. arithmetic average
b. middle score
c. score with the highest frequency
d. standard deviation

_____ 2. What percentage of the scores in a normal distribution will fall between the mean and +1.0 standard deviations?
a. 16
b. 34
c. 50
d. 68

_____ 3. For a normal distribution in which the mean is 80 and the standard deviation is 6, we know that
a. 95 percent of the subjects had scores between 68 and 92
b. the range is about 50
c. roughly 50 percent of the subjects achieved high scores
d. 95 percent of the subjects had scores between 74 and 86

_____ 4. Which of the following can be called a descriptive statistic?
a. confidence limits
b. the significance of a mean difference
c. the standard deviation of a distribution
d. the critical ratio of r

_____ 5. A scatter diagram with points running from the bottom left to the top right along a diagonal line will yield a(n)
a. negative r
b. negative *rho*
c. r close to 1.00
d. *rho* close to 0.00

_____ 6. Sue made a raw score of 90 on a psychological test. This means that
a. she exceeds 90 percent of the population who took the test
b. she answered 90 percent of the questions correctly
c. she is in the upper quarter of the distribution
d. more information is needed in order to interpret her performance

_____ 7. A convenient method of expressing a relationship between two variables is a
a. standard error
b. measure of variation
c. rank-difference
d. coefficient of correlation

_____ 8. For a sample, we derive a mean of 60.0. Assume that the standard error of the mean is 1.0. The probability is .95 that the population mean lies between these limits
a. 60 ± 1.0 or between 59.0 and 61.0
b. 60 ± 0.5 or between 59.5 and 60.5
c. 60 ± 2.0 or between 58.0 and 62.0
d. 60 ± 3.0 or between 57.0 and 63.0

_____ 9. The median is
a. obtained by adding the scores and dividing by the number of cases
b. that part of the scale where most cases occur
c. the score with the highest frequency
d. the middle score in a distribution

_____ 10. An obtained statistical relationship is generally regarded as statistically significant if it could have been obtained by chance alone less than _____ in 100 times.
a. 5
b. 10
c. 25
d. 50

_____ 11. If we wish to know whether the measure of variation for a distribution is small or large, we would compute the
a. median
b. standard deviation
c. critical ratio
d. mode

_____ 12. What is the mean of this distribution: 40, 60, 65, 35?
a. 65
b. 50
c. 35
d. 30

_____ 13. On a school achievement test, scores in city A have a mean of 78 and a standard error of the mean of 0.50. Scores in city B have a mean of 75 and a standard error of the mean of 0.40. Is the mean of 78 for city A significantly higher than the mean of 75 for city B?

a. we need the range in order to test for significance
b. there is no significant difference
c. the critical ratio barely meets the test of significance
d. the critical ratio is large and easily meets the test of significance

_____ 14. An analysis of the starting times of a commuting train that is usually on time in leaving, occasionally starts late, but never starts early would show a distribution of times

a. that would be symmetrical
b. that would be skewed, with the median and mode higher than the mean of the starting times
c. that would be skewed, with the median and mode lower than the mean of the starting times
d. the shape of which we cannot determine without further information

_____ 15. A correlation of $r = -.80$

a. cannot occur
b. means that increases in x are accompanied by decreases in y
c. means that increases in x are accompanied by increases in y
d. makes the relationship between x and y unclear

_____ 16. If the standard deviation of a distribution is 10 and the number of people in the sample is 100, what is the standard error of the mean ($\sigma_M = \sigma/\sqrt{N}$)?

a. 1
b. 5
c. 8
d. 10

_____ 17. A rank correlation

a. is a simpler method for determining

correlations than is the product-moment correlation
b. is designated by r
c. should probably be done on a computer
d. does not go below zero, because ranks are involved

_____ 18. Which of the following numbers approximates the standard deviation for this distribution of scores: 10, 8, 6, 4, 2?

a. 2.0
b. 3.0
c. 4.0
d. 1.0

_____ 19. The accuracy of statistical inferences depends upon the

a. critical ratio
b. size and representativeness of the sample
c. standard error
d. standard deviation

_____ 20. Craig made a score of 90 on a test that had a mean of 75 and a standard deviation of 15. On a second test, which had a mean of 50 and a standard deviation of 6, he achieved a score of 64. On which test did he do better?

a. he did equally well on both tests
b. he did better on the first test
c. he did better on the second test
d. more information is needed for interpretation

key to self-quiz

20. c	15. b	10. a	5. c
19. b	14. c	9. d	4. c
18. b	13. d	8. c	3. a
17. a	12. b	7. d	2. b
16. a	11. b	6. d	1. c

individual exercises

introduction

Although a mastery of statistical techniques requires time and training, the basic notions of statistics can be understood by those with a minimum of mathematical background. The following exercises use sim-

ple data in order to make computations easy. These exercises are designed to illustrate how the formulas work rather than to provide skill in their use; you should attempt the exercises only after you have read the Appendix in the textbook. (The answers to these exercises are given in the Appendix of this book, page 285.)

equipment needed

None

procedure

Read carefully the instructions given for each exercise and then make computations.

FREQUENCY DISTRIBUTION

Eleven applicants for an office job made the following scores on a typing test:

25 53 42 64 38 43 56 36 38 48 47

Complete the table below by counting the scores in each class interval; then plot the diagram.

FREQUENCY DISTRIBUTION

Scores on typing test	Number of applicants making these scores
20–29	———
30–39	———
40–49	———
50–59	———
60–69	———

FREQUENCY DIAGRAM

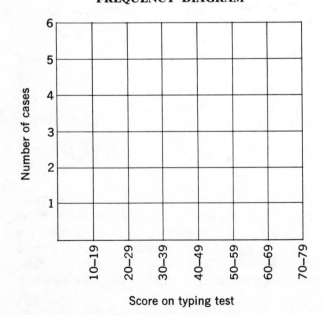

Score on typing test

questions

1. What is the class interval?

2. Is the distribution symmetric?

MEASURES OF CENTRAL TENDENCY

questions

3. Determine the *median* score for the above data by arranging the scores in order and finding the *middle* case (that is, the 6th from either end of 11).

   Median = _____

4. Calculate the *mean* for the above data by adding the *raw scores* and dividing by the number of scores.

   Mean = _____

5. Under what circumstances do the mean and median differ?

6. If the person getting the high score of 64 had in fact gotten a score of 75, how would it have affected the mean and the median?

MEASURES OF VARIATION

Consider the following weekly earnings reported by five part-time taxicab drivers:

Driver	Weekly earnings
A	$50
B	$60
C	$70
D	$80
E	$90

questions

7. What is the *range* of weekly earnings? _____ the *mean?* _____

8. Compute the *standard deviation* by completing the following table.

Driver	Weekly earnings	Deviation from mean (d)	Deviation squared (d^2)
A			
B			
C			
D			
E			

Sum of d^2 =

$\dfrac{\text{Sum of } d^2}{N}$ =

Standard deviation = $\sqrt{\dfrac{\text{Sum of } d^2}{N}}$ = _____

STANDARD ERROR OF THE MEAN

The more cases that enter into the computation of a mean, the more confidence we have that our obtained mean represents the total group from which our sample has been drawn.

Suppose that we draw successive samples of increasing size in order to measure some psychological characteristic, such as speed of reaction, among college students. How does our confidence increase with the size of the sample?

Suppose that the means of our reaction-time measurement fluctuate around 150 milliseconds (0.150 seconds), with standard deviations around 15 milliseconds. Where does the true mean reaction time fall?

These problems will be dealt with as you answer Questions 9 and 10.

questions

9. Let us compute the *standard error of the mean,* assuming different numbers of cases (persons) in our sample. Complete the following table, using the formula:

Standard error of the mean (σ_M) =

$$\dfrac{\text{Standard deviation } (\sigma)}{\sqrt{N}}$$

Number of cases (N)	$\sqrt{N}$	Standard deviation (σ)	Standard error of mean (σ_M)
25	5	15	
100	10	15	
400	20	15	

Note that the standard error of the mean decreases as N increases. How can we convert this into some kind of statement about the true mean?

10. *Confidence limits.* We can state that with repeated measurements we can expect our means to fall within the range from -2.0σ to $+2.0\sigma$ in 95 percent of the cases. Using the table below determine the confidence limits for the mean reaction times of the three different sample sizes.

Sample size	Mean reaction time (milliseconds)	95 percent confidence limits	
		Lower limit (mean less 2.0 × standard error)	Upper limit (mean plus 2.0 × standard error)
25	150		
100	150		
400	150		

Thus far nothing has been said about the true mean of the population. Setting the confidence limits as we have, we may infer that the true mean lies within our confidence limits 95 percent of the time.

SIGNIFICANCE OF A DIFFERENCE

Suppose that we are comparing the mathematics scores of boys and girls in the fourth grade, with the following results:

	Number of cases (N)	Mean	Standard error of mean (σ_M)
Girls	50	72.0	0.4
Boys	50	70.5	0.3

questions

Do the girls score significantly higher than the boys? To find out, we compute a *critical ratio,* but first we have to find the *standard error of difference,* according to the following formula.

11. The formula for the standard error of difference is

$$\sigma_D = \sqrt{\sigma_{M_1}{}^2 + \sigma_{M_2}{}^2}$$

where σ_{M_1} and σ_{M_2} are the standard errors of the means for girls and boys. Work out this formula using the data above.

$$\sigma_D = \sqrt{(\quad)^2 + (\quad)^2} =$$

$$\sqrt{(\quad)} = \underline{\quad}$$

statistical methods and measurement   **277**

12. Compute the critical ratio, using this formula:

$$\text{Critical ratio} = \frac{\text{Difference between means}}{\sigma_D} =$$

$$\frac{(\quad\quad) - (\quad\quad)}{(\quad\quad)} = \underline{\quad\quad}$$

13. If the absolute size of the critical ratio is over 2.0, we usually call the difference *significant*. In our example, is there a significant difference between the mathematics scores of boys and girls?

COEFFICIENT OF CORRELATION

Salesmen were given a test of sales ability before being hired. Then their scores were compared with subsequent performance on the job (as shown in first table below).

questions

The degree of relationship between scores and sales is expressed by the *coefficient of correlation*. This index may be computed from two different formulas.

14. The most frequently used method yields the *product-moment correlation, r.* What is the product-moment correlation between the salesmen's test scores and earnings? Complete the computations indicated in the table on page 279 and copy your result here: $r = $ _____ .

15. When there are few cases, an approximate method, known as *rank correlation*, yielding *rho* instead of *r*, is useful. The data are converted to ranks and then the following formula is used:

$$rho = 1 - \frac{6(\text{Sum } D^2)}{N(N^2 - 1)}$$

where D is difference in ranks for the measures and N the number of cases. Compute the rank correlation, using the table below.

16. On the basis of this correlation, what can be said about the cause-and-effect relations between test scores and sales performance?

	Anderson	Brown	Cook	Dodge	East
Test score:	50	60	70	80	90
Sales (in thousands of dollars):	$60	$80	$90	$70	$100

COMPUTATION OF RANK CORRELATION

Subject	(1) Sales test score rank	(2) Earnings score rank	Difference in rank $D = (1) - (2)$	Squared difference (D^2)
Anderson				
Brown				
Cook				
Dodge				
East				

$$rho = 1 - \frac{6(\quad\quad)}{(\quad)(\quad\quad)} = 1 - \frac{(\quad\quad)}{(\quad\quad)} = \underline{\quad\quad}$$

COMPUTATION OF PRODUCT-MOMENT CORRELATION (r)

Correlation between a sales test and later sales in thousands of dollars

Subject	Scores on the sales test and computation of σ_x			Sales success and computation of σ_y			Cross-products used in computing r
	Test score (x)	Deviation from mean (dx)* (mean = 70)	(dx)²	Sales score (y)	Deviation from mean (dy)* (mean = $80)	(dy)²	Product of deviations (dx)(dy)
Anderson							
Brown							
Cook							
Dodge							
East							
	Sum (dx)² = $\dfrac{\text{Sum }(dx)^2}{N}=$ $\sigma_x = \sqrt{\dfrac{\text{Sum }(dx)^2}{N}} = \sqrt{} =$			Sum (dy)² = $\dfrac{\text{Sum }(dy)^2}{N}=$ $\sigma_y = \sqrt{\dfrac{\text{Sum }(dy)^2}{N}} = \sqrt{} =$			Sum (dx)(dy) =

* Subtract mean from score: respect the sign of the difference.

Coefficient of correlation, $r = \dfrac{\text{Sum }(dx)(dy)}{N\,\sigma_x\,\sigma_y} = \dfrac{()}{()\times()\times()} = \dfrac{()}{()\times()} = \dfrac{()}{()} = \underline{}$

APPENDIX

Chapter 11 (page 137) RULE-LEARNING IN PROBLEM-SOLVING

The rule is that when the second digit of the number is "odd" assign the letter A, when "even" the letter B. Ignore the first and third digits.

Chapter 12 (page 146) MEASURING MOTIVATION

Score your completed sentences as follows:

P . . . . if your response indicates a positive, humorous, or hopeful attitude

C . . . . if your response indicates conflict, antagonism, pessimism, emotional disturbance

N . . . . if your response is neutral, that is, not clearly positive or conflictful

Examples of how your responses should be scored:

Boys ——————————————— .

P . . . . are friendly, are easy to get along with, are nice, are good sports, are considerate, are fun at a party, are good friends, are O.K.

C . . . . are a pain in the neck, get on my nerves, can't be trusted, bother me, give me a headache, think they are superior, are rude, are stupid.

N . . . . are human beings, are taller than girls, are stronger than girls, are the opposite sex, are the same sex.

Count the total number of P, C, and N scores. Your instructor may ask you to write these on a slip of paper so that he can determine the distribution of results for the entire class. (You may then complete the table below and determine the median score.) You need not identify yourself. Compute your score by adding fifty to the number of C responses and subtracting the number of P responses. Do not mark omissions if there are any.

Score	Number of students	Score	Number of students
96–100		46–50	
91–95		41–45	
86–90		36–40	
81–85		31–35	
76–80		26–30	
71–75		21–25	
66–70		16–20	
61–65		11–15	
56–60		6–10	
51–55		1–5	

Median score

Crime description to be read by the experimental subject:

Read the following paragraphs carefully and completely.

I have committed murder. . . .

It all began yesterday, the last day of school. I had taken all my exams—was beginning to get back those grades. The first two were flunks.

Well, to forget my troubles, I borrowed a car and began making the rounds of the bars. Sometime during the night I picked up a peroxide blonde wearing a red sweater. After the bars closed, we drove around on some of those lonely, deserted roads. She suggested we stop. We stopped. But when we had stopped, she insisted that I change places with her and let her drive. Frustrated and drunk, I refused and began to get sore. In fact we both became so angry, I grabbed her roughly. She squirmed loose, pulled a .32-caliber revolver from her purse, and ordered me to hand over my wallet and get out of the car. I grabbed for the gun and in the struggle it went off.

So there I was with the .32 in my hand and her still-warm body, with the blonde hair straggling and the blood slowly darkening the red sweater, on the seat beside me.

I felt for her pulse and, as I realized she was dead, I realized too that, even if I could prove it was an accident, my career would be ruined—not to mention the shock to my family.

But I ought to be able to escape detection. There's no reason anyone should connect me with her. There was nothing to do but pull her body from the car and drag it to a nearby pond. I weighted the body with stones, dragged it out into the water, and watched it sink out of sight into the slime and mud.

I carefully cleaned out the car, drove back to school, returned the car, slipped the keys into my friend's mailbox, and went back to my room. As I undressed and cleaned up, I checked back on possible clues that might lead to me. What about blonde hairs found in the car—or some yarn from that red sweater? Or could I have left something personal at the scene of the crime?

Then I noticed that my tie clasp was missing. My *initialled* tie clasp. Why didn't I autograph the body?

But maybe I dropped it earlier in the evening. Still, I could have pulled it loose and lost it between the car and the pond.

A few days later, the body was found and the bartender at the bar where the girl hung out was asked to name all the people who had been in the bar on the evening she disappeared. Unfortunately, I had cashed a check, and I, as well as a number of other patrons, was to be brought in for questioning by the police. The bartender doesn't remember whom she left with so I may still escape.

But I must appear innocent!

WORD-ASSOCIATION TEST FOR EXPERIMENTAL SUBJECT

Stimulus word	Response word	GSR reading	Reaction time
1. time			
2. yellow			
3. red*			
4. book			
5. check			
6. stones*			
7. vacation			
8. desk			
9. pond*			
10. building			
11. shoes			
12. thirty-two*			
13. type			
14. sky			
15. blonde*			
16. teacher			
17. paper			
18. tie*			
19. tree			
20. pole			
21. sweater*			

*key words

	Key words	Neutral words
Average reaction time	_____	_____
Average GSR deflection	_____	_____

WORD-ASSOCIATION TEST FOR CONTROL SUBJECT

Stimulus word	Response word	GSR reading	Reaction time
1. time			
2. yellow			
3. red*			
4. book			
5. check			
6. stones*			
7. vacation			
8. desk			
9. pond*			
10. building			
11. shoes			
12. thirty-two*			
13. type			
14. sky			
15. blonde*			
16. teacher			
17. paper			
18. tie*			
19. tree			
20. pole			
21. sweater*			

*key words

Key words Neutral words

Average reaction time   ___   ___

Average GSR deflection   ___   ___

Chapter 15 (page 176) INDIVIDUAL DIFFERENCES

The unscrambled sentences are as follows:

1. The good that men do lives after them.
2. Don't shoot until you see the whites of their eyes.
3. The most valuable thing in the world is the free human mind.
4. Tell your yarn and let your style go to the devil.
5. It is only at rare moments that we live.
6. Do not blame me too much for not knowing all the answers.
7. The greatest of faults is to be conscious of none.
8. It is better to understand a little than to misunderstand a lot.
9. The worst use that can be made of success is boasting of it.
10. Better a witty fool than a foolish wit.
11. First love is only a little foolishness and a lot of curiosity.
12. The power of laughter is astonishing.
13. Money cannot cure unhappiness.
14. Your reputation grows with every failure.
15. Talk to a man about himself and he will listen for hours.
16. The truth is the one thing nobody will believe.
17. My way of joking is to tell the truth.
18. It is not pleasure that makes life worth living.
19. A bluestocking is a woman who has a mania for intellectual subjects without having a ray of intellect.
20. Very simple ideas lie within the reach only of complex minds.

Chapter 15 (page 178) MEASURING INTELLIGENCE

Answers to computations of Stanford-Binet I.Q.

1. (a) Mental Age = 5 years (or 60 months)
   (b) I.Q. = 100
2. (a) Mental Age = 10 years (or 120 months)
   (b) Chronological Age = 12 years and 6 months (or 150 months)
   (c) $I.Q. = \dfrac{120}{150} \times 100 = 80$
3. (a) Mental Age = 6 years and 6 months (78 months)
   (b) $I.Q. = \dfrac{78}{72} \times 100 \approx 108$
4. Mental Age = 10 years (or 120 months)

Chapter 16 (page 189) MENDELIAN THEORY OF INHERITANCE

The descriptions of genetic make-up of offspring are as follows:

1. (a) *Example.* (b) All will have curly hair and be recessive carriers. (c) One-half (two) will have curly hair and be recessive carriers; one-half (two) will have straight hair. (d) Three-quarters (three) will have curly hair—two will be recessive carriers, and one pure dominant; one-quarter (one) will have straight hair.
2. (a) One-half (two) will be female, both normal, one a recessive carrier; one-half (two) will be male, one normal, the other a hemophiliac. (b) One-half (two) will be female, both normal and recessive carriers; one-half (two) will be male, both normal.

Chapter 20 (page 236) CLASSIFICATION OF BEHAVIOR DISORDERS

The cases are designed to illustrate the following disorders:

Case 1. Psychosis—manic-depressive reaction, manic phase (or hypomania)
Case 2. Psychosis—schizophrenia
Case 3. Neurosis—conversion reaction
Case 4. Neurosis—anxiety reaction
Case 5. Neurosis—phobic reaction
Case 6. Neurosis—compulsive reaction
Case 7. Psychopathic reaction (or psychopathic personality)

Appendix: STATISTICAL METHODS AND MEASUREMENT (page 275)

Answers to the *Individual Exercises.*

1. 10
2. No
3. Median = 43
4. Mean = 44.55
5. When the frequency distribution is not perfectly symmetric about the mean
6. Increased the mean, no effect on the median
7. Range from $50 to $90, or $40; Mean = $70
8. Standard deviation = 14.14
9. Standard errors: for 25 cases, 3.0; for 100 cases, 1.5; for 400 cases, 0.75
10. Confidence limits: for 25 cases, 144–156; for 100 cases, 147–153; for 400 cases, 148.5–151.5
11. Standard error of difference = 0.5
12. Critical ratio = 3.0
13. Yes
14. $r = .70$
15. $rho = .70$
16. No definite conclusions about cause-and-effect relations can be drawn from correlational evidence. See discussion of this topic in text.